W9-BER-701

contents

wow magazine may 1999 vol. 1 issue 1

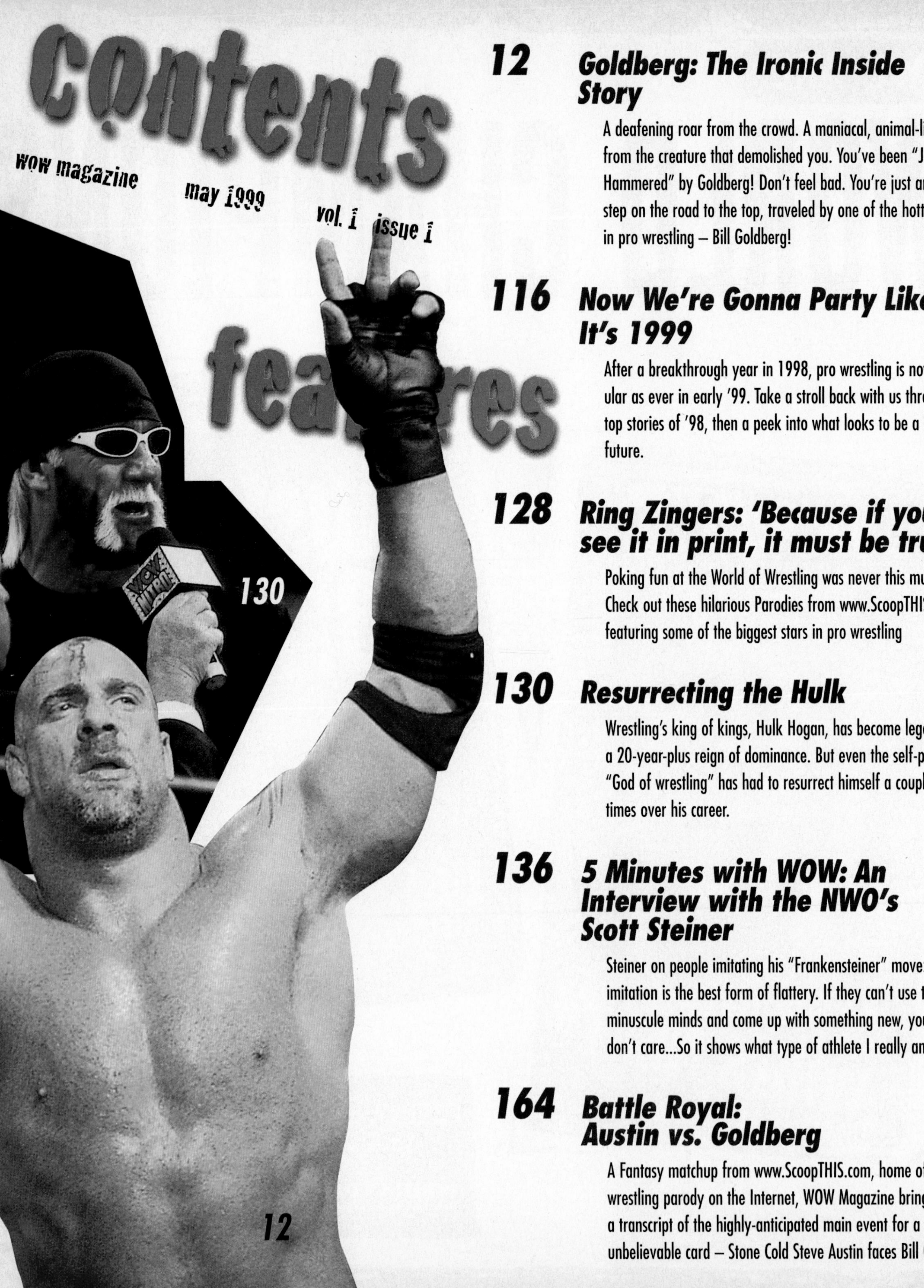

features

departments

32

168

columns

World of Wrestling Magazine

Michael M. Meyers .... Publisher
Mike Morris .... Managing Editor
Elliott From .... Managing Art Director
Rebecca Bruch .... Production Assistant
Brad Perkins .... Editorial Assistant

Contributors

Contributing Writers:
Blake Norton, "The Phantom of the Ring," Greg Saggese, Matt "Twiggs" Grill, Joe Bush, RichInKC, Jim DeRogatis, A. Rettinger, Larry Burnett, John Spangler, Richard Berger, David Conroy, Sammy Eanes, Marc Middleton, "Dirty" Dutch Mantel.

Contributing Photographers:
AP/Wide World Photos, Jack O'Shea, Bill Otten, A. Rettinger, Kaz Takahashi, Steve Dart, Mike Delany.

2121 Waukegan Road, Bannockburn, IL 60015
Phone: (847) 444-4880 • Fax: (847) 444-1153

Distributed by Warner Publisher Services and ADS Publisher Services, Inc.

H&S Media, Inc.

Harvey Wasserman .... Chief Executive Officer
Stephen D. Keen .... President
Michael M. Meyers .... Executive Vice President
Richard Pinder .... Vice President Controller
Bruce Jones .... Vice President of Sales & Circulation
Laura Grimaldi .... Director of Marketing & Promotions
Kathy Arthur .... Purchasing Coordinator
Kimberly Blair .... Production Coordinator
Jennifer Coyle .... Webmaster
Jill Djuric .... Corporate Imaging Manager
Rick Kieras .... Scanner Operator
Marketing Representative .... Timothy Towe
David Hagman .... Newsstand Circulation Manager
Jessica Vivirito .... Circulation Assistant
Patrick Julian .... National Advertising Director

Check out WOW Magazine on the Internet!

http://www.wowmagazine.com

Back orders of this magazine can be obtained by contacting:
World of Wrestling Magazine
ISI
30 Montgomery Street
Jersey City, NJ 07302
Phone: (800) 544-6748 Fax: (201) 451-5745
e-mail: isi@wwmag.com
The cost for a back ordered issue is the cover price of the issue + $2.50 postage and handling.

backtalk

Welcome to WOW

World of Wrestling magazine

By any name, a pro wrestling magazine like this has been a loooong time coming.

A magazine that's got the guts to tell it like it is. To give the fans what they want. A magazine like none other on the market today! Combining the best of what's truly great about the sport of pro wrestling – from interviews, profiles and action-packed coverage to inside news and rumors and the best color photography around – it's all here in World of Wrestling magazine. WOW, indeed!

We've assembled an elite staff of reporters, photographers, columnists, and experts in their field, and we're dedicated to produce the most exciting wrestling magazine you've ever seen. Complete coverage of the World Wrestling Federation, World Championship Wrestling, and Extreme Championship Wrestling, plus the indies and international scene. But that's just for starters.

Inside every issue of WOW, we'll give you an insider's perspective on some of the real people behind the ropes, the real stories behind the scenes, the real deals behind closed doors! It's what you've always wanted in a pro wrestling magazine! Now you've got it.

Check out our WOW profile of ***Bill Goldberg (see page 12)***! And you thought his tough-as-nails persona was some sort of gimmick! Pro football's loss was definitely pro wrestling's gain in the case of Goldberg. A true competitor. A true warrior. The true story. Don't miss this rare glimpse into the heart and soul of a real modern-day champion.

When you're done, take a peek at ***"Sable – Revealed!" (page 146)*** WOW's exclusive interview with one of the most provocative women in pro wrestling today. WOW's Women of Wrestling expert Marc Middleton sat down with Sable to talk about life, love, wrestling, and of course her highly-anticipated spread in "Playboy!"

Whether you crave features like the ***Hollywood Hogan story (page 130)***, the "Phantom of the Ring's" thoughtful review of the ***Bret Hart documentary (page 10)***, or just the hundreds of exclusive color photos, there's sure to be something for every wrestling fan in every issue of WOW.

But that's not all! Because we know wrestling fans tend to be a little extreme, we've included a ***"Raw Sports" department (page 168)***, jam-packed with news, notes and features of interest on all kinds of extreme sports! For you hardcore rock 'n' roll fans, don't miss Jim DeRogatis' review column ***"Testosterone Rock" (page 188)*** – enough said! And for you video game junkies out there, every month we'll roll out reviews of new and ***exciting games*** for you to check out ***(page 186)***.

After you put down this Premiere Issue of WOW (if you can!), take a look at our ***Web site (www.wowmagazine.com)*** – where you can keep up on what's new and exciting in the World of Wrestling, enter contests, purchase WOW merchandise, and MORE. While you're there, don't miss your opportunity to enter our "Grand Slam of Wrestling" Contest and win a trip for four to an exciting Pay-Per-View event.

The bottom line is this –WOW is determined to be THE BEST pro wrestling magazine you've ever seen. So let us know what you think!

Welcome to WOW.

Hope you like it!

Mike Morris

Mike Morris
Managing Editor

We want to hear from you!

Let us know what it is YOU want to see in YOUR wrestling magazine – WOW magazine. More interviews? More features? Different features? Got an idea? A thought? Gripe? Correction? Well, don't just sit there. Write to us. E-mail us. Yell out the window. Scream at your TV during "Nitro" on Mondays. But let us hear from you.

Here's how.

U.S. MAIL: H&S Media, Inc., 2121 Waukegan Road, Bannockburn, Illinois, 60015

E-MAIL: wowmagazine@hsmedia.com

Every issue, we'll publish the most interesting mail we receive in this very spot. Be sure to include a daytime telephone number, as we may need to verify identity or factual information prior to publication. NO MAIL WILL BE PUBLISHED unless it includes complete name, address and phone number. And, by all means, send pictures. We'll also publish photos of the "craziest" wrestling fans the World of Wrestling has to offer!

by Blake Norton

'Smart' is as 'smart' does

The entire wrestling industry has waited a long, long time for a "smart" magazine; one which deals with the sport for what it is. Yes, wrestling is generally pre-determined. Does that mean we enjoy it any less? Not in the slightest!

The difference between wrestling and boxing, football, basketball or any other sport for that matter is that wrestling promoters discovered a long, long time ago that people don't watch sports simply for "competition," but for entertainment as well. The fact that it's mainly the competitive nature of the sport from which they derive that entertainment is merely coincidental. There are many other factors which can be just as effective in capturing one's imagination.

Wrestling has always, and will always, keep changing the mix of what it provides in its sports entertainment programs to try and match the mood of the viewers – and hopefully attract more. Some would argue that in the current climate of wrestling promotion, through the barrage of screwjobs and far out angles, the original "competitive" nature on which the sport is based has been co-opted; but that's an argument for another day.

So what if you don't always find a contest that strictly meets the guidelines of what "competition" is? You also won't find off-seasons, walk-outs over billion dollar contracts or Pay-Per-Views with a 90-second main event. There's a little word known as "respect"; it takes an awful lot of respect to put a man over, to make your opponent look good, for the sake of the business, and that's the only difference between our sport and any other out there.

Perhaps wrestlers don't compete (or shouldn't, at least) to score more points or try to knock one another out – but they do compete just as passionately to put on the best performance, pull off the greatest moves and get the best crowd reaction.

Personally, I'd consider the motivation behind the latter endeavors to be at least as noble as its time-tested predecessors.

Are we proud of Shawn Michaels, of Shane Douglas, Ric Flair and Steve Austin? Are we proud to be fans of the sport, and admit to what it really is, the greatest combination of competition, athleticism, raw hard work and showmanship on the planet? Are we proud that boxers, football players, and everybody else is now actually jumping on the bandwagon we created, and laying out their interviews like wrestling, using entrance music like wrestling, showboating like wrestling, promoting like wrestling? Does

everyone want to be a part of the greatest show on earth?

As one prominent industry figure would say, "Oh Hell Yeah!"

Let me quickly introduce myself. My name is Blake Norton, editor of "The Bagpipe Report" (TBR) online wrestling newsletter (www.bagpipe-report.com). As many fans already know, there are numerous reports available from the so-called "sheets" – newsletters such as "The Observer," "The Torch," "The Figure Four," and many online publications including "TBR" (the largest!), "HWG" and others.

These reports bring a behind-the-scenes alternative to the so-called "mark mags," ("wrestling is real") which covers just about every wrestling magazine currently available in the U.S. Does that make the "smarts" better? Not necessarily, and here's why.

Because, smart is as smart does.

The strongest image which always comes to mind when I think of "the sheets" is that of Jim Duggan giving his retirement speech on "Thursday Thunder" shortly before he was to go under the knife to try and avert his bout with cancer.

In his teary-eyed address, at one point he referred to the sheets making fun of him, because of his low "workrate" and (self-imposed?) limited wrestling repertoire. At that moment, the thought that came to mind was this: "Here's a guy who started his career before any of us 'smart' guys were even around; a guy who has entertained fans for two decades; a guy who I've always respected and loved to see proudly walk the aisle with his American flag; and a guy who always had a smile for the kids and a warm attitude toward everyone I've known who've met him. And yet, he feels it necessary to refer to the callous criticism the 'sheets' have layed upon him."

It wasn't a feeling of regret on my part. "TBR" already knew he was announcing his retirement, and we gave our very best wishes, congratulating him on what had to be in anyone's book a phenomenal career. But I went surfing the Internet that night, and the majority of references to Duggan's retirement were laden with celebratory cheer. I couldn't, frankly, believe it! These "whiz-kids" were jumping up and down about a man having cancer! Why? Because of his supposed low "work rate."

Well, there's nothing "smart" about that at all.

But it did bring home, perhaps more profoundly than I would have liked, the fact that there are some aspects of the so-called "smart" publications I wish to be associated with...and some that I do not.

We write about the sport of pro wrestling because we love the sport. You, the fans, want to know what's really happening in the sport because you love the sport as well. We don't aim to "expose" anyone. We don't wish to criticize unnecessarily, or cause problems for anyone. We're just here to make our contribution.

So, on behalf of the staff of "The Bagpipe Report" and everyone else contributing to "WOW magazine," I invite you to form your own opinions. Any comments, suggestions, questions you may have are welcome; don't hesitate to send them in, we all hope you enjoy "World of Wrestling magazine!"

–Blake Norton
World of Wrestling Magazine
Blake Norton can be reached via E-mail at: editor@Bagpipe-Report.com

Jesse "The Governor" Ventura

Five years ago he was a play-by-play man for World Championship Wrestling. **Three years ago**, he had a bit part as a prison guard in one of the Batman movies. **Today**, Jesse "The Body" Ventura is the governor of Minnesota.

How did this 47-year-old former pro wrestler go from broadcasting "Wrestlemania" at the beginning of the 1990s to leading an entire state at the decade's end? His hardnosed, never-say-die attitude that carried him through the U.S. Navy, the WWF, the WCW and movie roles also carried him to this upset victory.

In defeating two major-party candidates, Ventura showed that anything is possible. "The Mind," as he now calls himself, showed the dedication that made him a great wrestler, broadcaster and actor and a fan-favorite throughout the 1980s and 1990s. Or, as he says,

"We've shocked the world."

AP/Wide World Photo

A&E's documentary on "Hitman" Hart really hits home

Having seen Bret Hart over the years on both TNT and USA, who would have thought we would get the best insight into his character on the A&E Network?

A&E (Arts and Entertainment Network) has discovered wrestling, or rather, that there are good ratings in wrestling programs. Its first entry into the field, "The Unreal Story of Professional Wrestling," fared surprisingly well, leading A&E to consider more wrestling programming. Not that we would see anything as ordinary as a wrestling show on the network—A&E is too highbrow for that. But we have seen such wrestling personalities as Jesse Ventura and Andre the Giant on A&E's "Biography."

And last December, this cable network treated us to an extraordinary documentary about a year in the life of a wrestler. That wrestler was Bret Hart.

Paul Jay's documentary, "Hitman Hart: Wrestling with Shadows," traces the life and times of Bret "Hitman" Hart leading up to that fateful day in Montreal at the WWF's "Survivor Series," where Hart, the champion of the WWF, was double-crossed out of his title. Little did Jay know when he began filming that he would stumble across the biggest controversy to hit wrestling in years, and the first time a wrestling champion has been double-crossed (or "hooked") since 1950 when Don Eagle got a fast three count in his defense against Gorgeous George.

But there is more to this film than simply wrestling. It's a chronicle of the day-to-day life of Hart, championship wrestler and one of Canada's most popular athletes. We meet the other members of the Hart family, the first family of wrestling: brothers-in-law Davey Boy Smith and Jim Neidhart, and brothers Owen and Keith. Only Keith is retired from the game. We also meet the parents, Helen and Stu Hart. Stu was a respected wrestler whose Stampede Wrestling promotion dominated Western Canada from the '50s to the early '80s, when he sold the promotion to Vince McMahon.

While we feel the love and

awe Bret has for his father, we also feel the distance between them—a distance that came from wrestling. Stu was on the road during much of Bret's childhood and Bret, despite other plans for his life, ended up going into the family business.

Bret tells us that wrestling was the last thing he considered doing, though as a child he participated in amateur wrestling. (It was his father's dream that Bret would make the Olympics.) But life has a strange way of working itself out. Stu needed wrestlers for his promotion and Bret became a professional wrestler. In fact, all Stu's sons worked in the business, either in the ring or behind the scenes. Stu's daughters all married or dated wrestlers.

Wrestling was more than the Hart family business—it was a way of life.

More importantly, we see the strains of this way of life on the family. Helen mentions that she hates wrestling. She didn't want her sons to become wrestlers nor her daughters to date them. This attitude is mirrored in Julie, Bret's wife of 14 years. She mentions the constant traveling that takes her husband away from his family, and while Bret sympathizes, this is his profession and it has its demands.

The demands of his profession are tearing Bret up inside. Should he leave the WWF, where he has worked for the last 14 years, and take a better paying contract with Ted Turner's WCW? It's not as easy a question as it looks. Bret has invested much time and loyalty in the WWF. We note during the course of the film that McMahon is a sort of father figure to Bret and that given his choice, Bret would like to stay put.

But other factors are at work. The WWF is changing. WCW, with former WWF superstars Hulk Hogan and Randy Savage in their stable, is making serious inroads into the WWF's dominance of wrestling. McMahon mistakenly allows two of his headliners—Diesel (Kevin Nash) and Razor Ramon (Scott Hall)—to sign with WCW. They join with Hogan to form the New World Order and cause WCW to skyrocket in popularity.

To keep up, McMahon has to do two things. One is to sign his biggest superstar, Bret, to a 20-year contract at $1 million per. The other thing is to change the course of WWF angles. They are leaning more toward sex than wrestling. Hart himself has had his character altered from good guy to bad guy, at least in the United States. In Canada he remains the hero.

This change of direction has Hart concerned. He criticizes what he sees as the WWF's descent into smut and voices concerns about characters like Shawn Michaels and Steve Austin being made into heroes by the American fans. He worries about Michaels, a wrestler he despises, taking his heat as lead heel. McMahon gives Bret permission to make a better deal. Hart accepts the WCW offer, which takes effect after the 1997 "Survivor Series."

Bret does not want to drop the title to Michaels, even though it's his last day with the WWF. He claims it would kill his character to do such a thing, to do a job to Michaels. What Hart did not mention was not only did he not want to drop the strap in Canada, he did not want to drop it to Michaels, a wrestler he personally despised. Hart preferred simply to do a successful defense and resign the title the next day. McMahon did not want that. His main objection was there was no guarantee Hart would do what he promised. McMahon already had suffered the humiliation of having his women's champion, Alundra Blaze (Debbie "Medusa" Miceli) suddenly turn up on WCW's flagship show, "Nitro," and toss her WWF belt into the trash as she announced she was now working for WCW. What would stop Bret from doing the same thing with the WWF title belt?

Bret's position was that he had been a loyal WWF employee for the last 14 years, at one point turning down a prior WCW offer to sign a longer-term contract at less money with the WWF. Now it was McMahon who was urging Bret to take the WCW offer. It was McMahon who wanted to let Hart out of his contract. Vince gives in to Bret and tells him the outcome will be a disqualification. The rest becomes another sordid piece of wrestling history.

Midway in the match, Michaels applies Bret's own sharpshooter to Bret. Bret is supposed to kick out, but before he does, McMahon orders the bell rung and Michaels declared the new champion on a submission. Hart is stunned. He spits on McMahon at ringside and later punches him out in his office before leaving. The film does an excellent job of not only showing us Bret's anguish, but also that of his wife, Julie, who can't believe her husband could be treated like that.

So who was really hurt in all this? Hart landed a contract paying him three times more a year for a reduced number of days. Meanwhile, McMahon was able to launch his most successful character to date—that of the evil Mr. McMahon, Corporate Promoter. In retrospect, letting Hart go was the best move McMahon had made in a long time. Sort of addition by subtraction.

Hart, however, may have been the biggest loser. Shortly after this documentary was released on A&E, his marriage to Julie ended in divorce.

In any case, no matter which side you're on, watch the documentary and decide all over again. It gives a rare, intelligent look into a game that has increasingly become a smutty cartoon. A&E will be repeating it in the future. Watch it. Tape it. It's a definite keeper.

***THE PHANTOM OF THE RING** column can be found on the Internet at www/angelfire.com.*
E-mail THE PHANTOM OF THE RING at phanring@aol.com

The music pounds. A solitary figure appears ... black boot ... black knee wraps ... black briefs ... black-padded gloves and black elbow pads – warrior accessories on a frame that has been ripped and chiseled from years of intense exercise, weight training, and dedication to excellence.

By Larry Burnett

You are standing in your underwear in front of thousands of raucous, rowdy fans. You turn around and a high-powered, bald-headed behemoth catapults into your rib cage. Your body crumbles and your lungs try not to collapse. You've been "speared" – planted in the canvas – by

GOLDBERG!

The Ironic Inside Story

You are exhausted, beaten up, barely standing.

Suddenly, your head is forced down, then crammed between bulging biceps, pumped-up pecs and a sweaty armpit. You feel a tug

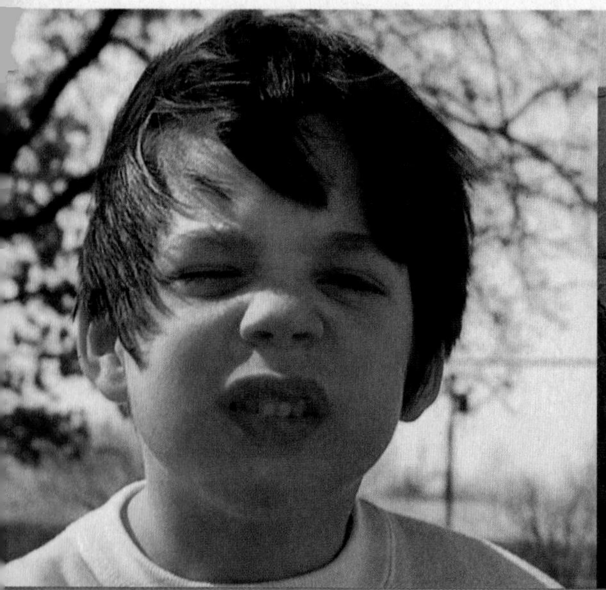

at your waistband. Before you know it, your head is down, your feet are up, your toes are tap-dancing in the sky. This mammoth mass of muscles dangles you there, upside down, toying with you. You cannot break free!

You are at his mercy, suspended, blood rushing to your head, awaiting your fate ... waiting ... waiting ... and then – BLAM!

Your opponent stands tall, then pivots. Your torso does a half twist in midair. Your back leads the way as your body tumbles and starts to drop. Your weight crashes to the mat and a 285-pound monster comes along for the ride, crushes the air out of you, forces your shoulders into the canvas, and yanks your leg for leverage. You vaguely hear a "1-2-3," a slapping sound on the mat, and a bell.

Finally, the attack is over. The bulky body sets you free. You are flattened and can't get up. There is a deafening roar from the crowd and a maniacal, animal-like roar from the creature that just demolished you. You've been "Jack-Hammered" and pinned by GOLDBERG!

Don't feel bad and don't bother getting up. You are just another step on the road to the top, traveled by one of the hottest shooting stars in the history of professional wrestling – Bill Goldberg!

Football Glory Days

His story is almost impossible to believe. In the late 1980s, Goldberg (yes, that is his real name) grabbed All-Southeastern Conference honors as a ruthless, predatory nose tackle at the University of Georgia. "Football News" named him second-team All-America behind Illinois' Mo Gardner, Notre Dame's Chris Zorich, and USC's Tim Ryan. Just for perspective, a pretty good lineman from the University of Miami, Russell Maryland, was a third-team pick that year.

Goldberg earned his accolades with hard-nosed play and tenacity. His powerful head-knocking play and his aggressive hand-to-hand combat in the collegiate ranks also earned the four-year letterman a reputation. Goldberg was the featured attacker in Georgia's "Junkyard Dogs" defense. He'd chase down, rough up, and bite into opponents. And when his teeth unclenched, Goldberg would bark right in their faces. His Georgia glory days were Goldberg's proving ground for attaining his life-long dream of playing in the National Football League.

Unknowingly, those Bulldog battles "between the hedges" may have also set the stage for Goldberg's current career in World Championship Wrestling.

Goldberg's grit and determination at Georgia got him drafted in 1990 by the L.A. Rams. He went in the 11th round, much later than he ever expected. When he finally got to play in the NFL, he didn't exactly tear up professional football, but he did manage to tear up various parts of his body on numerous occasions. In fact, his stints with the Rams and Atlanta Falcons were a blur of injuries, disappointments, and frustrations.

Finally, in 1994, major stomach surgery forced Goldberg to hang up his helmet and put his NFL dream to bed, way too early.

"Anybody who aspires to do something their entire life, then finally gets there and doesn't accomplish what they wanted to accomplish, you're gonna feel like you sold yourself short," Goldberg said in an exclusive interview for this article in WOW Magazine.

"In a way, I did, but, hell, once I look back on it, what is the percentage of people who even make it there? So that keeps me going."

At the age of 28, Goldberg's chase for a high-profile NFL career was over.

Professional wrestling was barely in his thoughts and definitely not on his short list of "things to do" to replace the thrill, excitement, and competition of NFL football.

"Throughout my entire life, I've known, and realized, that I AM NOT LIKE ANYBODY ELSE. I WANT TO BE DIFFERENT. I DON'T WANT TO FOLLOW THE SAME PATH."

Reality, though, was seeping in for Goldberg and was tough to face. His bank account was dwindling and his options were limited, at best.

"There really weren't any," Goldberg explained. "I could go back to school, could work as a personal trainer, which is a dead-end job, or I could get a regular job like everyone else.

"I had to try to find something that my football career could carry over to," he added. "All the years, all the blood, sweat and tears that I sacrificed to get where I was in the NFL game. I knew there had to be something out there that likened itself to pro football. It was very limited! To be able to compare something to professional athletics, it's quite hard. So, I had to search high and low. Wrestling was always an option. It was always an option. It was never in the back of my mind that I would actually take the option."

In fact, Goldberg was adamantly opposed to climbing into the wrestling racket at that time. During his college days at Georgia, and his NFL-playing days with the Falcons, Goldberg had rubbed shoulders in the Atlanta area with several professional wrestlers. Goldberg worked out at Main Event Fitness, the gym owned by Lex Luger and Sting, in Doraville, Ga. He impressed them with his size, strength, agility, and personality, but Goldberg made it clear – he wanted nothing to do with their sport.

"They always put it in my ear, 'Well, you'd be a good wrestler. You've got the look and you're athletic.' I just said, 'You've got to be kidding! I'd never do that!' I have a lot more pride in myself than to go out there in

my underwear and wrestle in front of millions of people."

Then Goldberg laughed and said, "Look at me now! When I made that statement, it was prior to me finding out how much money these goons make."

MY, HOW TIMES CHANGE

Fast forward to now.

This football guy who never wanted to be a professional wrestler is now in his second season with World Championship Wrestling. He has taken the sport by storm. Goldberg brings a "no-nonsense, take-no-prisoners" approach to the craft. His incredible crowd appeal and marketability have rocketed the former nightclub bouncer on the fastest track ever to wrestling superstardom.

Goldberg's goateed mug is a fixture on the covers of just about every wrestling magazine, and he has made his mark in the mainstream as well with a cover for "TV Guide," "People" Magazine, "The New Yorker," "Rolling Stone," and "Spin Magazine." "The New York Daily News" and "USA Today" jumped on his story and so did "EXTRA," the tabloid TV show. Last fall, Goldberg made his acting debut on "Love Boat: The New Wave," and the 32-year-old wrestler will be seen in the fall of '99 on the big screen starring opposite Jean Claude Van Damme in "Universal Soldiers: The Sequel."

Not bad for a reluctant wrestler.

Incredible for the WCW, which almost let Goldberg slip through its bare knuckles in 1996 – to its rival, the World Wrestling Federation.

"I came up with a wrestling idea that I thought was different. Nobody else had done it," Goldberg recalled. "With the package I brought to the table, I thought I could be different. I thought I could be successful, with my work ethic and my martial arts background, and me training so hard. If I put my mind to it, I think I can do just about anything. So, I finally put my mind to it."

Goldberg was in great shape, muscular from years of workouts and preparation for the wars of collegiate and professional football. He was 6'4," 285 pounds and "cut." His chiseled physique was tailor-made for wrestling, and his shaved head and trademark antlers tattoo on his left shoulder didn't hurt "the look."

Goldberg figured that his football background and training, combined with his hard-nosed tenacity and desire to learn the wrestling game, would give him an innovative approach to the business – one that,

Goldberg on the set of the Love Boat

Goldberg hoped, would land him a shot at professional wrestling's big paydays.

"I made a call to Eric Bischoff (President of World Championship Wrestling) and I inquired," Goldberg said. "Then I went to an event with Lex and Sting. I talked with Bischoff a little bit more and inquired more. They never called me back! And then I said, 'Time is running out here!' So I contacted the WWF. They made me an offer and it was terrific and everything, but it was just so hard."

Goldberg was offered a solid, seven-year, guaranteed deal by the WWF and was just hours away from signing it when the WCW finally called. He was miffed that Bischoff had taken such a long time to show interest in him, but Goldberg also had misgivings about hooking up with the World Wrestling Federation.

"Number one, I didn't know anybody up there (at the WWF)," Goldberg said. "Number two, I didn't want to move to Connecticut. I was in the process of trying to buy a house, so it just wasn't the right time for me to get up and move. So, finally the WCW gave me a call. The morning of my meeting with the WWF for my contract signing. They called me that morning!"

Goldberg postponed his WWF signing to hear what Bischoff had to offer, and in September of 1996, he signed a developmental deal with World Championship Wrestling. It basically came down to opportunity, familiarity, and location, location, location. The house that Goldberg was buying was located outside of Atlanta, the home base for the WCW.

"No question, that made all the difference in the world," Goldberg admitted. "That, and the fact that I knew so many of the people here. I felt like I was, kind of, at home."

But wait a minute! Wrestling? Goldberg's NFL career had been punctuated by a laundry list of injuries. How could he expect to survive, with no pads and no helmet, in the rugged world of professional wrestling. With all the travel, all the lifts, flips, and flops? In 1993, when he was with the Falcons, Goldberg suffered what appeared to be a severe groin injury, but he still limped his way through the entire NFL schedule. Then, during the offseason, he had surgery to repair the painful problem. Goldberg had to have the operation. It was a necessity, but it killed any chance he had of hooking on with the brand-new Carolina Panthers, who had picked him in the 1994 expansion draft.

"I decided right after the Falcons' season," Goldberg remembered. "Team doctors are team doctors. They're self-serving in the sense that they want to get you ready, or they want to do whatever they can to make you a part of the team, if you are valuable enough. I wasn't happy with their diagnosis. I found my own doctor and bing, bang, boom, he found out what the deal was. I got it operated on and got it taken care of."

"Unfortunately, it took me a long time to recover and I went to Carolina right after my surgery and I couldn't even walk. I couldn't even jog. So I was on this expansion team, but I was hurt and couldn't perform for about a month while they were trying to put a team together. It was the

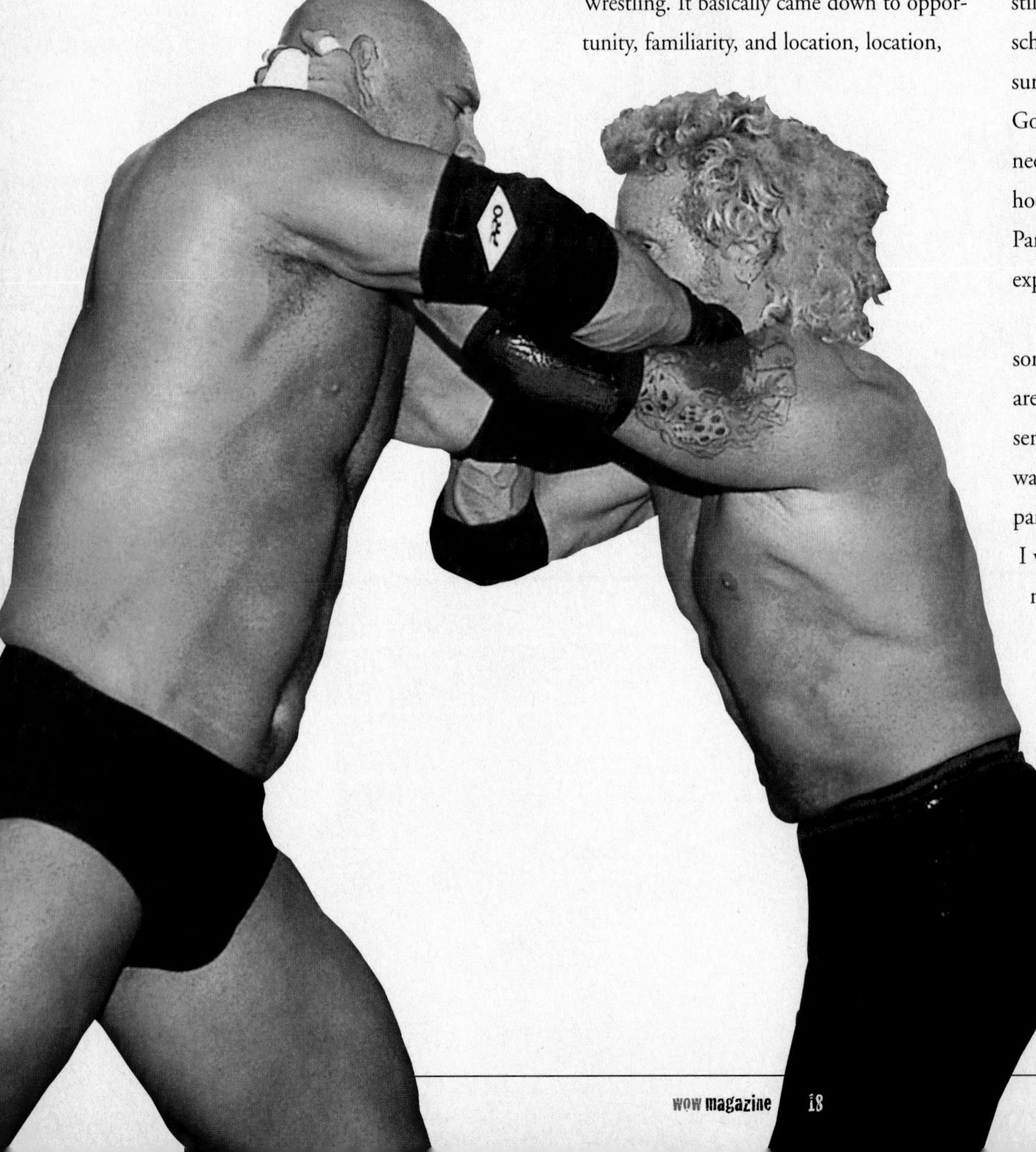

worst scenario I ever could have imagined!"

Get this! Goldberg's injury wasn't just a groin pull. He had torn the stomach muscle right off his pelvic bone. Dr. William Meyers, now the Chairman of Surgery for the University of Massachusetts Memorial Medical Systems, reattached the abdominal muscle with an innovative procedure that he had used on the NHL's Claude Lemieux, soccer's Eric Wynalda, and many others.

"People didn't understand it very well and thought if it wasn't a hernia, you shouldn't operate on the groin for this sort of thing," Dr. Meyers explained. "The main abdominal muscles insert on the pubis and the adjacent ligaments. Basically, there is a rip and they are torn away. What you do (to fix it) is create a broad band of attachment so you are reattaching and reinforcing the muscle so that it doesn't rip again."

Dr. Meyers has a 96 percent success rate with these procedures, but Goldberg's surgery happened so close to the Panthers' mini-camps that he didn't have time to recover and never got to show his true stuff. Carolina waived Goldberg. His NFL window of opportunity slammed shut in the spring of 1994.

The surgery, however, was a success!

Three years after the operation, Goldberg was a headliner for the WCW, leaving opponent after opponent in his wake, and putting more strain on his abs and groin muscles than the rigors of the NFL ever did.

His signature move, the "Jack Hammer," is a vertical suplex. Goldberg lifts incredibly large wrestlers (for example, the 550-pound "Giant"), turns them upside down, holds them in the air, then pivots, rides his opponent's chest to the canvas, and hammers him into the mat for the pin.

Holy abdominals, Goldberg! Even your surgeon can't believe what you're up to.

"Our aim is to get athletes back to previous performance status, or above," Dr. Meyers explained. "I've achieved that, fortunately, in most of the patients that I have operated on. But I still can't imagine doing the sort of stuff he (Goldberg) is doing. That's impressive to me, no matter who it is! Absolutely! It's very impressive!"

Goldberg learned the wrestling "ropes" during three months of intense training and workouts at the WCW's Power Plant training site in Atlanta.

Plant director Dwayne Bruce pushed Goldberg through concentrated, one-on-one sessions to get him ready for the ring. Those sessions led to practice (dark) matches in Orlando. With the help of Bruce, Goldberg caught on quickly and found that there wasn't much he couldn't do.

"(Bruce) is the leader of the Power Plant, and if it wasn't for him, I wouldn't be where I am now." said Goldberg, his voice tensing as he continued. "Bischoff just thought I was another football player who wanted to wrestle. Dallas Page has helped me along the way, but in no way, shape, or form has any one person molded me, molded my career moreso than Dwayne Bruce. Anyone out there who takes credit for it (and Dwayne wouldn't take credit for it) is full of it."

At The Plant, Goldberg soaked up all the wrestling technique and "know-how" he could handle. It was there that he answered any, and all, questions about his strength and durability by learning and mastering the "Jack Hammer."

"I picked up that big giant guy, Reese (who is close to 500 pounds)," Goldberg said. "He was the guy I originally formed the move on. I figured if I could do it to him down at the school, I could do it to anybody. You always worry about past injuries. Unfortunately, when people focus on that, they always get hurt! The thing I do is: I don't even think about it. I feel that if I'm prepared enough, physically, to go in there, then I'm prepared enough to do whatever it takes to perform."

THE DEBUT

Goldberg got his first chance to perform – on live national television – on Sept. 22, 1997 in Salt Lake City, Utah. It was WCW Monday Nitro on TNT. He was still called "Bill Goldberg" back then. There was no special introduction, no fanfare, no exciting entrance. Truth is, that night, when WCW announcer Tony Schiavone introduced Bill Goldberg for the very first time, he played up the fact that this new guy in the ring was a virtual unknown in professional wrestling circles.

"We have a newcomer, Bill Goldberg," Schiavone told his TNT viewers, "a man we know absolutely nothing about. He is making his debut here and from the looks of him, he is very determined and looks very powerful."

If there are pro-wrestling history books, let them

FOOTHILL
98

FOOTBALL

record that Bill Goldberg's first televised bout was against Hugh Morris (a.k.a. "Humorous").

Goldberg's first move was a forearm to Morris's head.

The new kid was down for a "two-count" early in the match but, later, he kicked out of Morris's signature move, "No Laughing Matter," a back flip made by the 300-pound wrestler off the top rope and right onto Goldberg, who was sprawled on his back in the middle of the ring. Goldberg did a standing back flip of his own later in the match and body-slammed Morris twice. That led WCW announcer Bobby Heenan to inject, "Hey, pretty agile for a big Goldberg!"

All right, it wasn't exactly a clinic, nor the most creative or technically-attractive match ever. Goldberg wrestled with little, or no, emotion. There was no "spear" (the football tackling move Goldberg later added to his devastating repertoire) but the raw rookie did get Morris up and down with a wobbly vertical suplex move (later named the "Jack Hammer") and pinned the veteran in 2:42. Goldberg turned to the camera and said "That's number one!"

"I WAS HORRIBLE!" Goldberg growled. "I'M STILL HORRIBLE! That first match was excruciating! I was more nervous than I think I've ever been in my life. You know, when you go out there, you want people to like you. If you force it, they're not gonna like you, so I just went out and did my job. Thanks to Hugh Morris, I got over pretty well in that first match and I started on my mystique right there. I came from nowhere. People didn't know who I was. That's what I wanted."

After his first bout, Goldberg blew off announcer, "Mean" Gene Okerlund, who wanted a television interview. The next week, he pushed the camera aside and stalked off during a similar request. The die was cast. Bill Goldberg's wrestling persona was evolving. Fans were catching on. World Championship Wrestling was taking notice, but the man who was once known as one of college football's best "quote machines" was keeping mysteriously quiet, almost silent.

"It was my idea, first of all," Goldberg said. "If my character is based on realism, then I'm not going to go out there and give your stereotypical wrestling, screaming, yelling, interview. That's the one thing I didn't want to do, is be molded as a 'professional wrestler.' That's what separates me. It creates intrigue. People don't know much about you, so therefore, they are intrigued. They come to their own conclusions. I'm letting my work in the ring do my talking. When I talk, it's like my work in the ring. It's short, it's sweet, it's to the point and it has a purpose!"

THE ENTRANCE

Pro wrestling fans took to Bill Goldberg in a hurry. As his popularity grew, so did his undefeated record, and so did his marketability. Crowds began chanting his name long before the wrestler ever entered the arena. Goldberg remembers the first time he heard it.

"Washington D.C., last year, during the hockey playoffs," he recalled. "I was standing, getting ready to go up on the stage for my entrance and I'm a bigger hockey fan than I am a football fan, and, to me, that was kind of like a hockey chant. It sent chills up and down my spine. It was just awesome! Its hard to describe. I was very honored."

Goldberg picked some pounding, ominous-sounding, almost dirge-like battle march music to announce his presence. Then, he teamed with WCW's pyrotechnic wizzes to create an entrance that makes Goldberg the focal point, the sizzling centerpiece of what has to be the hottest entrance in all of sports.

PICTURE THIS! You are Goldberg's opponent. You stand in the ring waiting. His music begins. Fans chant and cheer. Focus shifts to the WCW stage at the end of the arena. The music pounds. A solitary figure appears ... black boot ... black knee wraps ... black briefs ... black-padded gloves and black elbow pads – warrior accessories on a frame that has been ripped and chiseled from years of intense exercise, weight training, and dedication to excellence. As you stand there and wait, the specimen steps from the darkness towards his mark on the metallic stage. Spotlights hit him. The man's neck builds like a mountain, starting at the shoulders and rippling its way north to his bald peak. He stops. Head bows. Huge arms dangle at his sides. There is peace, momentary peace.

Then, THE PYROTECHNICS FIRE OFF! The noise is startling! Sparkling stars of fire shoot from left and right, directly at the wrestler until he disappears in flashes of light and smoke. Moments later, the figure reappears, looking even more formidable, more forbidding, more ferocious. Goldberg has swallowed up the fire. He breathes out the smoke. He's a human dragon wearing black jockey shorts.

Schiavone put it best, "You can't even set the man on fire!"

Goldberg loves his incendiary entrance so much it hurts – literally. So, what's his inflammable secret?

"I douse myself with as much water as possible so that I don't spontaneously combust or ignite, but it is such a unique entrance, it's something that I can withstand because of its originality and how it sets itself off from everyone else's entrance," Goldberg said. "I endure through it because of the effect. It hurts! It burns for sure! It's kind of like sticking a big sparkler up your nose. I try

You know, when you go out there, you want people to like you. If you force it, they're not gonna like you, so I just went out and did my job.

not to breathe very much of it at all. Unfortunately, you have to weigh the ill effects of it!"

When Goldberg steps out of the fireworks, his glaring eyes rivet on the target – YOU! The face twists and contorts. The massive neck flexes. The powerful forearms rise from his sides as if to lift the already-standing throng to its tiptoes, like a muscle-bound evangelist raising his flock. The goateed mouth roars open wide, fireworks blast off behind him, and Goldberg blasts out a primitive, guttural scream – "ERRAAAAAAAAAAAAAAAAHHHH!"

Tendons tense! Muscle fibers flex and activate. It's time to go to work. Goldberg's march to his roped office begins. Time to take care of business. With each heavy stride, there is a head slap, or a neck stretch, a spit, a slashing uppercut, or a series of boxing combinations all designed to prepare this warrior for battle. Barely a few feet separate the wrestler from the fanatics who reach, claw, and clamor to get close to him. The decibel level reaches the danger point. Distractions are all around, but Goldberg locks in on the task at hand, playing his role, pleasing the crowd, and putting away his opponent as quickly, powerfully, and dramatically as he can.

In Fargo, North Dakota, Goldberg made fast work of journeyman Barry Darsow, and broke the veteran's ribs with a "back-breaker" in the process.

In Colorado Springs, Goldberg got hit with a chair, hit in the head with a STOP sign, battled the entire "Flock," "Jack-Hammered" the gargantuan Reese, and still managed to pin Raven in 4:58 to win the U.S. Heavyweight Championship. Goldberg got up off the canvas, contorted his face into a maniacal mask, stuck out his tongue and roared like a mad walrus. He grabbed the championship belt, held it up for all to see and looked right into the TNT camera and yelled, "IT'S MINE!" His career record was 75-0.

On July 6, 1998, Goldberg went home to the Georgia Dome in Atlanta. More than 40,000 fans were there and a national cable television audience was watching on TNT. Goldberg did away with Scott Hall in 5:35 to earn the right to meet the reigning champ and head bad guy, Hollywood Hogan, that same night. Less than a year on the wrestling circuit and Goldberg was getting his first shot at the WCW/nWo World Heavyweight title.

He conquered "Hollywood" faster than Spielberg. Goldberg used just 8:11 to win the unified championship and run his record to 108-0.

The Atlanta crowd chanted "Gold-berg, Gold-berg" for a full three minutes until the Nitro show went off the air, and for several minutes more after that. Goldberg climbed up on the ropes, held the championship belts high, worked the Georgia Dome crowd, and realized he had found the "rush" that had been missing.

"It was like someone shot a lightning bolt through my body," Goldberg offered in

4
Life

"Seventy-five percent of the people in the world think wrestling is fake," he said

"Fifty percent of them think that they know it's fake.

I put a bit of doubt in every one of those people's minds.

That's my job!"

a reverential tone. "I wouldn't have wanted to be any other place in my life. It was a thrill to have all those people yelling for me. It was something I never got playing football. I guess it filled that void."

AH, THE SWEET SMELL OF SUCCESS!

WCW had found something, too. A new cash cow with which to stuff its already overflowing coffers! Goldberg's title bout with Hogan last July drew a 6.9 quarter-hour television rating, the highest ever for pro wrestling on cable. The replay of his October championship match with Diamond Dallas Page proved even better: a 7.2 rating, which made it the most-watched wrestling match ever televised on cable.

Goldberg's stock was taking off and his merchandise was moving out the door at an incredible rate. Goldberg action figures, sweatshirts, mugs, necklaces, jerseys, caps, collector cars, t-shirts, trading cards, posters, plaques, plates, blankets, and boxer shorts were ringing up huge sales. His appearance with Kevin Nash last fall on QVC helped the cable shopping channel haul in more than half a million dollars from WCW merchandise sales in just one hour.

According to Michael Weber, WCW's Director of Marketing, "Goldberg is the top-selling product that we have going. He is the No. 1 individual selling product out there. He is a big part of the overall success that we are experiencing right now in licensing and retail merchandising."

A big part of the more than 200 million dollars that the WCW raked in in 1998 was from merchandise sales alone. All this money, exposure, recognition, celebrity, marketability and success came quickly for Goldberg. It still has the wrestler a bit surprised, yet surprisingly humble.

"Hey man, I'm no different than anybody else," Goldberg said in a matter-of-fact way. "I'm just on TV twice a week. Its flattering! It obviously helps my career, but there's nothing that's been done, or nothing that can be done, that will change how I am. It's flattering! It's embarrassing! I'm just happy to be in the position I am in, to be able to get the credit that I do. It doesn't mean I'm more special than anybody, it just means that I'm lucky."

Lucky to be extremely successful at a job he never really wanted. Goldberg's meteoric rise, though, has not come without sacrifices. You see, he never, ever, wanted to shave his chest and body hair. Now he does it, regularly, to get that super-smooth, high-definition, body-builder look. It may be necessary, but it sure ain't fun!

"I've cut myself many times," Goldberg said, and then laughed. "It just adds to my number of scars. It makes me look like a warrior. Going out there looking like Wolfman doesn't carry over too well."

He never, ever, ever wanted to perform wearing wrestling briefs. Now Goldberg's black "trunks" are his everyday work clothes! That wasn't supposed to happen!

"No, I did everything I could to get away from that," Goldberg said. "I wanted to wear a wrestling singlet, football pants, or something. I was digging for anything to not have to wear my underwear out there."

Minor sacrifices, I think you'll agree, when you stack them up against Goldberg's enormous professional, and monetary, success so far. He should feel luckiest that wrestling fans across America have taken to him and taken him in so quickly. They accepted him right away and bought in to his Neanderthal character. Lucky, that WCW's brass picked up on the fan reaction and put Goldberg's career on a "smart" missile to the top of the profession. Fortunate, that he has taken his opportunity and made the very most of it.

Goldberg says his connection with wrestling fans is based on a simple formula.

"Seventy-five percent of the people in the world think wrestling is fake," he said "Fifty percent of them think that they know it's fake. I put a bit of doubt in every one of those people's minds. That's my job!"

Goldberg goes to great lengths to create that doubt. He really, and truly, beats up lockers and dents doors with his bald head as part of his pre-bout ritual/psych session.

"It's quite similar to what I did to psych myself up for football," he said as if this was, somehow, normal. "I hit a couple lockers, butt the doors with my head and I'm ready to go. I just kind of get in the zone. That's what does it for me. I've got to go out there and be an intense character from the get-go, not just when I get in the ring and get hit! From the beginning on, from when the fans see me on, I HAVE GOT TO BE ON!"

You want real? Buck Martin, the V.P. of Booking and Events Services at the Great Western Forum, got the true picture last summer in Los Angeles, when Goldberg was gearing up backstage for a WCW Cage match.

"Bill comes out and he's getting fired up, breathing heavy, and pumping his chest out," Martin recalled. "Right when they announced his name, he turned and put his head into the steel case fire door and put a dent in it that was probably about and inch deep and five inches in diameter. You see the strength and the girth of these doors, you can't believe that somebody human could do something like that. You'd have to take a bat to put a dent in a door like that. That's just not normal!"

But it is real! So was the stun gun, or cattle prod, that intruder Scott Hall used to "zap" Goldberg on December 27, during his championship defense match against Kevin Nash at "Starrcade" in Washington, D.C. Goldberg was 173-0 going into that match, but due to the electrifying circumstances,

he got pinned, suffered the first loss of his career, and Nash walked away with the championship belts.

Goldberg knew he couldn't go undefeated forever, but the man hates to lose at anything.

He also hates to hear people question his profession, his athletic abilities, or those of his wrestling colleagues.

Goldberg understands that he is part athlete-part actor, but he is constantly seeking reality in the fantasy land of sports and entertainment.

So, whatever you do, if you run into Bill Goldberg, don't ask him if what he does is fake, because you may find out first-hand!

"My answer is, if you think it's fake, stand 10 feet away from me," Goldberg challenges, "and let me hit you with my tackle. If you can get up and brush it off and laugh, then it's fake. Not too many people have taken me up on that!"

Nor will they!

Larry Burnett is a freelance writer from Agoura Hills, Calif. He was a sportscaster for ESPN Sportscenter for 5 years and currently does radio broadcasts of the Los Angeles Lakers.

by Blake Norton, "TBR" Editor

'Wrestlemania' Lives On

"Tradition" is seeping from this sport faster than Rey Mysterio running the 100-yard dash on a caffeine overdose.

Screw jobs, run-ins, hirings, firings, overpriced merchandise, pay-per-view two or three times a month, backstabbing, satanic rituals, suicidal stunts and death-defying leaps, 20 hours of wrestling television a week, feuds that start on a Monday and conclude within a week while never making much sense to begin with...the list goes on.

We are indeed experiencing a roller-coaster ride of revolutionary proportions in the wrestling business, and a major change in how the public and media view our sport.

Even insiders will acknowledge we are witnessing a metamorphosis in the basic principles that drive the industry. This began only recently, forcing a business that seemed reluctant to evolve from the status quo to shift into high gear. But beneath all the rubble, the changes, the development and discarding of talent, one modern tradition has managed to stand the test of time—"Wrestlemania."

For the 15th time, "Wrestlemania" fever has swept the industry as fans and journalists alike gear up for "The Granddaddy of Them All." Last time around, we were treated to one match of epic proportions. However, the rest of the afternoon proved entirely forgettable. The undercard included a tag team battle royale (a mess by anyone's standards), another frustrated attempt by Ken Shamrock to win the Intercontinental championship from Rocky Maivia, and an injured Owen Hart failing to put away Triple H for the Euro strap.

It may well have qualified as one of the worst "Wrestlemanias" of all time, until the main event. At that time, Shawn Michaels walked the aisle a champion and left the ring a legend.

Before the match, rumors were flying that the world champ wouldn't show up; some even said he'd never wrestle again. Three months earlier, Michaels had destroyed his lower back taking a hellacious bump when the Undertaker dumped him awkwardly on the casket in their "Royal Rumble" gimmick match. In the buildup to his title match with "Rumble" winner Steve Austin, Michaels missed several weeks of TV tapings.

At no point along the way did he involve himself physically in any of the angles played out on "Raw." When the February "In Your House" main event rolled around, (an eight-man tag booked to build heat between team captains Michaels and Austin), Michaels didn't even make it to the arena.

Yet, coming off the farcical "Starrcade" of 1997 (which saw Bret Hart restart the main event when Sting lost via pinfall to Hulk Hogan), the world champ put his career on the line to put Austin over. By so doing, Michaels passed along the torch, cleanly establishing his conqueror as the top man in the federation—a role injury forced upon him. Michaels' actions would ultimately lead to the WWF stealing back the pole position in the almighty Monday night ratings war.

What led to Michaels' actions? Perhaps he was concerned about what people would say about him. Maybe he was afraid that not putting Austin over would make him look bad. Possibly, he thought he had something to prove. Or, did he do what he did because under the ego and self-promotion beats the heart of a true champion? Whatever the reason, it happened at "Wrestlemania." The tradition of providing a unique moment in wrestling history was again intact.

On March 20, 1999, the talent of the World Wrestling Federation returns to Philadelphia, as once again a large roster of wrestlers pick their numbers and take their places. After their seeding is determined, they will partake in the most-recognized annual Pay-Per-View event in the world. Can they again live up to expectations? Can they provide that one moment that will make "Wrestlemania XV" memorable? It's hard to say.

The tradition of excellence almost died in 1997—in fact, it would have if it wasn't for Hart and Austin. If you recall, they tore the house down in a wild brawl in front of a hot Chicago crowd. This was backed up by a physically brutal six-man tag match involving hometown boys The LOD and Ahmed Johnson taking on the Nation of Domination in a violent no-D.Q. pier 6'er. If not then, it came very close to ending in 1998, when the whole evening lacked originality and electricity until the final event.

With the overall quality of PPV wrestling at an all-time low, the newfound emphasis on Monday TV, and an increasingly short amount of time available to prepare for every PPV broadcast, can Titan pull it out for the big one? History would suggest the answer is "yes." For the first time in the past 12 months, will we enjoy a PPV that doesn't end with: "For the answers to these questions, tune in Monday Night?"

Modern booking tells us "no." Whether it's Austin, The Rock, Mick Foley, The Undertaker, or Kane, the real main event at "Wrestlemania" won't be about titles or competition. It will be about tradition, and will offer us a glimpse into the future of the business.

Who's going to be at Wrestlemania?

The New Age Outlaws

During "In Your House XIV" in '96, Billy Gunn appeared as "Rockabilly" and Jesse James was a child-hugging country singer. Obviously, they both needed help. But nobody ever imagined when they first got together that The New Age Outlaws would dominate the Legion of Doom. They would go on to win three tag team titles and become the "PWI" Tag Team of the Year for 1998. Now, with Jammes having won the Hardcore Champion and his partner vying for the Intercontinental belt, the future of the team is in doubt. But at the end of "Wrestlemania," we should know if they're still a team at all.

The Rock

Three months after his WWF debut, he emerged as the most hated face in the business. Nine months later, he was a successful heel. And 15 months after that, he was a champion. Then two years after entering the WWF, he became heavyweight champion of the world. The Rock is now one of the key players in the WWF. Look for him to make a big impact on "Wrestlemania." Could The Rock enter his first "Wrestlemania" main event at the age of 27?

Steve Austin

The man who defeated Savio Vega for the Million Dollar Belt in his first outing, competed in the match of the year in the '97 installment with Bret Hart and dethroned Shawn Michaels in the main event last year hopes to make it four great "Wrestlemania" performances in a row. You can bet Austin's looking to get his World Title back. If so, he'd be the first WWF star to become World Champion three times in a year.

Mick Foley

After his performance at the "Royal Rumble," can anyone be sure of what the former world champ has in store for "Wrestlemania?" Foley has never been a "main event" personality. Many thought he'd never win a world title because his style was so anti-politics, anti-ego, anti-muscleman and showboating. Who on earth could ever have pictured Mankind as a world champion and on the cover of magazines? As a face? But now Foley is on top, so be afraid—be very afraid, because the most controversial world champion of all time is headed to "Wrestlemania!"

Hunter Hearst Helmsley

Until it became apparent that back surgery would keep his former DX Stablemate Shawn Michaels out of action, Helmsley was on the verge of facing his former mentor in a technical marathon. Now it's all about the Corporation—will the former European and IC champ be looking for gold? Or are his intentions strictly personal, since Vince McMahon's Corporation has declared war on DX?

The Undertaker

Reuniting with Paul Bearer, (his former manager for six years) and redefining the WWF's definition of "hardcore" with Mick Foley, the WWF's most consistent wrestler of the '90s looks to be making a big impact at "Wrestlemania." And why not? It's the same event where he pinned top stars such as Jimmy Snucka, Jake Roberts, King Kong Bundy, Sid and Diesel. Without a doubt, The Undertaker's attitude for "Wrestlemania XV" will prove as bad as ever. Right now, don't be surprised if he's not out for titles, but for blood!

exposed...wwf

by Blake Norton, TBR Editor

"Royal Rumble"

January 24, 1999 / Anaheim, Calif.

Hardcore Champion "Road Dog" Jesse James vs. Big Bossman (Hardcore Title not on the line)

The Background: Road Dog won the Hardcore title from Bossman several weeks ago on "RAW." Degeneration X and The Corporation are feuding heavily; this match is an offshoot.

The Action: The crowd was into it from the start, though Armstrong's intros always get a good reaction; the match would tell the tale.

Both seasoned veterans worked the crowd really well to start with. Bossman held character, screaming at Dogg in the corner and arguing with the ref about open hands. Working the crowd to cover for sub-standard in-ring wrestling on a PPV is always dangerous, because it works for the live crowd but generally not for those at home.

The tempo slowed after the initial five minutes; Bossman took control, and just didn't interest the crowd with his punches. It's not that he didn't put the effort in; he did well in working the moves he did use, and took a top rope bump which isn't easy for a 275-pounder. However, the crowd didn't get back into it until James took control and hit his typical offense, including the "wiggle elbow drop." Bossman caught him with a sudden Bossman slam.

The Finish: Bossman hit the slam at 12:15 for a clean pinfall.

Intercontinental Title match: "Bad Ass" Billy Gunn (challenger) vs. Ken Shamrock (champion)

The Background: Gunn defeated Shamrock in a non-title match a few weeks before on "RAW"; he also exposed his Mr. Ass to Shamrock's "sister" leading into the match.

The Match: The match started fast; Gunn went for a series of clotheslines and brawled with pace, taking control of the champion. He's added a delayed vertical suplex to his repertoire. Two minutes in, Gunn charged at Shamrock in the corner and missed, nailing his shoulder into the ring post. Shamrock took control with kicks, slams and a kneelift. At this point Shamrock's weak offense was exploited; he's primarily a defensive wrestler and shouldn't be given time to expose his one-dimensional brawling-based offensive moves.

Shamrock took to the left ankle, using a pressure-based offense and a series of stiff kicks to set up his ankle lock finisher. Gunn continued to play underdog, scoring with rare shots, generally dominated by his powerful aggressor. Shamrock hit a fisherman's suplex with a sound bridge for the two, then inadvertently took out the referee with a clothesline. Gunn and Shamrock then clotheslined each other, resulting in all three men being laid out on the canvas.

Val Venis ran in and hit a DDT, planting Shamrock into the mat with the referee knocked out. Gunn slowly crawled over to the semi-conscious champion and made the cover, as we witnessed the "groggy ref" spot; the crowd counted "One...Two...Thr - No!" The spot really worked here, and the ref regained his senses soon after.

Gunn took control, hit a slam and went to the top. Shamrock ducked out of the way as the challenger sailed into the mat, re-aggravating his ankle; that was all the opportunity the champion needed, as he circled his prey and viciously locked in the ankle lock. A helpless Gunn was forced to tap out at 14:30, and put his dream of being champion on hold for another night.

The Finish: Another clean finish. Shamrock's offense is generally limited, and while he can really go, it takes a Shawn Michaels, Steve Austin or otherwise to encourage him to display his repertoire of suplexes.

European Championship Match: X-Pac (champ) vs. Gangrel (challenger)

The Background: Not much to speak of. Two great lightweight wrestlers, one title; works for me.

The Match: X-Pac started off fast, as both men displayed their speed. The tempo of the match was high, with lightning-like kicks coming from the Kid (Sean Waltman). Waltman can really work a match well, so while he has the necessary buzz-moves (X-Factor, Bronco Buster), he can really wrestle all the way through a match. He also has a tendency to bust his ass and take major bumps, and this was no exception. Gangrel is also a very sound wrestler, with tremendous execution and a sound repertoire of good looking moves in the ring.

X-Pac hit a belly to back suplex, and followed it up with a lightning legdrop for the two. He went to work on Gangrel in the corner, but missed when charging in after an Irish whip. Gangrel hit a splash on the exposed champion in the corner and came back with a double-arm belly to belly suplex. Great start to the match.

After a brief resthold, Gangrel tossed Waltman six feet in the air, with his hapless foe left to smack with a sickening thud into the canvas. He missed a senton splash from the top rope, and the Kid came back with a series of great kicks and a flying clothesline. Double reversals, another kick from X-Pac, with some real hang time on the spin. The crowd popped big for the Bronco Buster.

Another spinning heel kick, X-Pac went to the top but was crotched by the challenger who climbed up to attempt a superplex. Waltman sent him flying backwards into the mat, and launched himself with a flying bodypress. Gangrel reversed it with a roll-though, and the ref counted three by mistake; The crowd chanted "You f**ked up"; the crowd on this night seemed particularly "smart."

X-Pac hit a series of kicks in the corner and charged, but was caught in a powerslam. Whipped off the rope, Waltman came back and nailed the "X-Factor" face buster to retain the gold.

The Finish: Six minutes the match lasted; how can the WWF allocate almost 13 minutes to Road Dog vs. Bossman and cut an encounter like this with such incredible potential down to six? I did like the fact that it was another clean pin, which was incredibly refreshing. Very sound bout, with a lot of hard work from two of the most capable wrestlers in the WWF today.

Women's Title Strap Match: Luna (challenger) vs. Sable (champion)

The Background: Luna turned on Sable out of nowhere after the two had been friends for several months.

The Match: Luna took the majority of the bumps to be had, as Sable whipped her left, right and center. Ultimately, the challenger came back with a back-breaker, to re-aggravate the back problems the champion had due to a sneak attack earlier in the evening. The "match" was bland, as most strap-rules encounters are, and involved little psychology.

The Finish: One could smell this one coming. It seems that the WWF only holds a strap match every year or so because it refuses to do any but one finish; Luna touched the first three turnbuckles, but Sable touched them behind her; so the first to touch the 4th turnbuckle would be the winner. The spot didn't come off as hokey as it usually does, but why did Luna insist on pulling the strap stout when she could just run to the 4th turnbuckle, leaving Sable standing at the third? Ultimately, Sable's "stalker" jumped the rail and beat up Luna as Shane McMahon distracted the referee (trying to help Luna), and Sable won the match.

Originally plans were to have Luna win the title here, but the WWF decided to keep Sable as champion until after her "Playboy" spread comes out on the 7th of March.

WWF World Championship Match: Mankind (champion) vs. The Rock (challenger)

The Background: At "Survivor Series," Vince McMahon double-crossed Mankind and helped The Rock win the championship. At "Rock Bottom" a month later, Foley was again screwed out of his opportunity by McMahon and Co. However, on "RAW" several weeks ago, Mankind kidnapped Shane after being screwed out of a "Rumble" spot, and tortured the son of the WWF owner until his dad granted him a title shot that night; with the help of Steve Austin, Foley's dream finally came true, and he defeated The Rock for the world heavyweight championship.

The Match: More mic games involved, as there had been seen at house shows recently; Foley nailed Rock in the head with a live mic, which reverberated around the arena like thunder, asking him time and time again if he quit; but neither "The Rock says you can kiss his ass!" nor "The Rock is gonna kick your fat ass!" were quite what the champion was looking for.

The action went to the outside and the damage toll started to rise; Foley was whipped into the steel steps and really took it out of his knees. Mankind stopped him in the middle of a conversation with Jerry Lawler to nail him with a major chair shot to the lower back.

Back in the ring, Foley hit the double-arm DDT and went for the mandible sock. "I'm gonna split open that ridiculous eyebrow!" proclaimed the champion. Foley kicked The Rock to the outside, and over the barricade. Foley charged at the former champ Rock from the crowd side, but his fatigued opponent hit a beautiful Belly to Belly over the barricade back onto the padded concrete at ringside. Rock took the timekeeper's bell and hammer, ringing it in his Foley's ear, and in golden tones proclaimed "Bells will be Ringing!"

The duo fought on to the Spanish announcer's table, but the table collapsed beneath them. Rock covered it up well by jumping back on the microphone. "Say 'I quit' now, you piece of monkey crap!" "Up yours, Rock!"

The match went right back to the ring entranceway for more brawling. The Rock planted Mankind with a major DDT on the concrete, and grabbed a ladder from the back, but soon lost it as Foley took the advantage and planted him on the ground. Mankind charged along the ground and threw himself at the ladder balancing on Rock's chest; the challenger moved, and Foley ended up planting himself on the steel.

The Rock placed the ladder vertically against the concrete wall, several feet down from the entrance way, and climbed up to the fans on the second level; Foley followed him up, as they fought precariously dangling over the concrete and electrical equipment below, hanging on by one arm each on the steel railing. Rock hit a low blow and jumped into the fans; getting up a head of steam, he charged Mankind and knocked him into the air, to have him come crashing back down to earth on the planted electricity board, which provided no give whatsoever.

His torso smashed off the metal as the sparks flew, and he rolled off and collapsed onto the concrete floor below. The lights went off briefly, as Cole suggested that he had landed on the lighting controls for the whole building.

"That son of a bitch will scream 'I quit' and I'll be damned if he doesn't!" exclaimed the obsessed challenger, who made his way back down to ground level and went back to work on his foe's quivering ribs. The Rock beat Mankind back to the ring, where he handcuffed the semi-conscious champion behind his back, continuing his assault.

After Foley mounted a brief comeback, Rock nailed a really powerful clothesline. For all intents and purposes Foley suffered a double-arm bar slam. Rock brought in a chair and placed it on the champ's head, giving the sign for the Rock Bottom; he nailed it to perfection, crushing Foley's skull.

A massive chair shot to the head followed, a second one made most viewers turn away.

"SAY I QUIT!" "You'll have to...kill me..." Rock hit another three chair shots in quick succession; each more vigorous than the last. Foley collapsed to the outside. Another shot, another shot, pure hellfire behind each one, breaking records for power and pain. Red crimson flowed freely down the face, in the hair, all over Foley's body. Again, again, more chair shots, in one of the most disgusting scenes in mark wrestling history. All fans of Mick Foley, including myself, squirmed in our chairs. Rock dropped to his knee, and was asked for what would be the final time if he would quit; "I quit I quit!" The voice had been pre-recorded; it came from an interview earlier on Sunday Night Heat.

Referee and paramedics rushed to aid Foley's beaten carcass, plopped unceremoniously at the top of the aisle. He hadn't moved for several minutes. As always, a record-breaking performance; but true fans will look at Shawn Michaels, they'll look at Foley, they'll wonder if it was all worth it. One way or the other, Mick Foley has put on another performance which will be remembered forever in wrestling history; and unlike the King of the Ring, not only did he deliver a suicidal performance, he also delivered a top class match. Kudos have to go to both stars. No company does PPV like the WWF; and nobody does a match like Mick Foley.

The Finish: After 15 minutes of hardcore mayhem and suicidal spots, The Rock walks away the new WWF World Champion. It's only the third World Title change in "Royal Rumble" history, after Sgt. Slaughter defeating the Ultimate Warrior in '91 and Shawn Michaels besting Sid in '97.

ROYAL RUMBLE

Austin and McMahon kicked it off in style; payoff, as the disgruntled employee got his big opportunity to attack his evil boss. Golga ran down to ringside, but then waited until Austin was on top to come in and try to claim the $100,000 bounty on his head. He failed; Austin sent him flying over the top rope.

McMahon escaped the ring, but the former champ wasn't finished with him. The two fought up into the balcony, and into the women's bathroom. It was all a plot, Austin was punked by the corporation and ultimately wound up unconscious on the floor of the ladies' bathroom. Edge ran in and the crowd really came alive. He and Droz threw themselves around, as both youngsters can really go.

With Dan Severn and Tiger Ali coming in, the pace in the "Rumble" slowed down considerably. Tiger Ali Singh and the Blue Meanie failed to add much interest in the proceedings. The pace didn't pick up again until Mable entered, throwing out five men.

Soon after, the lights dimmed as the Undertaker made his way down to ringside. His Acolytes rushed the ring to take out Mable. Donned in a black cloak, he stalked down the isle and glared into the eyes of the mammoth athlete, apparently putting him under his control.

As with Golga, the crowd immediately started throwing their hands back and forth when Kurrgan approached – you gotta love that kind of fan involvement, whether they were just making fun of him or not. It was a really rowdy crowd that night. Road Dog came in, and the entire arena said his "Oh you didn't know?..." lines for him as he ran to ringside.

Kane appeared to a major pop. He proceeded to destroy all

ORDER ENTERING THE RUMBLE

1. Steve Austin
2. Vince McMahon
3. Golga
4. Droz
5. Edge
6. Gillberg
7. Steve Blackman
8. Dan Severn
9. Tiger Ali Singh
10. Blue Meanie
11. (Mosh) – Mable
12. Road Dog
13. Gangrel
14. Kurrgan
15. Al Snow
16. Goldust
17. Godfather
18. Kane
19. Ken Shamrock
20. Billy Gunn
21. Test
22. Big Bossman
23. Hunter Hearst Helmsley
24. Val Venis
25. X-Pac
26. Mark Henry
27. Jeff Jarrett
28. D-Lo Brown
29. Owen Hart
30. Chyna

ELIMINATED

Person	By
1. Golga	(Austin)
2. Gillberg	(Edge)
3. Severn	(Mable)
4. Blackman	(Mable)
5. Tiger Ali Singh	(Mable)
6. Blue Meanie	(Mable)
7. Droz	(Mable)
8. Edge	(Road Dog)
9. Mable	(*1 Undertaker)
10. Gangrel	(Road Dog)
11. Al Snow	(Road Dog)
12. Road Dog	(Kane)
13. Kurrgan	(Kane)
14. Godfather	(Kane)
15. Goldust	(Kane)
16. Kane	(*2 Kane)
17. Ken Shamrock	(Austin)
18. Billy Gunn	(Austin)
19. Test	(Austin)
20. X-Pac	(Bossman)
21. Jeff Jarrett	(Hunter)
22. Mark Henry	(Chyna)
23. Chyna	(Austin)
24. Val Venis	(Hunter)
25. Hunter	(Austin)
26. Owen Hart	(Austin)
27. D-Lo Brown	(Austin)
28. Big Bossman	(Austin)
29. Steve Austin	(Vince McMahon)

Rumble Performance Records

1. **Steve Austin** (Eliminated 9)
2. **Mable** (Eliminated 5)
3. **Kane** (Eliminated 4)
4. **Road Dogg** (Eliminated 3)

Footnotes: *1. The Undertaker came to ringside. Farooq and Bradshaw entered the ring and took out Mable, it's assumed; the lights were out. None were official Rumble participants. *2. Men in white coats came to the ring to get Kane, who fled through the crowd after stepping over the top rope.

competition in the ring until standing solo. The men in white coats hit ringside, but before Kane could be subdued he disappeared into the crowd, eliminating himself.

Vince McMahon hit ringside once more, to provide color commentary as Ken Shamrock walked the aisle. Billy Gunn came out next, selling his ankle, and had a great run with Shamrock which had solid pace while still selling the injury.

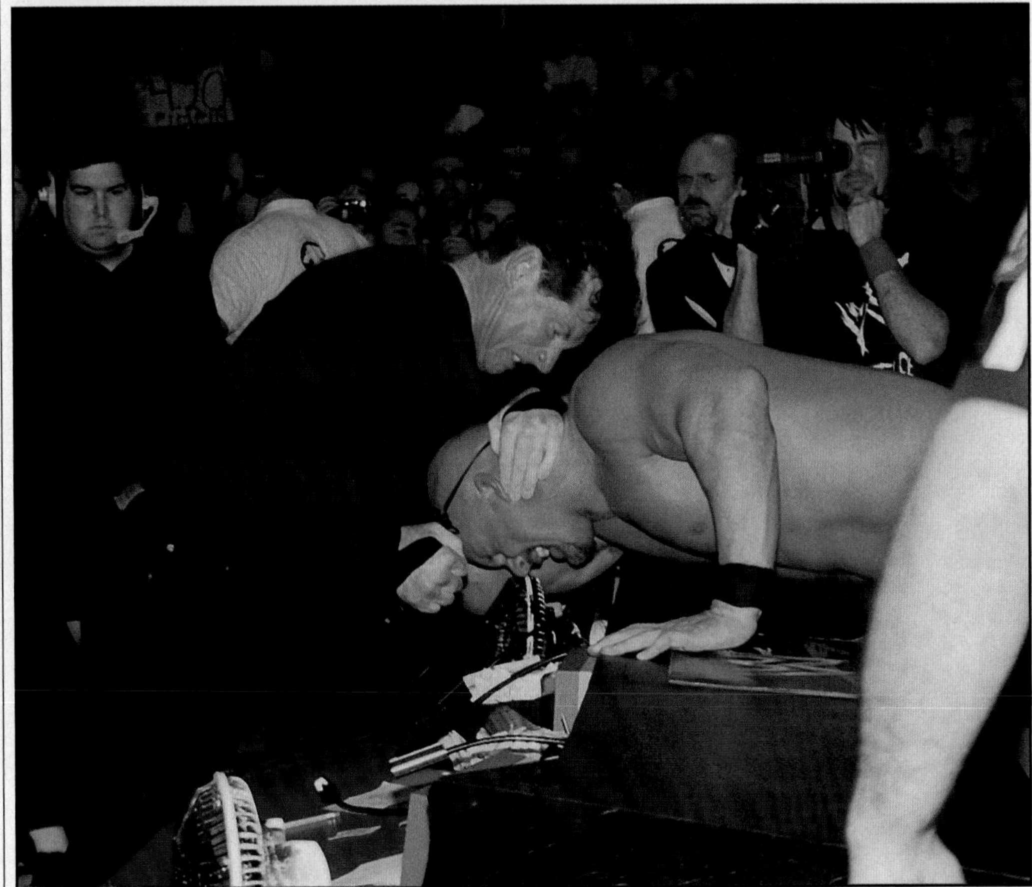

McMahon's face lit up as the camera jumped to outside; Stone Cold had commandeered the ambulance and driven right back into the building. Wasn't he unconscious and strapped into a stretcher 20 minutes ago? Austin made his way to ringside and chased McMahon into the ring, but the Corporate members beat him down to the ground as McMahon slinked away. Austin went on to beat everyone else in the ring, right up to No. 30.

He jumped out of the ring and started to pound on McMahon, throwing him into the crowd and beating him around ringside. A cracking chair shot later, the boss was semi-conscious as Austin pulled him back into the ring. He hit the Stunner, but rather then send him over the top, dropped the elbow to inflict more pain.

The Rock sped down to the ring to divert Austin's attention, as the two started to argue on the apron; one quick recovery later, and Stone Cold's chances of winning the World Title at "Wrestlemania" had taken a major turn for the worst. Vince McMahon was the winner.

The WWF bought a lot of ground back with me with this Pay-Per-View. This time, the WWF combined its angles with some solid wrestling, and a very welcome lack of run-ins. In terms of sheer excitement, the event blows away all WCW's efforts of the last six months and beyond – even "Souled Out," which was extremely solid from the fourth match on. For the first time in the last year, I can walk away from a WWF card and say that was truly 30 bucks well spent.

wwf in the house

By Tony Yannuzzi and Blake Norton

RAW 12-7-98

D-Lo Brown def. Jeff Jarrett (pinfall)

Jarrett continued his losing streak against D-Lo, who was at the benefit of Goldust flashing his valet Debra, sidetracking his attention while Brown pinned him.

Headbangers def. The Brood (DQ)

Tiger Ali Singh caused the Brood to be disqualified.

Goldust def. Owen Hart (pin)

Debra distracted Hart to give Goldust the pin. Hart was returning after injuring Dan Severn on RAW.

Val Venis/Godfather vs. Acolytes (double DQ)

They brawled all over the outside.

Tiger Ali Singh vs. Steve Blackman (no decision)

Blue Blazer & Owen Hart attacked Blackman.

Mark Henry def. Droz (pinfall)

Chyna attacked Droz, giving Henry the win.

Triple H & X-Pac def. Shamrock & Boss Man

Billy Gunn ran in and hit Shamrock with a chair, breaking his ties with the corporation.

The Rock & Undertaker vs. Steve Austin & Mankind

The bout was a total hardcore mess. Undertaker managed to knock Austin unconscious. He then dragged him to the big wooden cross at the top of the ramp. The Druids had placed him on it, and raised it all the way up. Austin had woke up, and was cursing Undertaker as the show ended. It was possibly the most disturbing RAW stunt ever pulled.

RAW 12-14-98

Godfather & Val Venis vs. Christian & Edge

Venis fights back and takes the win for his team with a suplex.

Blue Blazer vs. Goldust

Goldust nailed the Curtain Call and set up the Shattered Dreams, however Jeff Jarrett ran out. Steve Blackman then ran out and kicked Blazer. Blackman then unmasked Blazer and it was revealed to be Owen Hart. Jarrett then tried covering Owen's face with his shirt.

Mark Henry & D-Lo Brown vs. Scorpio & Bob Holly

Jacky hit a top rope dropkick which let Henry nail a powerslam for the win.

New Age Outlaws vs. Ken Shamrock & Big Bossman

Michaels nails Gunn with a nightstick, which enables Shamrock to get the ankle lock for the win.

Jeff Jarrett vs. Steve Blackman (guitar on pole match)

Debra teased a strip to Blackman, as Jarrett grabbed the guitar. Jarrett couldn't capitalize with it. The referee got knocked out, and as Blackman got set to win, Owen ran out and nailed Blackman with a guitar to give Jarrett the win.

Tiger Ali-Singh vs. Gangrel

The lights go off and Tiger tries to run off, but is cornered by the Brood. After the lights go off, Tiger is beaten and covered in blood.

Mankind vs. Kane (no-holds-barred match)

A physical match between both men. Kane gets clotheslined to the outside, as Vince comes out. Vince says that if Mankind wants it, he will meet him in the parking lot for a good old-fashioned street fight. Mankind then goes after Vince to the back. Kane is attacked by Shamrock & Bossman. Mental Hospital orderlys come out and put a straightjacket on him. In the parking lot, Mankind is beating on Vince. Patterson & Brisco try to interfere but get thrown into the gate. As Mankind tried to stuff Vince in a car trunk, The Rock came out. The Rock then beat on Mankind and put a dent on the hood of the car by hitting the Rock with the Rock Bottom. HHH vs. The Rock. The match goes to the outside. Rock grabs Cole's headset and berates HHH and slams his face in. They both go back inside, and Rock gets a swinging neck breaker. Rock then slows the match with a chin lock. Rock hits the People's Elbow but only got a two count. Chyna came in and gave Rock a low blow. HHH hit the Pedigree, but the referee was distracted by Chyna. Michaels came in and hit HHH with the belt. Andrew Martin then ran in and nailed HHH with a powerslam to give Rock the win. RAW ends with Rock, Michaels & Martin celebrating.

RAW 12-21-98

Al Snow def. Gangrel

Snow catches the Snowplow for the win. The Brood suddenly attacks and Snow is covered in blood, ala Tiger Ali Singh.

Billy Gunn def. IC Champ Ken Shamrock

Gunn wins the belt. However, commissioner Michaels spoils the party, and claims that he never announced a title match. Gunn then moons Shawn.

Steve Blackman vs. Blue Blazer

Owen comes out after the Blazer, is introduced and says that he is not the Blazer after all. Owen jumps in the ring for a DQ and stomps Blackman. Goldust comes in and unmasks Blazer, who turns out to be Jeff Jarrett.

Road Dog def. Boss Man (Hardcore title)

Mankind comes up and throws a net over Boss Man, enabling Road Dog to get the win, and the title!

Acolytes vs. Scorpio/Holly

The Acolytes totally dominate as usual. They're so brutal the match is thrown out and awarded to the JOB Squad.

Shane McMahon vs. Mankind

Patterson & Brisco intervened, but got hit for their troubles. Shane then got a taste of Mr. Socko, as the Corporation hit the ring, followed by DX.

D-Lo/Henry vs. Headbangers

D-Lo comes out by himself for a handicapped match. Footage is shown of an angry Terri & Jackie, whipping a helpless Henry. D-Lo is overwhelmed, and eventually beaten by the Headbangers. An exhausted Henry comes out and argues with D-Lo.

Triple H/X-Pac vs. The Rock/Test

In the end, Kane's music fires up as he comes down to the ring. He chokeslams HHH and the rest of DX. Kane is revealed as the "Bonus" as he joins the Corporation.

RAW 12-28-98

Road Dog vs. Val Venis (Hardcore Title):

Test bulldogs Val from behind and the ref calls for the bell. DX comes down for a save. Vince takes the mic and informs Road Dog that he'll face Mankind.

Edge def. Al Snow

Al uses "Head" and is disqualified, then attacked by the Brood. The JOB Squad soon followed.

Sable (champ) vs. Spider Lady (Women's Title)

Spider Lady is revealed to be Luna. She yells "It's about ME, and what I DESERVE!"

X-Pac (champ) vs. Big Boss Man (Euro Title)

Test comes in, but is intercepted by Val Venis, and the match is thrown out.

Goldust/Blackman def. Owen Hart/Jarrett

Owen gets Steve in the Sharpshooter, as Dan Severn walks in! Debra distracts Severn as Owen gets rolled up by Blackman for the win.

Triple H vs. Shamrock (IC Title)

Hunter finds himself in the ankle lock after a distraction from the Boss Man. He catches the rope, but Shammy won't let go. A DX/Corporate brawl ensues.

Billy Gunn def. Kane (DQ)

Shamrock runs in and locks the ankle lock on Gunn on the outside. Kane then brings him in and chokeslams him. X-Pac comes in for the save.

Road Dog def. Mankind

Mankind eventually landed Socko in Road Dog's mouth. The Rock interfered enough, so that Road Dog managed to keep his title.

Shawn Michaels Fired

Vince gets serious and gets down to business. He shows Shawn black-mailing footage from last March, saying that "McMahon needs him." He tells him he sucks as commissioner, and that he's fired. Shawn then superkicks the WWF owner to a huge pop. He escapes through the crowd as RAW fades.

RAW 1-4-99

Steve Blackman d. Shamrock (pin)

Shamrock was irked by Dan Severn's presence, which allowed Blackman to get a pinfall from behind.

Mark Henry d. Goldust

Chyna comes down with her friend Sammy, and they distract Henry to the point where Goldust can recover. He capitalizes with the "Shattered Dreams" which gives Henry a DQ victory.

Godfather n. Test (Double DQ)

Match ends up in double count out as Val beats on Test. Officials try to separate the two.

Triple H. d. Mankind (Referee: Shane McMahon)

HHH rolls him up for a fast three count. Helmsley apologizes and Pedigrees Shane.

Edge n. D-Lo Brown (no contest)

PMS come out to taunt D-Lo. Terri tripped and fell off the steel stairs. Everyone is shocked as medical attention is brought out.

Kane d. Brisco/Patterson

Brisco and Patterson try to appease Kane, to no avail. He totally destroyed them.

wwf in the house

By Tony Yannuzzi and Blake Norton

Road Dog d. Al Snow (Hardcore Title)

After a vicious piledriver on the concrete, Road Dog retains his belt.

Mankind d. The Rock (pin) (WWF Title, No DQ)

When Mankind comes out, DX follows to watch his back. The Rock comes out, and they brawl on the outside most of the match. All of a sudden, Stone Cold comes out to a huge pop and clobbers Rock, enabling Foley to get the win! Mankind becomes the new WWF champ!

RAW 1-11-99

Jeff Jarrett and Owen Hart d. The New Age Outlaws (pin)

Debra McMichael stepped up to the apron and showed her stuff. Billy Gunn said, "Suck It." Jesse James was distracted and got pinned by Owen Hart, giving them a Tag Team Title shot.

Luna d. Gillberg (Duane Gill) (Pin)

After a Goldberg-esque entrance, the LHW champ took on Luna. Gillberg attempted the Jackhammer, but Luna landed on him and made the pin.

X-Pac d. Al Snow (pin)

An exciting match. Goldust came down and showed Al Snow his Head. Goldust nailed Snow with Head, which let X-Pac make the pin for the victory.

Kane n. Mankind (no contest)

Kane Tombstoned Mankind and went for the pin, but The Rock ran in and hit Kane. The Rock ended up hitting them both with a chair. Austin came down and chased Rock out. Austin stunned both Mankind and Kane.

Triple H d. Edge

Triple H won with the Pedigree. The Brood attacked him and the lights went out. Jesse James ended up receiving the blood-bath.

Team Corporate vs. D-Generation X Battle Royal (Chyna wins)

Triple H and The Big Bossman were the only ones left. Vince surprisingly entered the battle royal, and knocked out both Triple H and Bossman. Vince thought he was the winner, until Chyna made her way in. Austin made his way down, and distracted McMahon, which let Chyna eliminate the WWF owner.

RAW 1-18-99

A tribute to Martin Luther King kicked off the show.

Jesse James def. Gangrel

James won after two chairshots to Gangrel's head.

Billy Gunn def. Test (DQ)

Ken Shamrock interfered. Shamrock destroyed Gunn, slamming his head into the table and staircase, and putting him in the Ankle Lock.

Steve Blackman def. Dan Severn by Disqualification.

Steve Blackman called for the Lethal Kick, but Dan Severn was disqualified after giving him a low blow.

Hardcore Rules: Mankind def. The Big Bossman (retains Heavyweight Title)

Bossman was about to submit, but The Rock interrupted with a chairshot on Mankind. The Rock hit Mankind with the Rock Bottom on a chair.

Al Snow def. Goldust (Pinfall)

Goldust got back up, and nailed Snow with Shattered Dreams. Goldust grabbed Head, hit Snow with it, and stole it again.

Handicap Match: Chyna def. Gerald Brisco and Pat Patterson (pinfall)

Brisco put powder in Chyna's eyes. She was blinded, as Brisco and Patterson patted her rear and breasts (censored). Chyna DDT'd Patterson and Brisco, placed them on top of each other, and made the pin.

Kane and The Rock went to a No-Contest.

Team Corporate members began to attack Kane. The Rock asked Team Corporate members to leave the inside of the ring, because he decided to wrestle the match. Mankind made his way down to the ring with a chair, and took out everyone with it. Stone Cold Steve Austin popped out from behind. When The Rock turned around to see Austin, he was nailed behind with a chair by Mankind, as the show went off the air.

RAW 1-25-99

Billy Gunn d. Goldust (rollup)

After a distraction by "Bluedust" (Blue Meanie), who stole Head back, Gunn took advantage for a rollup pin.

Droz d. George Steele (pinfall)

Droz makes quick work of "The Animal." He gets carried away, snapping on refs

Jeff Jarrett/Owen Hart d. Ken Shamrock/Boss Man (new tag champs)

Shamrock & Boss Man weren't fazed by Debra's antics this time. They actually had the match well in hand, until a black Blue Blazer pasted Shamrock with a guitar. Jarrett pinned Shamrock for the win.

Test d. Val Venis (pin)

After a screening of Val's new "movie" starring Ken Shamrock's sister, he took on Test from the corporate team. Shamrock attacked Val with a chair from the outside, enabling Test to easily pin Venis.

Hardcore Rules: Road Dog/Al Snow d. Gangrel/Edge (pin)

"Bluedust" (Blue Meanie) gave Al Snow his Head.

The Rock d. Triple H ("I Quit" rules, for WWF Title)

The Corporate team took Chyna hostage, and Kane threatened to Chokeslam her unless he said the two little words. He obliged, but then Chyna turned on Helmsley, and joined the Corporation.

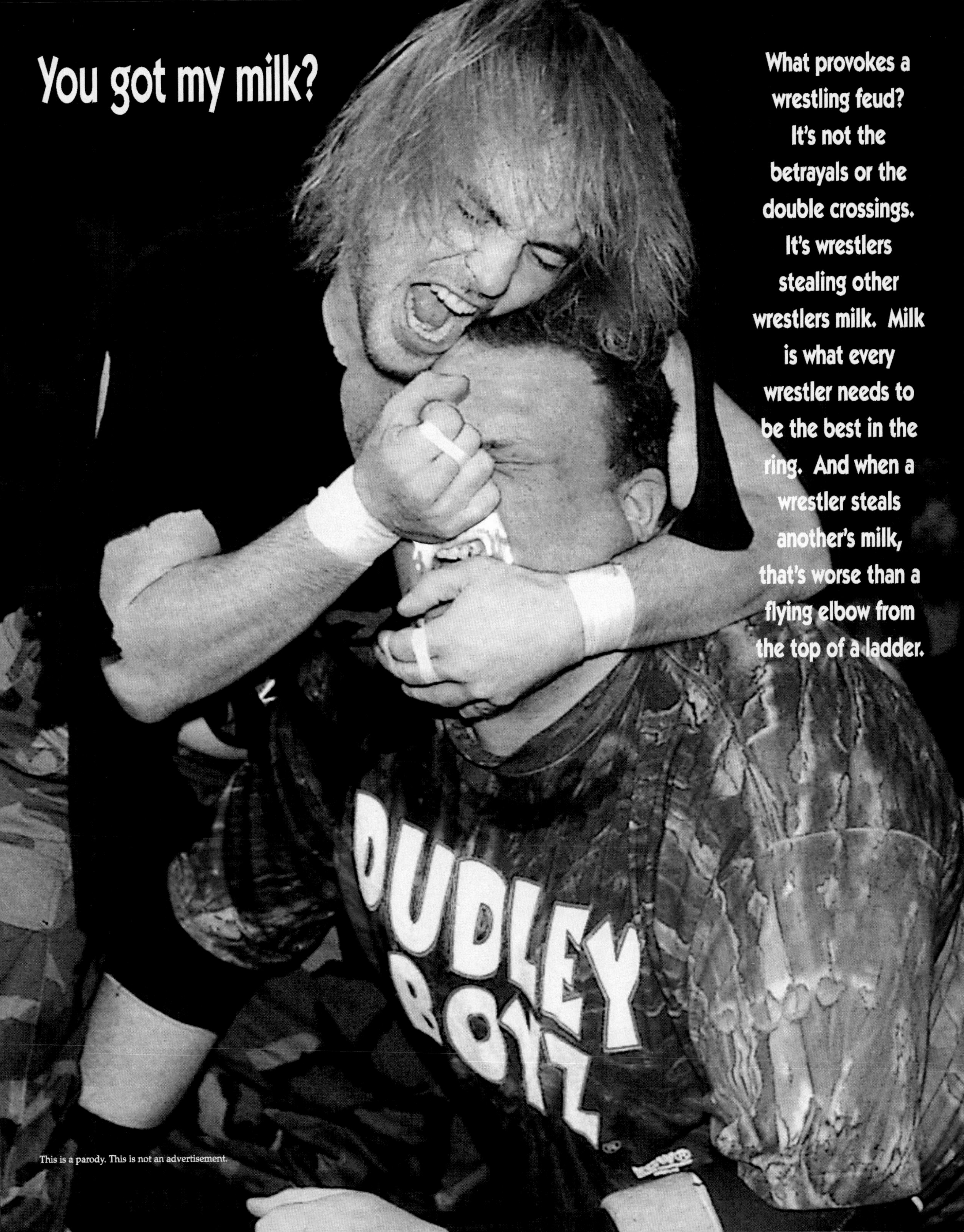
You got my milk?
What provokes a wrestling feud? It's not the betrayals or the double crossings. It's wrestlers stealing other wrestlers milk. Milk is what every wrestler needs to be the best in the ring. And when a wrestler steals another's milk, that's worse than a flying elbow from the top of a ladder.
DUDLEY BOYZ
This is a parody. This is not an advertisement.

Shawn Michaels announces his retirement

Shawn Michaels, recognized by many as the most versatile performer in WWF history and the personification of wrestling in the '90s, announced his retirement after he underwent surgery to correct back problems stemming from a major bump he took at the "Royal Rumble" last year. However, the operation to fuse two of the discs in his back has left him in a weaker physical state overall, despite the surgery being a success. We hope that there are further, positive developments in the near future, but the future looks bleak for the three-time former champion of the world.

From everyone here at "WOW magazine," a sincere "Thank You" to Shawn Michaels for making such a profound positive impact on wrestling the last 10 years, and putting out time and time again the greatest matches in wrestling history. We'll have a further, larger update in the next edition of "WOW magazine." Michaels, 33, is expected to remain an active participant in the wrestling industry. Some of his best work may be seen in the following widely-available matches:

- ***Survivor Series '92***
  (vs. Bret Hart, WWF title match)
- ***Monday Night Raw in '93***
  (vs. Marty Janetty, PWI match of the year)
- ***Wrestlemania X***
  (vs. Razor Ramon, Ladder Match, IC title match)
- ***Royal Rumble '95***
  (Royal Rumble)
- ***Wrestlemania XI***
  (vs. Diesel, World Title Match)
- ***Summerslam '95***
  (vs. Razor Ramon, Ladder Match, IC title match)
- ***Wrestlemania XII***
  (vs. Bret Hart, Ironman match, WWF Title match)
- ***King of the Ring '96***
  (vs. British Bulldog, WWF Title match)
- ***Survivor Series '96***
  (vs. "Psycho" Sid Eudy, WWF Title match)
- ***In Your House Badd Blood***
  (vs. Undertaker, Original Hell In A Cell)
- ***Survivor Series '97***
  (vs. Bret Hart, WWF Title match)
- ***Wrestlemania XIV***
  (vs. Steve Austin, WWF Title match)

Rumor Killer – Brian Lee to return to the WWF

There's rumors flying around again that Brian Lee (formerly of the DOA) will be part of the new Undertaker angle. It's well known that the two are friends, and it was in fact Lee that played Ted DiBiase's "evil Undertaker" when the original (Mark Callaway) disappeared off camera for several months in '94. Well, all rumors are false, as Lee told "WOW magazine" that all the plans he has for the immediate future are to keep working on the new wrestling school he's established in Tennessee.

If you want to get into the biz, it sounds like a great place to start to me; if you're over 18, they take all comers and assess your in-the-ring potential. Interested? Give "Lee's Professional Wrestling Academy" a call at (615) 213-2500.

Funk still with the WWF

Terry Funk is still with the WWF, and should be returning at some stage in the near future. He was set to have a really hardcore World Title match with Mick Foley – remember their first brutal no-DQ match on "RAW?" – when Foley was champion, but many sources said he had contracted Hepatitis A and was unable to make the card. Depending on how his angle with Tommy Dreamer goes, he should be back soon.

And the new champion of the world...

Kudos to Mick Foley for winning the WWF World Championship. One of the most touching moments in my 1998 calendar was witnessing the crowd chanting "Foley" after super-heel "Mankind" literally obliterated his body in taking on the Undertaker at "King of the Ring." Foley clearly has the ability to touch some hearts. Call him crazy, call him unpredictable, just call him champion. Two time champion. What's more, he's actually still alive after his performance at the "Royal Rumble." Uncanny. Please Mick, stop taking the insane bumps! We don't want you to end up like the Dynamite Kid!

Titan into Chris Jericho?

The WWF are said to be focused entirely on Chris Jericho now, according to the "Observer" newsletter. It's been suggested that because of their focus on luring The Giant into the fold, they couldn't free up the money to make real offers to Chris Benoit, Eddy Guerrero or Dean Malenko, who have now been offered deals worth a cool half million per year to re-sign with the company. Does the WWF really need another big man, with the Undertaker, Kane and Giant Silva on the roster? Apparently so.

Kaientai disbanded

Kaientai are being disbanded, apparently. Most of the group are going back to Japan, and Taka Michinoku has been talked into staying and may be getting a stint in ECW (ala Al Snow). Dave Scherer came out with that first, I believe. How the WWF could underuse such exciting stars is beyond me. In fairness to WCW, if they had these guys, they'd at least make them wrestle each other!

Thrasher injured

Thrasher of the Headbangers has suffered a knee injury; he's been spotted recently in tag matches where he hasn't actually tagged in. He won't be back for at least three months.

Mable back with the WWF?

At press time, the former King Mable joined the Undertaker's ministry on "RAW," after making his return to the federation at the "Royal Rumble," beating up Mankind and falling under the Undertaker's spell. When he did the one-shot deal last year the day after the "King of the Ring" and jobbed to Ken Shamrock, the big man was looking for a new contract with the federation. He originally left at the end of '95, and was said to be a natural hazard to wrestle. At "Summerslam '95," he injured then-world champion Diesel's lower back when he literally jumped on him, which caused the big man to miss several calendar dates. Have the WWF lightened up on their concerns?

Wrestlemania Update

"Wrestlemania IV" is coming to Philadelphia, Pa., on Sunday March 28.

As far as predictions go, my bets are still on Rock vs. Austin. For that to happen, Rock would have to have won the WWF title three times in under four months. Wow! Those were definitely the plans as of "Survivor Series," but since Foley won the WWF title, he's actually gained the popularity to be considered viable for the main event of the biggest supercard of the year.

Until the last 12 months, the kind of psychotic characters he plays would never have been considered mainstream championship material; but with the WWF insisting on shoving "hardcore" down everyone's throats to the nth degree, I wouldn't overlook a "Wrestlemania" main event involving Foley either. Money's still on Rock vs. Austin, though. I've been promised a raise if that happens, so WWF bookers, don't fail me now!

The WWF's next PPV after "Wrestlemania" is scheduled to be "In Your House," on Sunday, April 25. Mark your calendars (better yet, TEAR OUT OUR WOW PULLOUT CALENDAR in the middle of this issue!).

Excerpts from AOL chat with Steve Austin prior to "Royal Rumble"

(Note: This chat was conducted mostly in Kayfabe, and the questions were all mark. Some answers are still interesting, while others are more interesting still by how they're answered considering the Kayfabe nature of the chat.)

Q: How long do you plan to stay part of the WWF?

Austin: I think I always want to be associated with the WWF in some capacity. Will I be able to wrestle forever? Of course not. But to me, being a part of the WWF is something special. And to me, I just like being associated with it. That's about it.

Q: Who was the toughest opponent you've ever faced?

Austin: Ricky Steamboat. The guy was just so good. He never got tired. As far as here in the WWF, it would be a toss-up between Undertaker and Mankind. Speaking of Mankind, if Mankind keeps the title I'd love to wrestle him at "Wrestlemania." Like he said on "RAW," we'd blow the roof off the place. "Wrestlemania" is the biggest show of the year. Whether it's the Rock or Mankind, it will be a hell of a deal. I guarantee you that.

Q: Who influenced you?

Austin: I didn't really have any influences as far as interview style. The only person that really influences me interview wise would be Brian Pillman. As far as people I respected in the ring. Harley Race, Jake "The Snake" Roberts, Dick Murdoch, and Bob Orton, Jr.

Q: Do you really bleed?

Austin: When I really get cut. Check out the Blood from a Stone shirt.

Q: Would you ever want to wrestle Dennis Rodman?

Austin: No I wouldn't want to wrestle him. But I would consider dating him. I might consider shooting baskets with him or something like that. But he's not in my league.

1. Mick Foley

Foley has finally achieved his dream of becoming World Champion, and the whole business was elated to see him on top (with the exception of Tony Schiavone, who is rumored to be a remote-control droid created by Eric Bischoff to replace the original Schiavone, who died suddenly in 1993). Not only did he overcome the seemingly impregnable Corporation to defeat The Rock for the World Title, but also successfully defended the championship up and down the country all through January. His match with The Rock at The Royal Rumble combined not only suicidal spots but solid hardcore wrestling with as much transition and psychology as one could hope for. A great star, a great champion, No. 1 in our first-ever WWF rankings. Mick Foley.

2. The Rock

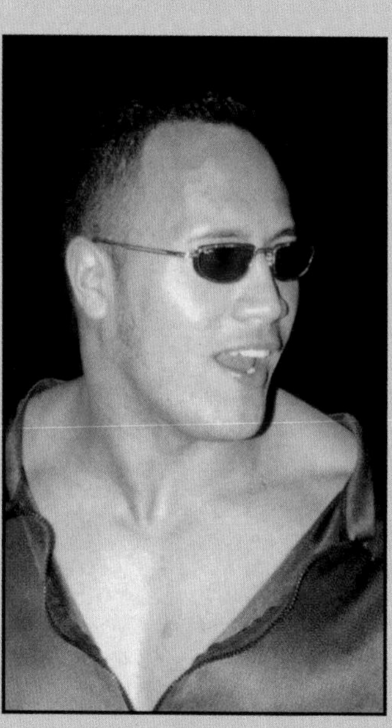

The Rock has been on a roll ever since "Summerslam." First, he became one of the most popular stars in wrestling, and as such, he fought to several major victories (including a major Shotgun battle royal and a brutal triple-threat cage match against Ken Shamrock in Canada last October). At "Survivor Series," his main-event status was confirmed, as the man still in his second year of wrestling made a major heel turn and captured the World Title with the aid of the Corporation. He now turns in really consistent performances, and his interviews have become nothing short of legendary.

3. X-Pac

First entering the WWF in 1993, the 28-year-old X-Pac managed to come back from yet another major concussion last year and establish himself as one of the top stars in the business. He remains the European champion, and as such, has had excellent, clean matches with D-Lo Brown, Gangrel and Val Venis in the last several months. Not only does he bust his butt every time he gets in the ring, but he can wrestle with transition and excellent execution. The WWF's closest in-ring substitute to Shawn Michaels right now.

4. Edge

Underwent curious transition to heel and joined the Brood. Incredibly exciting young star to

watch in the ring. Has been in the WWF 10 months now—where did the time go?

5. Steve Austin

After dominating 1998, Austin tore a stomach muscle at "Rock Bottom" in December, making his return at the "Royal Rumble." Look for him to move swiftly up the chart once back in action, likely winning the World Title at "Wrestlemania XV" against The Rock.

6. Ken Shamrock

After going 15 months without a WWF championship victory, he won the 1998 King of the Ring and subsequently picked up the IC belt in a tournament, defeating X-Pac in the final.

7. Owen Hart

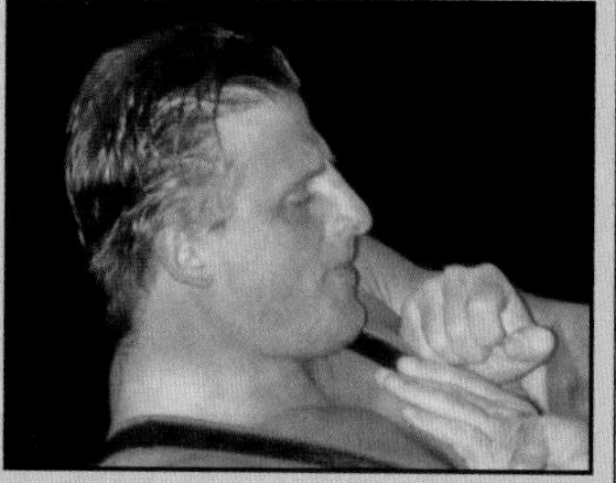

He's been vastly underused since the breakup of the Hart Foundation. Looks to be getting a major push with Jeff Jarrett in the tag ranks, could really do some damage. One of the greatest wrestlers on the face of the earth.

8. Val Venis

Venis has worked hard to break into the WWF's roster and survive after the initial push. At 6-foot-5, his "money shot" splash is one of the best in the business.

9. Road Dogg

Earns his spot from a series of top-notch hardcore matches on "Raw" recently. Defeated Al Snow and Gangrel, among others. One of the famous Armstrong brothers.

10. Undertaker

Hasn't wrestled many shows recently, working on the new angle. One of the very best big men in wrestling today.

The Rock (real name: Duane Johnson)

Age: 27
Fed: WWF
Height: 6-5
Weight: 232 lbs
Style: High Flying/Bump Taker
Highest Accolade: WWF world champion
Native Country: U.S.

exposed...wwf

1995

Started as a football player in Miami, his hometown. Initially wrestling as a hobby, he entered the USWA in 1996.

1996

Under contract to the WWF, he made his federation debut at "Survivor Series" in November, winning as sole survivor.

1997

In a shocking victory, defeated Triple H for the IC championship on "Thursday Raw Thursday" in February, the same broadcast where Shawn Michaels forfeited the WWF world title. After surviving subsequent rematches, he went on to "Wrestlemania" to defeat The Sultan (Fatu).

Due to his green naivete and instant success, the same resentful crowd mentality that made Hulk Hogan unpopular in WCW took hold. Fans started chanting "Die, Rocky, Die" in one of the most regrettable periods in modern wrestling history. A discouraged Maivia dropped the IC title cleanly to Owen Hart on the April 28 edition of "Raw" and disappeared after being somewhat buried on TV.

Returned near the end of the year to join Farooq's (Ron Simmons) Nation of Domination heel stable. He started employing talented microphone work and soon stood out as the most-recognized member of the Nation. He entered a huge feud with IC champion Steve Austin, who was just returning after his infamous "Summerslam" neck injury. Unable to unseat the champ, Austin forfeited the title to Maivia to go after the world title.

1998

Loses IC strap to Hunter Hearst Helmsley in a ladder match on Aug. 30 at "Summerslam." Soon after, the Nation of Domination dumps him and he becomes a mega face. Became WWF champion at the 1998 "Survivor Series," thanks to help from McMahon's corporation. After two months as a face, he had gained a huge fan base. So, when McMahon's interference gave him the win in the World title tournament over Mankind in the finals, the fans were shocked. On "Raw" the next night, he cited the fans' hatred during his first run in the federation as the reason for his actions. Lost the title to Mick Foley Dec. 28 on "Raw."

1999

Won the title back on Jan. 24 at the "Royal Rumble." He lost it again during the "Half Time Heat" match with Foley during the Super Bowl. Don't be surprised if Rocky becomes a three-time champ in the near future.

–by
Blake Norton,
TBR Editor

Owen Hart (real name: Owen Hart)

Age: 32
Fed: WWF
Weight: 226 lbs.
Style: High flyer/technical
Highest Accolade: WWF Intercontinental Champion
Native Country: Canada

1988

Debuted in the WWF as the Blue Blazer. The talented high-flyer won "Pro Wrestling Illustrated's" Rookie of the Year for 1987.

1992

After the briefest of stints in WCW, he made it to Japan in the early '90s before returning to the WWF to team with Jim Neidhart as "The New Foundation," which received a substantial push in '92. Despite being a popular and capable team, they soon broke up as Neidhart left the federation and Hart formed the mid-card tag team "High Energy" with Koko B. Ware. Hart had already teamed with Ware several times when he was the Blue Blazer.

1993

At "Survivor Series," Hart teamed with his brothers against Jerry Lawler and his Knights. A falling-out with Bret during the bout led to a heel turn and a long-awaited push for Hart as a singles star.

exposed...wwf

1994

Defeated Bret cleanly in the opener of "Wrestlemania X" at 20:21. The match remains one of the greatest encounters in "Wrestlemania" history. That June, Neidhart returned to the federation and helped Owen Hart defeat Razor Ramon in the finals of the 2nd annual "King of the Ring" tournament, after Hart had already put away Tatanka and the 1-2-3 kid (X-Pac) in opening rounds. Hart feuded with Bret over the world title for the rest of the year as the pair put on a string of excellent matches, including a steel-cage encounter at "Summerslam" that marked the return of the "British Bulldog" Davey Boy Smith to the federation. Smith teamed with Bret against Owen and Neidhart on "Raw," and headlined cards around the U.S. and in Europe.

1995

Teamed with Yokozuna to win his first world title, the WWF tag belts, at "Wrestlemania XI." The team, managed by Jim Cornette, rolled through '95, dominating a feud against the British Bulldog and Lex Luger while holding teams such as The Smoking Gunns and Men on a Mission at bay.

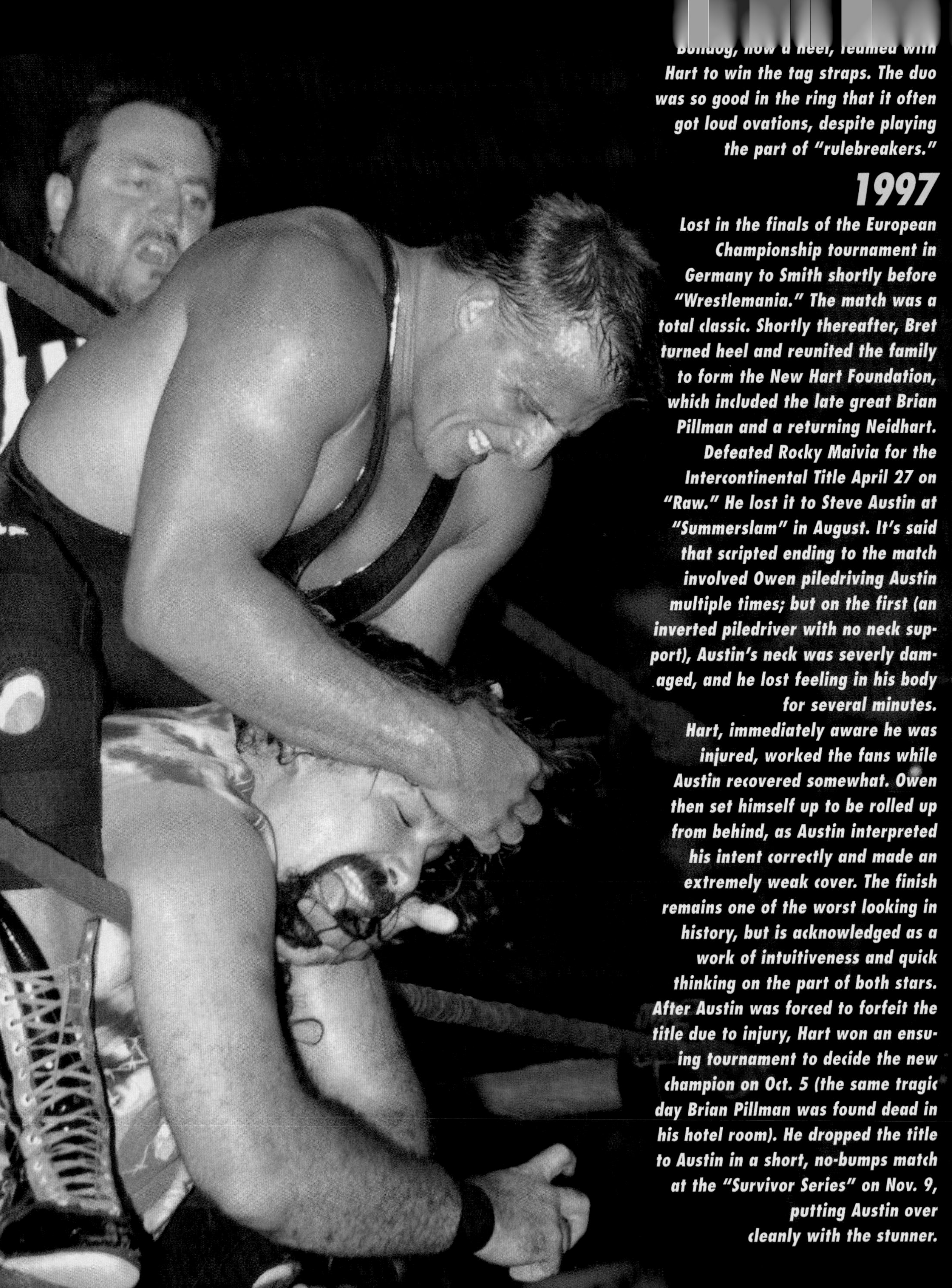

Bulldog, now a heel, teamed with Hart to win the tag straps. The duo was so good in the ring that it often got loud ovations, despite playing the part of "rulebreakers."

1997

Lost in the finals of the European Championship tournament in Germany to Smith shortly before "Wrestlemania." The match was a total classic. Shortly thereafter, Bret turned heel and reunited the family to form the New Hart Foundation, which included the late great Brian Pillman and a returning Neidhart. Defeated Rocky Maivia for the Intercontinental Title April 27 on "Raw." He lost it to Steve Austin at "Summerslam" in August. It's said that scripted ending to the match involved Owen piledriving Austin multiple times; but on the first (an inverted piledriver with no neck support), Austin's neck was severly damaged, and he lost feeling in his body for several minutes. Hart, immediately aware he was injured, worked the fans while Austin recovered somewhat. Owen then set himself up to be rolled up from behind, as Austin interpreted his intent correctly and made an extremely weak cover. The finish remains one of the worst looking in history, but is acknowledged as a work of intuitiveness and quick thinking on the part of both stars. After Austin was forced to forfeit the title due to injury, Hart won an ensuing tournament to decide the new champion on Oct. 5 (the same tragic day Brian Pillman was found dead in his hotel room). He dropped the title to Austin in a short, no-bumps match at the "Survivor Series" on Nov. 9, putting Austin over cleanly with the stunner.

turned face after brother Bret was screwed at the "Survivor Series," but quickly reverted to heel after a feud with Hunter Hearst Helmsley for the Euro title, which he held for two months.

1999

Formed a successful tag team with Jeff Jarrett and won the tag team titles the day after the "Royal Rumble." Combined, the new champions have the potential to be the best since Hart teamed with Davey Boy Smith and before.

–by Blake Norton, TBR Editor

exposed...w

marc mero

Will he ever get BADD again?

al snow

Finally hit the Big Time!

Gangrel
Fresh WWF talent

exposed...

exposed... wwf

shawn michaels

Wrestler of the '90s

stone cold "I want my belt back!"

edge Creature of the Nigh

gold dust You'll never forget the name

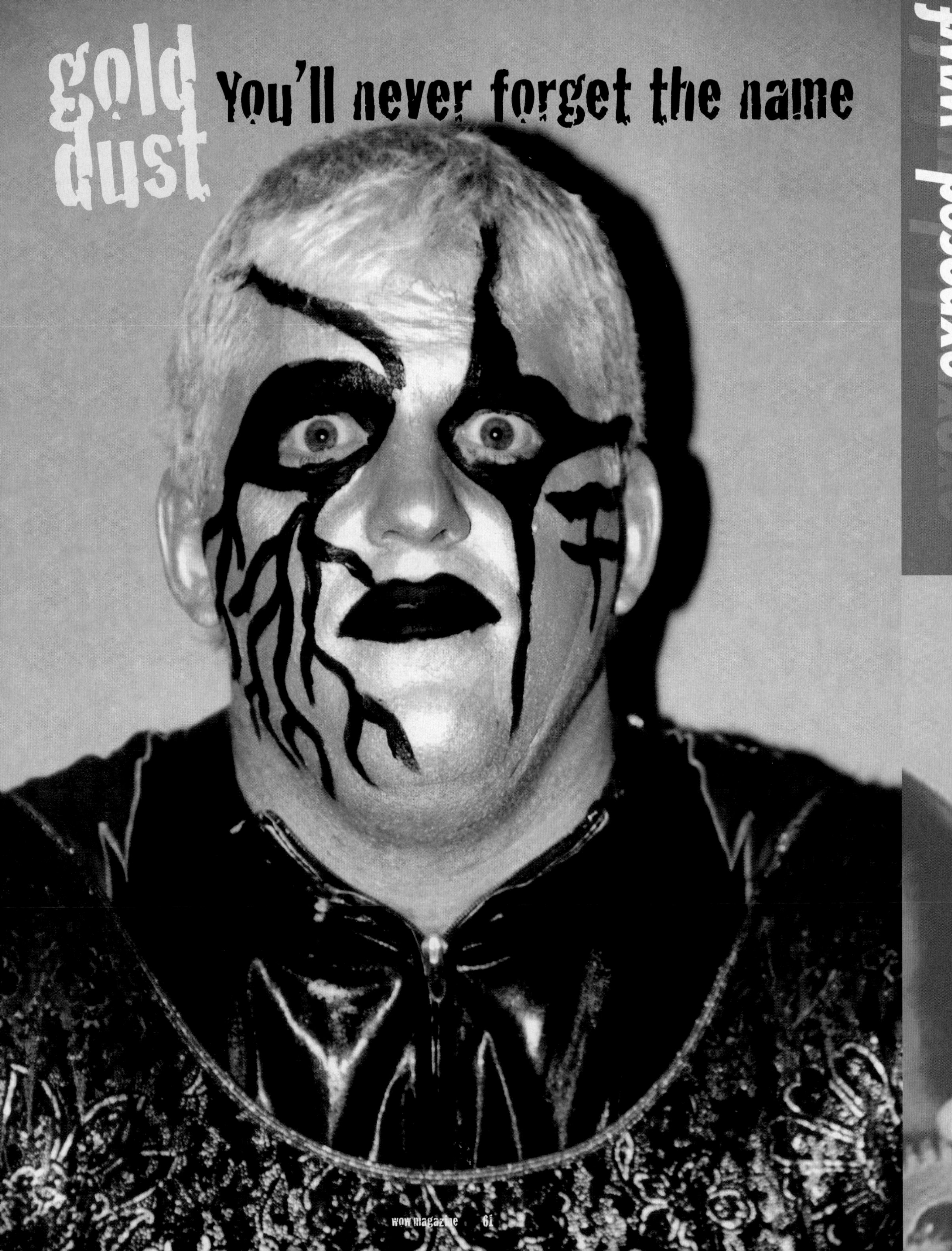

 by Chris Sabga

The Black and White Attack is Back

The New World Order…Well, It Worked the First Time!

The familiar black limousine pulled into the back entrance as crowd noise died down in the main arena. The air grew silent, and through an open window came the sound of excited chatter, several voices murmuring in unison. When the car door opened,the recognizable figure of Kevin Nash appeared from the shadows, a wicked grin etched across his broad face. The arena exploded into whistles, catcalls and wild screams. One by one, members of the new New World Order—the original NWO—made their way out of the vehicle and into the arena.

"We're here to take no prisoners!" exclaimed Scott Steiner, strutting through the catacombs of the locker room area. "Now, get that camera out of my face before I break you in half!" The arena was littered with signs, all conveying the same message: "NWO 4 LIFE," "We're back!" and "Black and white attack!" No matter what dastardly crimes were committed or how many fan favorites were mauled, beaten and tortured (not to mention how stupid the booking became since the splitting up of the original NWO), WCW had lost something. And the fans of WCW were glad to have that something back.

Why Did the NWO Come Back?

When the NWO formed at "Bash at the Beach" in 1996, Hulk Hogan, Nash and Scott Hall considered it an inside joke that would last no longer than a few months. Almost three years later, the NWO remains the biggest ongoing angle in wrestling, resulting in huge merchandise sales, different factions of the now-legendary stable and a worldwide fan following. Nobody really thought the "WWF Invasion" (designed to aid Nash and Hall in maintaining the momentum their WWF characters had in this new company while still evading Titan copyrights) would give WCW the upper hand in Monday night ratings and catapult it to North America's leading wrestling federation. But that's exactly what happened—WCW Vice President Eric Bischoff knew he was on to a good thing.

With the increasing popularity of the rogue stable, each weekly broadcast dedicated more time to the NWO. New members joined the revolution, such as: "Million Dollar Man" Ted DiBiase (introduced as a wealthy heel), The 1-2-3 Kid (now Syxx, 1+2+3, get it?) and Mr. Perfect (called by his real name Curt Hennig and adorned in the same attire he used in the WWF).

The NWO became a franchise. Ultimately, the notion of this being a WWF invasion into the WCW became silly. Hall and Nash already had established their personalities in the new federation. With more and more members, each successive addition made less impact and diluted the talent pool. Consequently, the stable lost focus and continuity, degenerating into a group of thugs. They were no longer Outlaws; with the addition of Eric Bischoff, they made the law. Monday nights had turned into NWO parties.

Rifts began to break out. Spearheaded by Randy Savage and Nash, the group broke into the NWO Black and White and the NWO Wolfpack in 1998. Meanwhile, Hall was having some personal problems and in the middle of a heartbreaking divorce. When he finally returned, he was booked to turn on Nash at "Slamboree" in a serious case of questionable booking. Almost immediately the pair wanted to get back together, which they spent the better part of six months trying to do on stage.

By then, nobody was really sure what NWO meant—what it stood for, even what the words "New World Order" were supposed to convey. As WWF began to catch up in the ratings, the company spent more and more on guest stars such as Dennis Rodman and Jay Leno, who wrestled in the main pay-per-view events to prevent buy rates from slipping. Meanwhile, many undercard superstars such as

Chris Jericho and Chris Benoit remained underexposed and underused. Morale within the company slumped to an all-time low. Ultimately, Hogan left WCW television after the buy rate for "Halloween Havoc" turned out lower than expected. It was decided the federation was moving in the wrong direction, and fast. So, eight days after Nash won the world title from Bill Goldberg at "Starrcade," WCW wiped the slate clean by bringing Hogan back in to take the world strap. It was a classic case of NWO deviousness: reuniting Hall and Nash, and once again bringing back the strongest players to form the new NWO Wolfpack.

The new version is, for all intents and purposes, the same lineup as in 1996: Hogan, Hall and Nash are the top guys. Only this time, the WWF isn't involved. And the theme is "tradition." Ric Flair—the man WCW has had to rely on so many times—has been brought back with his Horsemen to fight the ultimate battle of good vs. evil. Arguably, this is the strongest NWO and Horsemen lineups of all time.

Will the same angle that catapulted WCW "Nitro" into the slot of "coolest Monday night show" work a second time? Bishoff is betting it will.

NWO: The Start of a Tradition

In 1996, the climate between the WWF and WCW was chillier than ever.

Both companies went back and forth trying to strike the knockout blow. WCW gave away taped "Raw" results on its "Nitro" program. The WWF struck back by poking fun at several main-event stars down South with its "Huckster," "Nacho Man" and "Scheme Gene" skits. The battle was on. Fast forward to Memorial Day, May 27. During a relatively unimportant Mike Enos/Steve Doll match, "Razor Ramon" appeared out of nowhere. He emerged from the crowd, his hair slicked back and toothpick in tow. The fans gasped in shock, millions around the world were calling their friends and loved ones. The former WWF Intercontinental champion had "invaded" "Nitro" and talked of a dangerous "hostile takeover." WCW on Monday nights quickly became "must-see TV" with the later emergence of Kevin Nash and talk of an ominous "third man" coming to back the renegade crusade dominating WCW storylines for several weeks afterwards.

Fans were buzzing. The WWF was thrown by a fastball for which no batter could prepare. Two of its top stars were now on enemy lines. Razor and Diesel were once again the talk of the wrestling town, but this time Titan wasn't attracting all the publicity. The night Hall knocked both Enos and Doll out of the ring changed the sport forever. Now, WCW was on the road to dominating the North American wrestling market.

The "black and white" of the early NWO quickly translated into major "green" for all parties involved. There was no turning back. Mark wrestling reality had turned a corner and set precedent—one which led to the top federations regularly badmouthing each other and getting the upper hand by any means necessary. It's an exciting new storyline that is still being written today.

by Blake Norton, TBR Editor

"Souled Out"

January 17, 1999 / Charleston, W.V.

Chris Benoit vs. Mike Enos

The Background: Enos is a very talented wrestler, but never made it over in the States; besides his mid-card tag team with Wayne Bloom (a.k.a. The Beverly Brothers), there's been little to talk about. Nonetheless, he's a strong competitor who I can see being put on a PPV as part of a major push. However, when he's just one of a plethora of mid-card wrestlers on the PPV, many of which you wouldn't expect to see on "Nitro," it simply looks bad.

Benoit is just incredible. While the vast majority of stars going today use mic work and unrealistic angles to get over, and nine out of 10 times end up putting out heatless, dull matches, Benoit can walk to the ring stonefaced without a gimmick of any kind, and the moment he acknowledges the crowd with a look they go absolutely ballistic; such was the case on this particular evening.

The Action: The problem with PPV events is that because of the longer time slots given to matches, and the fact that there's no WWF product on the other channel to contend with, there's far less incentive to really push up the workrate. In this particular scenario, it would have worked out far better on "Nitro" with a faster tempo. Enos dominated the middle stages of the bout, and while he's a solid wrestler, there was little transition or psychology involved. We were mainly treated to brawling interspersed with suplexes. There is no way that Mike Enos should be able to dominate Chris Benoit for so long, or hold him to this long a match. The two guys can work, but in their current roles this just didn't pan out.

Finish: Chris Benoit won via pinfall at 10:05 with the Crippler Crossface.

Norman Smiley vs. Chavo Guerrero, Jr.

The Background: Smiley decapitated Guerrero's hobby-horse, "Pepé"; obviously there was need for revenge. Smiley's been experiencing a major push recently, but is in jeopardy of being cast as a one-move wrestler, like several WWF stars including the New Age Outlaws; it seemed as if all match long the fans were waiting for "The Jiggle," and popped huge for it, but they weren't as excited about the really top-class wrestling involved. Guerrero has been in semi-limbo since the collapse of the L.W.O.

The Match: It started out fast, Smiley ducked through the ropes to escape a charging Chavo, eager to defend the honor of his recently-departed hobby horse. The match was in danger of being a stalling-fest, falling prey to the same PPV trap that Benoit's opener did; but both stars, particularly Chavo, really bust their ass to put on not only a fast-paced but incredibly well-executed match.

It soon went outside, as Chavo launched himself with a cross body over the top rope. Back in, he nailed a springboard bulldog, but was caught with a cheap shot as Smiley took the advantage for the first time in the match. Guerrero was right back on top, however, absorbing an Irish whip and coming back with another cross body from the top rope which went so high he nearly missed Smiley completely.

The match slowed down some, and it was hard to resist thinking about the $30 spent on an event which had so far provided two "Thunder" matches. All these guys are very talented, and the matches are generally leaps and bounds better than those on a WWF Pay-Per-View – but until some of the mid-card talent get involved with the top guys, and fare favorably, it's hard to be happy with paying money for a product inferior to that available often several times a week on free television.

Chavo, 50 pounds lighter than Smiley, discreetly played up to a David and Goliath scenario. He did a lot of work, and took a consistent series of painful bumps, driven home with precise and painful execution.

At 14 minutes in, Smiley locked on the "Gory special;" he lifted Guerrero up into the Razor's Edge position, then Guerrero wrapped his feet around Smiley's legs as his aggressor pulled his arms and bent over forward to apply the pressure. It was a great looking move, like a standing inverted surfboard submission (used far more in Japan than in the States), but looked weak due to the fact that Chavo had to very obviously lock his own ankles into place to make the move work. Chavo broke his arms free and rolled forward into a sunset flip; Smiley grabbed his throat and hoisted his lighter foe off the ground, but Chavo again broke free in mid air and rotated his body 180 degrees, locking onto Smiley's torso in a hand-standing body scissors. Smiley proceeded to spank Guerrero's exposed rear. Norman then grabbed him around the waist and powered him up into the air again, this time in front of him; Chavo rolled forward, and followed through into a roll up for two-and-a-half. The pace at light-weight speed, the ever vengeful Chavo leapt onto Smiley's shoulders and rolled through again for a full victory roll. These guys should be much higher up the card.

Shortly thereafter, Chavo again went for the springboard bulldog, but this time Smiley had learned his lesson and blocked it on the way down. You have to love that kind of attention to detail. The aggressor now went for a back suplex, but the resourceful Guerrero followed through and landed on his feet. A waist lock was reversed via a standing switch by Smiley, who was reversed in his attempt to put on the chicken wing. Guerrero went for his own move, the Tornado DDT, but was blocked; he then tapped out to the cross-face chicken wing body scissors after being blinded by Smiley's urn full of wood chippings.

The Finish: The finish was slightly annoying, as the ref clearly saw Smiley use the chippings. If no rules are going to be enforced, it begs the question, why not just bring a gun and shoot the other guy? It was a top-class match, but the way WCW played its cards, it's crazy that we'd have to pay to see it. We see matches of this caliber on

"Thunder" every week. At least it got 16 minutes.

Fit Finlay vs. Van Hammer

Background: Next up on "WCW Saturday Night," er, "Souled out," is Fit Finlay. Again, is this really the place for him to take on Van Hammer? WCW proved the widely-held theory correct with this PPV – that WCW has the greater talent but the WWF knows how to use it. I didn't think I'd ever see the day that there were three semi-squashes between mid-carders, two of which had no history whatsoever, on WCW PPV. Hammer isn't even used on "Nitro," and now he's in the third match on PPV?

The Match: As with most of Finlay's matches, it was a cross between a submission-oriented match and a straight-out brawl, which didn't get over too well with the fans. It was reasonably smooth, but dominated with punches, kicks and clotheslines. Finlay hit the finish out of nowhere; after a rolling Samoan drop, he locked his larger opponent right into the Tombstone. Eight-minute match.

Wrath vs. Bam Bam Bigelow

The Background: This match was the first of the night which caught one's imagination. Not only are they two of the most talented big men in the sport today, who often work spots that middleweight stars have trouble with, but Wrath is also in the middle of a push where Bam Bam seems to be slowly slipping down the ladder after making a big impact in WCW after jumping Goldberg on "Nitro" two months ago. This result would speak volumes about both stars' careers.

The Match: Wrath is well over, in a similar way to Benoit, because of his wrestling style. He uses a lot of charismatic power

moves, and while his actual wrestling ability isn't comparable to that of the former Canadian superstar, his size makes what he does in that ring all the more impressive.

The match started fast, with both men showing their agility. Wrath hit a big jumping boot to send Bam Bam to the outside right off the bat. His offense was impressive, especially a wonderfully executed clothesline/body-block from the top rope which couldn't have been executed better by Rey Mysterio himself. However, the pace was ultimately slow; both guys work better with smaller opponents, and Bigelow, approaching 40, looked a little ragged. During a three-minute resthold we were entertained by Tony Schiavone and Bobby Heenan trying to get Mike Tenay to comment on Bigelow's head tattoos. Finally Tenay crumbled; and attention went back to the match.

Finish: The finish came when Bigelow hit the "Greetings from Asbury Park;" it was badly executed, however, as Wrath's head was obviously several inches away from the mat on "impact." It was hard for the commentators to call the replay. A disappointing performance from the big man, who nevertheless seems to be getting back on track with a renewed push.

Konnan vs. Lex Luger

Background: Konnan and Luger "rode together" for many months as part of the NWO Wolfpack; however, when Hulk Hogan returned to re-unite the original NWO, the Mexican wonder was left out in the cold. Wade Keller recently reported that Konnan and Kevin Nash have legitimate heat over the situation.

Luger was always better as a heel. It was terrific to see him back to his old arrogant self at the start of the match. The fans were digging him as a heel too; "Some guys make it...the elite, the very best, and some don't. You can take the easy way, or I can beat your brains out. You want to 'speak on this?'" Luger is just so funny sometimes, in a cult sort of way. It's all in the delivery.

The Match: The match started fast. Usually I'd be the first one to switch off during a match involving either men; but taking into account the crowd's interest, Konnan's pace and Luger's heel turn, this one held my attention for the first few minutes. Konnan went straight for the payoff, hitting a series of

clotheslines and takedowns before knocking his opponent to the outside; redemption was long overdue for the big man.

Back inside, Konnan hit a series of really stiff kicks to Luger's exposed abdomen before beating him senseless in the corner. Luger hooked the top rope on the whip-in, as the pool was empty for Konnan's attempted drop-kick. Luger just kicked away at Konnan's head as the chorus of boos grew increasingly more intense, climaxing with Luger slapping his foe's head in a sign of total disrespect and provoking the crowd even further. This kind of heat can make any match worth watching, it's impressive to see stars manipulate the crowd like that.

However, the pace soon slowed, as Luger knocked Konnan around the ring and to the outside. He dominated the next five minutes with his predictable brawling style. It picked up near the end, with Konnan ultimately locking in the Tequila Sunrise.

Finish: Elizabeth walked down with her new pair of implants; was that really necessary? Sigh. The interference wasn't the best either. She sprayed paint in Konnan's eyes; you can figure out the rest.

Chris Jericho vs. Perry Saturn

The Background: Looks like this may have been Jericho's last victory in a long, long time. His contract comes up in July, and he hasn't re-signed yet. His issues with Saturn are a great excuse for a series of top matches.

The Match: In contrast to all the matches so far, this one started slow, and just seemed to build and build until the last exchange. As could be expected, both guys delivered an incredible performance, which literally blew away everything on the card up until that point in the first couple of moves. The pace just kept building up until the last few minutes.

Saturn hit a major splash from the top and came close to the three. There was a standing switch, and a series of unsuccessful roll-ups. Jericho hit a German suplex and held the bridge, but couldn't get the three. Irish whip by Jericho reversed, Lionheart sent head first into the corner, leaping on to the top turnbuckle. He stood facing out towards the crowd, as Saturn punched the pad beneath his feet, resulting in Jericho being crotched on the top turnbuckle. The aggressor now climbed up behind his foe, and attempted a super belly to back suplex; Jericho rolled through with it and landed on his feet, and charged at his opponent.

However, it was telegraphed, as Perry ducked down and hoisted his man up onto the shoulders for the DVD. Jericho escaped, grabbing his opponents legs, pulling them out from under him. He teased the Lion Tamer; the crowd popped big for it, he really has the move over. Jericho attempted a vertical suplex, which Saturn blocked and turned into an inside cradle of his own. The ref grabbed Saturn's leg and pulled it over so that it was his shoulders that were down on the mat, and one fast count later Jericho had a victory.

The Finish: According to MiCasa wrestling, Saturn asked the booking committee if he could lose this one; for some reason, he felt wearing a dress would get him over more with the crowd. Otherwise, surely, Saturn would be given the victory, as Jericho's future is in doubt right now. As for the renegade referee? It's been done.

Cruiserweight Title Four Corners Match

Kidman (Champ) vs. Rey Mysterio vs. Juventud Guerrera vs. Psychosis

The Background: There was some criticism on the Internet about "Starrcade," in that the triangle

match between Kidman, Rey Jr. and Juvi was put first on the card, and the rest of the matches seemed to drag afterwards; this time around, it was the fifth match in, which worked much better.

The Match: Both Kidman and Rey Mysterio looked "on" this night, playing the faces, against Juventud and Psychosis. Kidman and Rey locked up and jumped into action, with Kidman hitting a shoulder block, skipping a drop-down, ducking a leapfrog, leaping a monkey flip and winding up flat on the mat via a flying headscissors. No way I'm going to call this one. Psychosis and Juventud were paired off next. They didn't seem to be as hot in their first exchange, though the action was generally of the highest caliber.

It's interesting to see how Lucha wrestlers seem to take turns, ironically meaning that Lucha matches are usually far more organized than their heavyweight counterparts despite being a lot faster. Having Rey/Kidman and Juvi/Psycho pair off during the match, each tandem working with a running mini-storyline between the two groupings which greatly aided organization. There were a lot of really well thought out spots involving two-on-one and two-on-two situations.

The match took to the outside, which saw Juvi and Psychosis arguing over who should perform the asai moonsault on Rey and Kidman. Eventually the latter two recovered and came back with a pair of leaping waist-locks into sunset flip powerbombs from the ring apron to the concrete.

The only problem with the match seemed to be the crowd; Kidman was super-over, Rey was over, but neither Juvi nor Psychosis had much heat going. Either of the heels could have teleported across the arena, and Kidman would still get a bigger pop just by running his fingers through his hair.

The Finish: Kidman hit a slightly awkward Shooting Star Press, landing with one knee jammed into Juvi's gut. Rey tried to break the pin, but was too late running in from the outside. The timing in the match was of a very high standard. Bad timing can kill a match entirely. Top quality action, a lot of hard work that paid off in this one, and Kidman remains on top.

Ric Flair & David Flair vs. Curt Hennig & Barry Windham

The Background: The crowd was hot for the feature tag match of the evening; Hennig and Flair can work great together, they've always done so since hooking up in the WWF in '91. Windham turned on the Horsemen, bad dude.

The Match: After the

traditional "Rookie Luck" (Dave countered a slam with a head-scissors, then a hip toss), Windham took the advantage; Flair soon tagged in and took charge as stinging chops echoed all around the arena. Flair chased Windham into his corner, and Dave actually tried to talk to his arch enemy before remembering he was on the opposite team. Hennig took control. A chop for David sent the crowd swearing profanity at the former "Mr. Perfect," who continued to dominate Flair, who remained in the ring most of the match.

Near the end, Flair came back and slapped the figure four on Windham, only to have it broken up by Hennig. Hennig went for the Fisherman's Suplex on David, but Anderson came in and knocked him silly. The younger Flair collapsed on Hennig for the cover and the pin.

The Finish: After the match, the whole NWO came out and whipped David, with Flair handcuffed to the ropes. It was a highly emotional scene, with Flair crying, screaming obscenities and threatening to kill Hogan. It was a terrific, if predictable, buildup to their recent match at "Superbrawl."

Scott Hall vs. Goldberg

Background: Hall cost Goldberg the WCW title at "Starrcade," so revenge was in order. This is Goldberg's first gimmick match, and Ladder is one of the most difficult. Hall was involved in what are commonly regarded as the two greatest Ladder matches in modern wrestling history, against Shawn Michaels at "Wrestlemania X" on March 20, 1994, and then "Summerslam" in August of 1995.

One aspect that all the commentators praising Hall for his two other ladder matches failed to acknowledge is that Michaels is the greatest wrestler in North America. He could carry a broomstick to a great main event; Hall definitely had something to prove here on this night.

The Match: Both big men are extremely underrated as wrestlers, and neither had to resort to mind-numbing brawling. Goldberg did a fabulous job of selling the left knee that was attacked by the NWO earlier in the evening. It was really believable.

Ten minutes in, the ladder was set up. Hall nailed a great elbowdrop from the ladder, on his first attempt to make it to the top. Goldberg came back to batter his opponent with the giant steel ladder, striking him in the abdomen and over the head repeatedly. Goldberg made the climb, but Hall drop-kicked the ladder and pushed it over on an opponent now splattered in blood from a gash over the head. Hall went for another Michaels-esque move when he took the "groin on a rope" bump while falling from the ladder, but fell a little short of the mark (it probably hurt him a lot more this way). Goldberg climbed the ladder, but Disco Inferno came out for his second non-scheduled PPV main event appearance in a row and knocked him down.

Hall got the tazer, and missed two charges; his mammoth opponent ducked the weapon twice, and nailed him with a superkick. Goldberg recovered the weapon before nonchalantly sending Disco flying to the floor with a single jab.

Back in the ring, Goldberg held the stick high in the air as Hall begged for mercy. The crowd came alive, and the stars in the ring really drew in the heat well. The former world champ finally threw the stick to Hall, which diverted his attention long enough to spear him to the mat before the former "Razor Ramon" could catch it. One Jackhammer later and Hall was prone on the mat, and tasting fresh cattleprod in the gut.

Finish: The 18-minute match really illustrated the underrated talent of both stars. After Goldberg won, Bam Bam rushed the ring and took him out; but Hall grabbed the stick in the confusion and proceeded to shock them both down to the mat. Hall really bust his ass to live up to expectations in this match, and achieved that. He deserves a lot of credit for stepping up a gear in the absence of Shawn Michaels.

Epilogue

Overall, the Pay-Per-View was highly enjoyable. Chavo, Benoit, Flair, Hennig, Goldberg, Hall, Jericho, Saturn, Kidman, Rey all put on great performances. One can seldom find a list that long to rave about on a WWF show, which usually makes up the ground by the use of over-booking, which was somewhat pleasantly absent tonight. All the same, the show suffered from being void of enough quality, original, big-name matches.

by Tony Yannuzzi and Blake Norton

The Nitro Report

December 7, 1998 NITRO

The show's introduction is an interview with Scott Steiner.

Diamond Dallas Page def. Kendall Windham

Pinfall with the Diamond Cutter.

Norman Smiley def. Prince Iaukea (submission)

Smiley uses his new Chicken Wing Crossface for the win.

Rey Mysterio Jr. def. Silver King

Mysterio wins by pinfall.

Wrath def. Renegade

Wrath uses the Meltdown to get the victory.

Chavo Guererro vs. Disco Inferno

Match turns into a tag match between Disco and Chavo vs. Stevie Ray and Horace. The latter team earns victory via a spike piledriver.

Glacier vs. Saturn

Earnest Miller hit the ring, and the match was given to Saturn by DQ.

Lex Luger vs. Emery Hale

Luger wins using the Rebel Rack.

Chris Jericho def. Bobby Duncum Jr.

Jericho is dominated, before mounting a comeback and pinning Duncum with his feet on the ropes.

The Giant def. Scott Putski

The Giant chokeslammed him and pinned him in record time. Then he takes the mic and rips on DDP about their upcoming "Starrcade" match.

Kanyon & Raven vs. Benoit & Malenko

Raven refuses to wrestle, so Kanyon challenges Benoit or Malenko for Thunder.

Konnan vs. Booker T.

Stevie Ray came down to the ring and hit Konnan, causing a DQ.

Scott Hall vs. Scott Steiner

Big Poppa Pump intimidates the WCW referee to the back and the Wolfpack comes out to even the odds for Hall. No decision was made.

Goldberg vs. Bigelow vs. Nash

Bigelow runs to the ring first, Nash then beats on Bigelow, Goldberg runs in and beats both of them. It's so chaotic, that security throws the match out.

December 21, 1998 NITRO

Fit Finlay def. Scott Putski (pin)

As Putski was going for the Polish Hammer, Finlay hit Putski with the Tombstone for the win.

Chavo Guerrero Jr. def. Kaz Hayashi (pin)

Chavo gets the win with the Tornado DDT.

Wrath def. Lizmark Jr. (pin)

Wrath defeats Lizmark Jr. with the Meltdown.

Eddy Guerrero def. Rey Mysterio Jr. (pin)

Eddy tells Rey that the LWO is about all of us and not about one of us. Kidman cost Rey the match in the end.

Norman Smiley def. Prince Iaukea

Van Hammer vs. Barry Windham

Flair comes out and attacks Windham. Members of the NWO try to make the save, but Arn Anderson comes out to beat up Vincent. The police spray mace into the eyes of Malenko and Benoit and put the cuffs on them. Bischoff then tried to get ahold of Flair, and told the police to take Flair away.

Booker T def. Jerry Flynn (pin)

Booker T. won with the missile dropkick.

Lex Luger def. Kenny Kaos (sub)

Kaos' tag partner Rage comes out, and tells Kaos that he is his partner, not Rick Steiner.

Konnan def. Alex Wright (sub)

Tequila Sunrise.

The Giant vs. Disco Inferno (pin)

Giant chokeslammed Disco off the top and earned the three.

Goldberg vs. Scott Hall

Chaos breaks out; Nash pulls Hall out of the ring, Bam Bam attacks Goldberg. It ends there.

December 28, 1998 NITRO

The Cat vs. "Jericho's Friend"

Miller is mouthing off when Jericho challenges him to face his friend; Cat accepts, and finishes off the new guy quickly.

Norman Smiley def. Chavo Guerrero Jr.

Smiley took Pepe, upsetting Guerrero. He won with the "Norman Conquest."

Booker T. def. Fit Finlay

Booker defeated Finlay by pinfall in short order.

Barry Windham def. Prince Iaukea

Squash match for Windham.

Guerrero vs. Mysterio vs. Juventud

Top class match. Eddy gets the pinfall with the Frogsplash.

Disco Inferno vs. Bam Bam Bigelow

Bigelow hits the "Greetings From Asbury Park" Michinoku Driver for the pinfall.

Scott Steiner def. TV Champ Konnan

Lex Luger comes out while Konnan has the Tequila Sunrise half crab finisher on. Luger tries to prevent Buff Bagwell helping Steiner, but manages to inadvertently break up Konnan's finisher. Luger nails Bagwell, who pulls down the top rope as he falls, which Konnan falls over. Luger chases Buff away from ringside, and Scott Steiner gets the victory with the "Steiner Recliner" Camel Clutch.

Scott Hall vs. Bryan Adams

Hall wins it with the Outsider Edge.

Ric Flair vs. Eric Bischoff

Horace and Vincent came from the back but the Horsemen kept them away from ringside. Next, Hennig, Steiner, Giant and Scott Norton come out to join in on the Horsemen attack. Arn Anderson and DDP come in next on the side of Flair. "Macho Man" Randy Savage walked out with his new valet, and was wearing a NWO Black and White shirt. He told the Giant he was going to finish Flair, only to low blow the Giant, and toss him out of the ring. Flair slammed Bischoff, and applied the Figure Four Leglock. Flair gets the submission win. Konnan, Benoit, Mongo, Arn Anderson, DDP, Booker T., Larry Zbyszko, Dusty Rhodes, and Tony Schiavone all joined Flair in his celebration.

January 4, 1999 NITRO

Hugh Morrus d. Glacier (pin)

Morrus then finished off Glacier with the No Laughing Matter Moonsault.

Booker T. vs. Emery Hale (pin)

Eric Bischoff would not say a word during the match. Booker T. easily and quickly won the match with the Missile Dropkick.

Chavo Guerrero, Jr. d. Norman Smiley (pin)

After Chavo Guerrero, Jr. finished off Norman Smiley with a Sunset Flip, Smiley attacked Chavo Jr. afterward.

Chris Benoit d. Horace (submission)

Horace gave Chris Benoit a tough time, but after Benoit got the Crippler Crossface going, he took the win.

Chris Jericho d. Saturn (due to crooked ref)

Jericho executed the Lion Tamer, and the referee called the bell. Jericho got the win, even though Saturn should've gotten the DQ victory.

Juventud Guerrera and Psychosis d. Kidman and Rey Mysterio, Jr. (pin)

After Kidman accidentally nailed Rey Mysterio, Jr. with a missile dropkick, Psychosis finished off Mysterio with the Guillotine Legdrop.

Konnan d. Scott Steiner (DQ)

Bagwell interfered, causing a Disqualification. Steiner threw out the other referee, as the NWO Referee made his way down. NWO Hollywood members continued to attack Konnan.

Wrath vs. Bam Bam Bigelow (no contest)

After the referee was knocked out, Wrath and Bigelow brawled outside of the ring. The referee called the match.

Diamond Dallas Page d. Brian Adams (pin)

Vincent tried to knock Diamond Dallas Page from the top rope, but DDP knocked Vincent right out. DDP then executed the Diamond Cutter from the top rope for the win.

Hollywood Hogan d. Kevin Nash (pin)

Hogan touched Nash with his finger, and Nash went down. Hogan made a successful pinfall, to become the new Heavyweight Champion. Hogan and Hall spraypainted "NWO" on Goldberg and then the Heavyweight Title.

January 11, 1999 NITRO

Ernest Miller d. Saturn (DQ)

Jericho ran in and hit Saturn with a shovel. Dickinson called for the bell, and ended up giving Ernest Miller the victory.

Rey Mysterio, Jr. n. Kaz Hayashi (no contest)

Luger then attacked Mysterio. Luger racked Mysterio and totally destroyed him.

Booker T. d. Lenny Lane (pin)

Booker T won easily with a Sidekick.

Scott Steiner d. Diamond Dallas Page (submission)

Steiner nailed DDP with a chair, and then strapped on the Steiner Recliner to take the win.

Bam Bam Bigelow d. Scott Hall (pin)

During the match, Disco Inferno made his way down with a tazer. Wrath shoved Bigelow from the top rope, as Disco handed the tazer to Hall. Bigelow was shocked with tazer. Hall fell down on top of Bigelow, and made the pin.

Ric Flair d. Curt Hennig (DQ)

Curt Hennig had Ric Flair in the Figure-Four Leglock, but Ric got out. Ric strapped Hennig in the Figure-Four Leglock, but Windham interfered, causing a disqualification.

Kevin Nash vs. The Giant.

Scott Hall came in during the slow match, but The Giant took on the both of them. The Giant later chokeslammed Hall. For some reason, the wrench Eric Bischoff used earlier to set up the ring, was still at ringside. Kevin Nash used it on The Giant to take the win. The NWO stunned and spraypainted The Giant.

January 18, 1999 NITRO

Booker T. def. Chris Jericho (Missile Dropkick)

After Booker hit a sidekick and the Missile Dropkick, he took the win.

David Flair def. Eric Bischoff (KO)

David came out with a one-punch knockout for the win. David revealed he had a roll of quarters when he executed the punch. The Horsemen came down, and they then cut Eric's hair. It was revealed after the match, with a replay, that Anderson was the one that gave David the roll of quarters.

The Faces of Fear vs. Bobby Duncum, Jr. & Mike Enos (tag tourney)

The Wolfpac-NWO made their way immediately to the ring. They destroyed both tag teams.

Disco Inferno defeated Wrath with the Chartbuster

When Wrath was about to execute the Meltdown, Hall attempted to stun him, but Wrath just knocked him out. Disco caught Wrath with the Chartbuster to take a surprising victory.

Scott Steiner def. Saturn (Steiner Recliner)

Saturn was about to execute the Death Valley Driver, but Bagwell was a distraction. Steiner then strapped on the Steiner Recliner to take the win.

Rey Mysterio, Jr. def. Lex Luger (Disqualification)

Nash came down, both Wolfpac members continued the attempt to remove the mask, but Mysterio fought back. Nash and Luger Powerbombed and Torture-Racked Mysterio. Finally, Konnan made the save, and scared off The Wolfpac with a chair.

Goldberg defeated Bam Bam Bigelow and Scott Hall (DQ)

Goldberg then was set to Jackhammer Hall but The Wolfpac-NWO interfered. All teamed up on the attack on Goldberg, until The Four Horsemen made the save. The Four Horsemen and Goldberg were the ones left standing in the ring, while Ric Flair ran after Hogan and his limousine outside of the arena, as the show went off the air.

January 25, 1999 NITRO

Disco Inferno d. Al Greene (pinfall)

Sporting the Red 'n' Black, Disco was confident in this match. He hit the "Chartbuster" and won without a problem.

Scott Hall vs. Bam Bam Bigelow (Ladder/Tazer match – No Contest)

Bigelow finally grabbed the stun-gun, but Disco came back out with his own. Enter Goldberg, who caused the match to be tossed.

Meng/Barbarian d. Fit Finlay/Dave Taylor (pin)

WCW wrestlers were lumberjacks for this tag tourney, just so NWO interference was nil. Barbarian powerbombed Taylor and got the win.

Perry Saturn d. Norman Smiley (pin)

After Perry did his own "Big Wiggle" dance, he hit the DVD for the pin.

Booker T. d. Bret Hart (US Champ) by DQ (Non Title)

Jean Claude Van Damme & Chuck Norris hyped in the audience. Booker wins by DQ after Hart hits him with his U.S. belt.

Goldberg d. Scott Norton (pinfall)

The NWO Black and White member fell victim to a spear and Jackhammer. The fellow NWO Black and White team tried to ambush Goldberg, but to no avail. Van Damme & Norris celebrated with Goldberg in the ring.

Flair/Benoit/Mongo d. Hogan/Nash/Scott Steiner (DQ)

A great, classic match. A wonderful showing by Benoit, especially. It was cut short when Nash hit Flair with a foam finger loaded with a metal pole, given to him by Bischoff. This caused a Horseman DQ victory.

By Sam Jerry, TBR Reporter

Injury Update

Scott Steiner has had injury trouble as of late, with a weak back which prolonged his feud with Rick last winter.

Steiner's partner in crime, Buff Bagwell, should be returning to regular action this month too. His comeback from paralysis due to a mis-timed top rope bulldog by Rick Steiner on "Thunder" last fall has been nothing short of miraculous.

With any luck, Eddy Guerrero will be returning to your screens in the next two months. Eddy was involved in a car crash around New Year's, which destroyed his vehicle and threw him over 40 feet through the air. The fact that he's still alive is incredible, and when his broken hip heals he hopes to return to WCW action. Whether he'll make an appearance before then, with the LWO now history, is up in the air right now, but you can guess that Rey Mysterio will have something to do with it.

Taylor Quits WCW

Terry Taylor quit WCW on the 18th of January. Taylor is said to have been responsible for a lot of great booking on "Nitro" when it was winning (coincidence, I'm sure) last year over "RAW." The 'net has been abuzz with speculation that the 43-year-old may get back in the ring, where it must be said he is brilliant. One might remember his "Red Rooster" gimmick several years ago in the WWF; the Rooster music; the streak of gelled, red-died hair; the "chicken strut;" the feud with the Brooklyn Brawler; it killed his career, full stop. He did wrestle as "Terrific" Terry Taylor in '93, and spend a little time in the WCW mid-card before and after that, but he was never the same guy in front of the cameras.

Whipwreak in WCW

Also on the Cruiserweight scene, Mikey Whipwreak is on his way to Atlanta after signing a deal with WCW for a reported $150,000 a year. The former ECW world champion and Kidman are rumored to start up a major feud upon his arrival; that's a match I'd pay to see.

Two former ECW associates have also come to WCW recently; Bam Bam Bigelow made a big initial impact, but now seems to be petering out. Perhaps his win against Wrath at "Souled Out" on January 17 will push him in the right direction. Bigelow, 37, could now spend the next three years in the mid-card. He may be one of the most agile big-men in wrestling history, but WCW has a huge talent base. Whether or not he'll regain the same form which saw him defeat Shane Douglas for the ECW heavyweight championship remains to be seen.

Fullington entering WCW – As Sandman?

Dave Scherer reported just before press time that Jim Fullington will be hitting WCW with his ECW persona "The Sandman" intact. For the last several months, it's been thought that the former ECW champ and all-around hardcore icon would be used in a different capacity, since Sandman is a beer-swilling, cigarette-smoking, foul mouthed, blood-spurting, hardcore hooligan, and WCW has very strict censorship policies. However, a friend of his, Scherer reported on 1wrestling.com that he'd be continuing on his previous persona after all.

Fullington has already debuted in WCW as the childhood friend of Raven in vignettes. The plan was originally to have Fullington himself turn into a degenerate like Raven, and for The Flock to come back to full strength. The last time around, it was a hostel for mid-carders without heat and/or a gimmick; this time, it was being given more consideration.

Exactly what effect this apparent change in plans will have on Raven and/or the Flock is anyone's guess, and how Sandman would be introduced was also up in the air as of press time. However, it could be suggested that WCW has upped its tolerance for the "extreme" in recent weeks already. Goldberg openly bled on television (which would have resulted in firing or at least wide-angle shooting a few years ago), Ric Flair cursed heavily at "Souled Out" and Hollywood Hogan himself threatened to kill Flair on an edition of "Nitro." Although by no means as racy as the WWF's product, Bischoff may be re-thinking the heavy emphasis on family values as he continues to lose the Monday Night ratings war.

Giant headed to Titan

The Giant should be a WWF employee by the time you read this. He spent the last several months of his WCW career bragging about a big offer from Titan, though some (including myself) thought he may have been bluffing in order to create some leverage for negotiations in a new contract with WCW; but one way or the other, he decided that the WWF was the place to be. Since Nash and Hall jumped to WCW in '96, few, if any, of their major stars have left WCW for the WWF, undoubtedly thanks to larger paychecks and easier travel schedule.

Where was Sting?

Steve Borden, a.k.a. Sting, was out for three months over the Christmas holidays. Apparently he has family issues which need some attention. He's competed at several house shows since then under his "Crow" gimmick, but not on television. Until that happens, it's hard to say exactly when he'll be back or what gimmick he'll use. Some have said that he'll be back to face Bret Hart at "Superbrawl;" you'll know by the time you read this. Bookers are still deciding on what role he should play in the company now that the old NWO has reformed and the Wolfpack now includes Hollywood Hogan.

Hart himself is looking towards a big potential feud with Chris Benoit in the near future; they had a less than memorable encounter on "Nitro" a few months ago, but there's incredible potential for great matches between these two. Let's hope it comes to pass.

NWO Heat

The "Torch" is reporting that there's legit heat between Konnan and Nash over how the Wolfpack was re-invented. One of the dangers of having a star who both books and wrestles. Hennig injured.... again!

Curt Hennig missed a recent "Thursday Night Thunder" taping. After returning at "Starrcade" after several months off because of the leg injury which he says has caused him most of his time off from WCW since his arrival in '96, he again cites his bad wheel as the reason for his absence. Rick Martel attempted a comeback last year and re-retired after a series of leg injuries. Hennig, now in his 40s, might want to consider doing the same if his leg isn't getting any better.

"Uncensored" Update

The WCW's next PPV is scheduled to be "Uncensored," on Sunday, March 14 in Louisville, Ky., with "Spring Stampede" set for April 11 in Tacoma, Wash.

Mark your calendars (better yet, TEAR OUT OUR WOW PULLOUT CALENDAR in the middle of this issue!).

Chris Jericho headed to Titan, too?

A second WCW member who may be leaving the federation in the near future is Chris Jericho. Just one year ago he was in the midst of a major heel turn; as a result, he is now one of the hottest young properties in wrestling. Although a verbal deal was reached between he and WCW last summer, since then the situation has changed, and political reasons as much as anything else seem to be weighing heavily on the mind of the former ECW and WCW TV Champion;

"It's been a crazy week as things between myself and the powers that be in WCW are slowing eroding. I'm seriously pondering my future in WCW. I really want to stay but I guess we just have to wait and see. Hopefully everything will work out," said Jericho on his Web site (www.chrisjericho.com). "Nothing new on the WCW controversy front" he said at press time, "Still at a deadlock standstill. I don't really know what the final verdict is going to be." He also made an appearance on Derek Gordon's "And Justice For Brawl" show on pseudo.com where he expressed his frustrations with how WCW booking is geared towards the older generation of stars.

1. Billy Kidman

Former student of The Wild Samoans, Kidman debuted in WCW in 1996 as a daredevil Saturday Night jobber. Got a major break when joining "The Flock" in '97, and was seen in the Stuck Mojo video "Rising" (along with Raven, DDP and others) doing a shooting star press into the crowd...broke away from the flock by drop-kicking Raven at "Fall Brawl" last year, captured the Cruiserweight title from Juventud Guerrera on "Nitro" the following night to the delight of the crowd in attendance...Has since become the hottest Cruiserweight in North America, continues to dominate the scene in WCW, despite often wrestling more than one guy on more than one occasion in the same night.

2. Bill Goldberg

After suffering his first announced defeat at "Starrcade," the former World Champ has stayed focused to defeat Scott Hall in the "Souled Out" main event. Still the top heavyweight in WCW. The Internet fans love to hate the "Steve Austin impersonator," despite the fact that the only similarities are purely physical. Perhaps he just wanted to prove to Bischoff beyond all doubt that a guy in black trunks and black boots CAN get over. He seems to get better every time he wrestles.

3. Scott Hall

Underrated big man, can actually wrestle as well as brawl. Put on a brilliant performance at "Souled Out" in the Ladder Match. Had a very rocky 1998, with personal and family problems. We hope he can come back to reaffirm his spot as one of the brightest veterans in wrestling.

4. Ric Flair

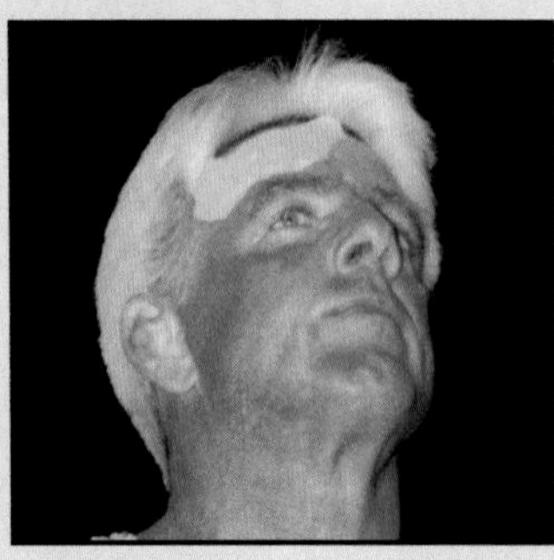

Back in top form, Flair has proven time and time again that despite whatever time has taken from him, he's still one of the very best in North America, in the ring and on the microphone. Turned 50 in February. Finally getting back to wrestling real matches, after fighting with his son David and taking on Eric Bischoff.

5. Chris Jericho

Uncertain waters lie ahead for the former cruiserweight and television champion, as his contract expires in July and he has yet to decide on his future. Was dominated by Konnan in December in their TV Title feud. Recently defeated Saturn at "Souled Out," and had consistently good matches across syndicated shows after carrying newcomer Bobby Duncum at World War III last year.

6. Perry Saturn

First YMCA getup, now a dress? Some would ask questions – not us. Saturn is one of the top stars in the sport whatever his attire. Came back from what seemed a career-ending leg injury to 100 percent in the space of weeks. The doctors said he'd be out a year when he first entered WCW in 1997.

7. Rey Mysterio Jr.

Always consistent, always great in the ring. Suffers somewhat from a lack of charisma. Making a strong run in the cruiser division since coming back from injury at "Bash At The Beach" last year.

8. Kevin Nash

Very agile for a big man. Heel or face, he always earns major heat from his legion of fans. Nash is now one of only five men to have captured the World Title in both the WWF and WCW.

9. Chris Benoit

After an arm injury held him back last Summer, Benoit is now back on track in the Horsemen. Although has been untested as of late, a potential feud with Bret Hart on the horizon could push him up the rankings in the near future.

10. Curt Hennig

Returned from yet another leg injury at "Starrcade" to re-ignite his feud with Ric Flair, six years after it started in the WWF. When he can go, he's one of the best. Great mic work, one of the best heels of the '90s, and that's the way he likes it.

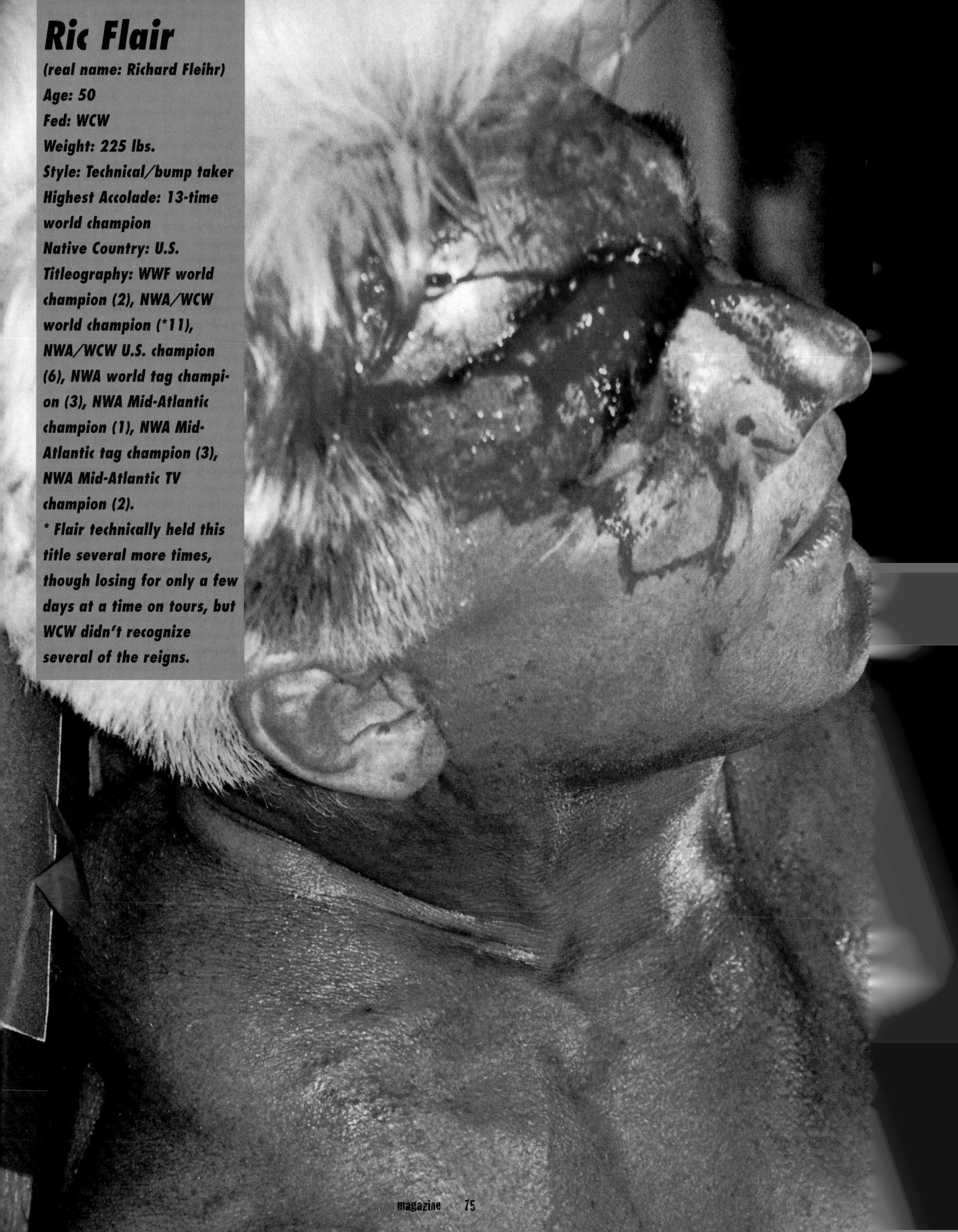

Ric Flair

(real name: Richard Fleihr)
Age: 50
Fed: WCW
Weight: 225 lbs.
Style: Technical/bump taker
Highest Accolade: 13-time world champion
Native Country: U.S.
Titleography: WWF world champion (2), NWA/WCW world champion (*11), NWA/WCW U.S. champion (6), NWA world tag champion (3), NWA Mid-Atlantic champion (1), NWA Mid-Atlantic tag champion (3), NWA Mid-Atlantic TV champion (2).
*** Flair technically held this title several more times, though losing for only a few days at a time on tours, but WCW didn't recognize several of the reigns.**

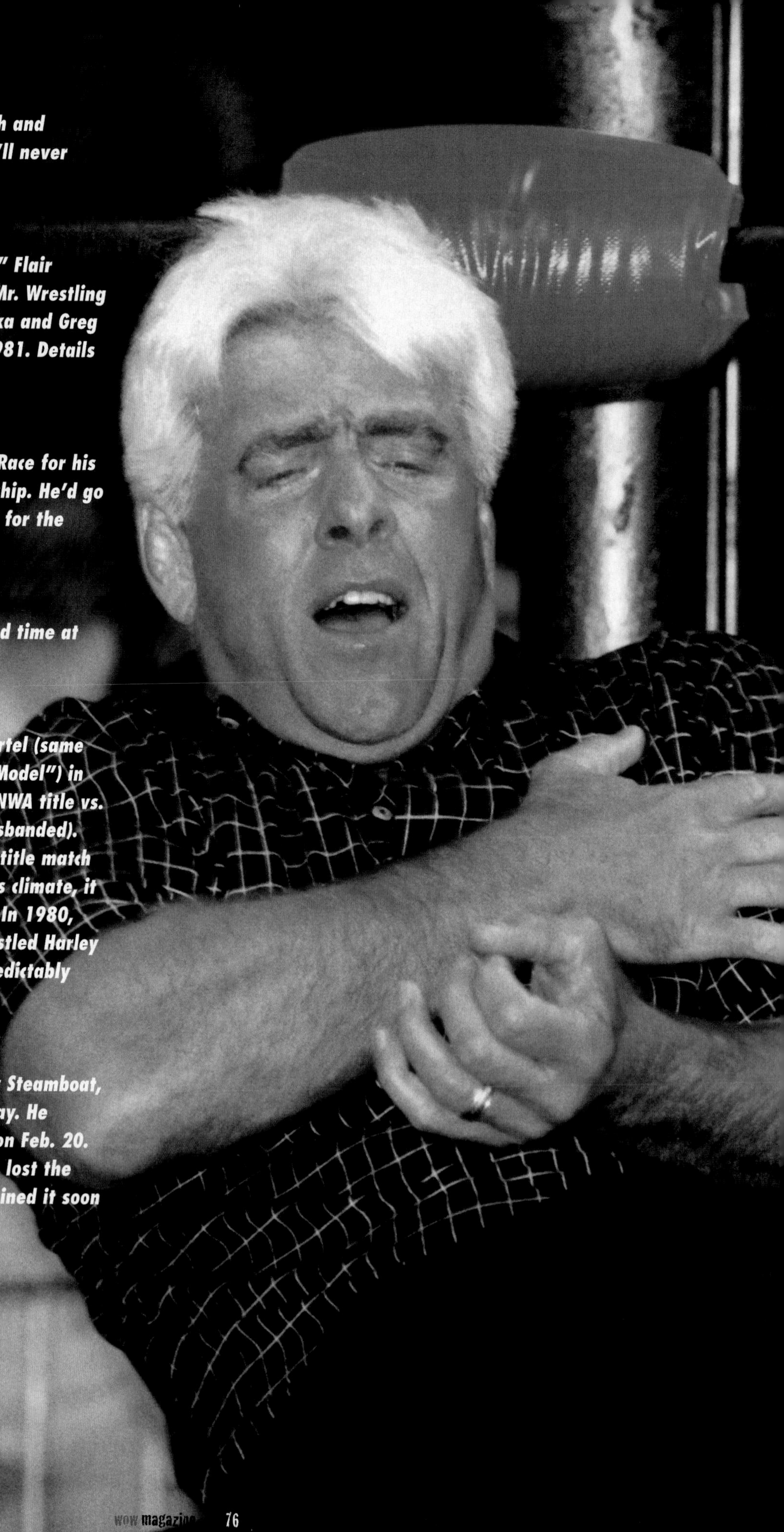

1975
Flair is involved in a plane crash and breaks his back; doctors say he'll never wrestle again.

1977
According to the "PWI Almanac," Flair defeated the late Bobo Brazil, Mr. Wrestling II, Ricky Steamboat, Jimmy Sunka and Greg Valentine between 1977 and 1981. Details from this period are sketchy.

1981
On Sept. 17, Flair beats Harley Race for his first-ever NWA world championship. He'd go on to feud with Race on and off for the next several years.

1983
Flair wins championship a second time at the first "Starrcade."

1985
On Oct. 21, he wrestles Rick Martel (same Martel who later became "The Model") in Tokyo in a title vs. title match, NWA title vs. AWA title (the AWA was later disbanded). While such an interpromotional title match is virtually impossible in today's climate, it wasn't uncommon decades ago. In 1980, Bob Backlund (WWF champ) wrestled Harley Race (NWA champ), though it predictably finished in a draw.

1989
Had a series of bouts with Ricky Steamboat, which are still talked about today. He dropped the belt to Steamboat on Feb. 20. But as with every other time he lost the title the last few years, he regained it soon after on May 7.

1990

Sting won his first world title from Flair at "The Great American Bash" and called Flair the greatest of all time afterwards.

1991

Flair won back the title on Jan. 11. However, when his contract came up for renewal that summer, he was offered a smaller role within the company. Flair, who'd been the main guy for the last eight years, balked at the idea and took off before he had the chance to lose the title. That summer, he brought the NWA heavyweight title to the WWF, in an angle where he insisted to Hulk Hogan that he was the "real world champion." In the storyline, WWF President Jack Tunney distorted the NWA belt on TV. The belt Flair held was actually the authentic version; he owned the belt already, and it wasn't until several months later that Ted Turner (who acquired WCW in 1988) bought the belt back off of him. Hence, it disappeared from TV. Flair hooked up with Curt Hennig (who had been forced out of the ring due to a back injury at "Summerslam") soon after entering the WWF.

1992

Flair won the "Royal Rumble" after drawing number 3 and wrestling more than 60 minutes in the ring. In doing so, he won the vacant WWF title. It's widely considered the best "Rumble" of all time.

1993

He returned to the WCW after losing a "loser leaves WWF" match to Hennig on "Raw" in January. Flair wanted to leave, and WWF owner Vince McMahon didn't feel Flair was part of his game plan for the forseeable future. They parted amicably. Sid Eudy was to defeat Vader for the WCW title and become the company's top man at "Starrcade" that year. But after a hotel brawl with Arn Anderson, he fell out of favor with the company and was fired. Flair was brought in to take his spot, despite the fact that he was inked in to have lesser role. He ended up winning the title.

1994

Flair put Hulk Hogan over clean at "Bash at the Beach" for the strap. He did so several times after that as well, including at a retirement match at "Halloween Havoc."

1995

Reunites the Four Horsemen after luring Sting into a trap. His fellow new Horsemen are Brian Pillman, Anderson and Chris Benoit. With their help, he wins the WCW title at "Starrcade" from Randy Savage.

1998

Was sued by WCW when he missed a "Thursday Thunder" to watch his son wrestle in a tournament. Reportedly, he'd already informed WCW of the tourney months before. When ratings began to drop, Flair was convinced to return with the Four Horsemen, and played up his real-life feud with Eric Bischoff. His quarterly ratings on "Nitro" are generally the highest on the show. At 50, Flair is still going strong.

–by Blake Norton, TBR Editor

Chris Benoit

Age: 31
Fed: WCW
Height: 5-10
Weight: 222 lbs.
Style: Technical/impact/high flyer
Highest Accolade: ECW Tag Champ with Dean Malenko (also won WCW TV title twice against Booker T. in '98, but the WCW acknowledged neither reign.
Native Country: Canada (Edmonton)

WOW
World of Wrestling
magazine
wowmagazine.com
Konnan
nWo
new world order

WOW
World of Wrestling
magazine
wowmagazine.com
lex luger

1985

Trained in "The Dungeon," Stu Hart's legendary training room in Calgary. Others to have done so include Chris Jericho, Bret and Owen Hart and Ken Shamrock. He idolized the Dynamite Kid as a young boy and would watch tapes of him wrestling for hours on end. Benoit debuted in 1985, and would win two tag team championships in "Stampede" wrestling before moving on to Japan.

1990

After "Stampede" wrestling folded in '89, Benoit returned to Japan to compete in NJPW, where he was known as Pegasus Kid and wrestled under a mask. Here, he perfected his high-flying and submission styles, as can be seen in his wrestling today. Pegasus defeated Jushin "Thunder" Lyger, a Japanese legend, in August for the IWGP junior title.

1991

Went to Mexico, won the WWF lightweight title (that version was long since disacknowledged by the WWF, not the modern-day version as worn by Taka Michinoku). He later returned to Japan.

1993

Signed a one-year contract with WCW, but was unsuccessful both in singles and as a tag team with Bobby Eaton. He returns to Japan that summer to win the "Top of the Super Junior" tournament, defeating El Samurai in the finals.

1994

Wins Super J cup, beating Great Sasuke in the final. Benoit joins ECW, where he earns the moniker "The Crippler" after injuring Sabu, and later Rocco Rock.

1995

Joins forces with Dean Malenko to defeat Sabu and Taz for the ECW tag team championships in February. Their reign lasts six weeks. Competed in a non-televised tryout with the WWF, but wasn't signed. Shortly thereafter, he joined with Ric Flair, Arn Anderson and Brian Pillman in a new incarnation of the Four Horsemen in WCW. Malenko and Guerrero also head to WCW.

1996

Feuds with Kevin Sullivan, taking up the slack on a feud that Sullivan had with fellow Horseman Brian Pillman, who leaves the federation unexpectedly. With Sullivan's real-life wife, Woman, leaving him for Chris Benoit on camera, the feud rages to epic proportions. The feud finally comes to a head at the 1997 "Bash at the Beach," with Benoit defeating his arch nemesis in a retirement match.

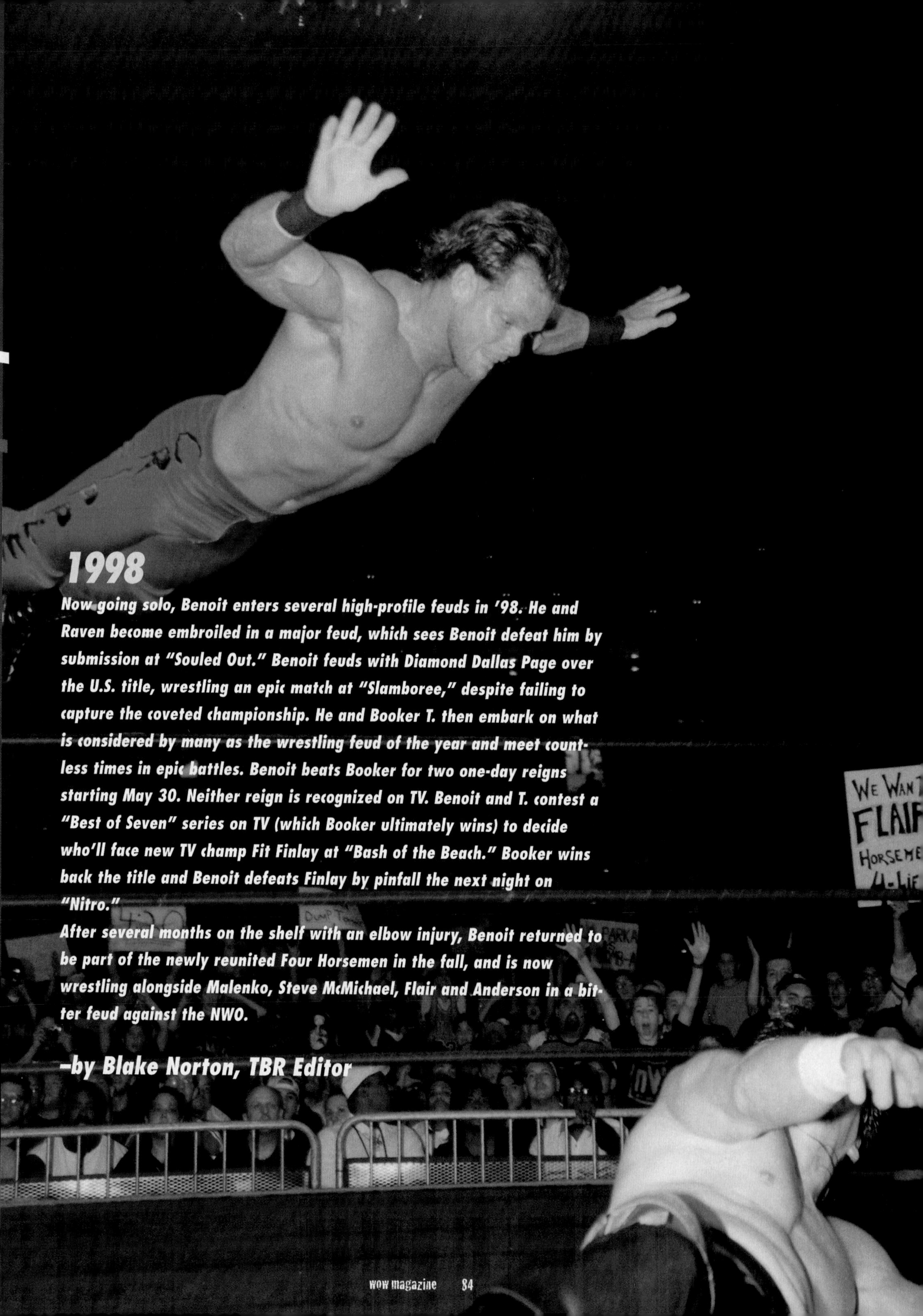

1998

Now going solo, Benoit enters several high-profile feuds in '98. He and Raven become embroiled in a major feud, which sees Benoit defeat him by submission at "Souled Out." Benoit feuds with Diamond Dallas Page over the U.S. title, wrestling an epic match at "Slamboree," despite failing to capture the coveted championship. He and Booker T. then embark on what is considered by many as the wrestling feud of the year and meet countless times in epic battles. Benoit beats Booker for two one-day reigns starting May 30. Neither reign is recognized on TV. Benoit and T. contest a "Best of Seven" series on TV (which Booker ultimately wins) to decide who'll face new TV champ Fit Finlay at "Bash of the Beach." Booker wins back the title and Benoit defeats Finlay by pinfall the next night on "Nitro."

After several months on the shelf with an elbow injury, Benoit returned to be part of the newly reunited Four Horsemen in the fall, and is now wrestling alongside Malenko, Steve McMichael, Flair and Anderson in a bitter feud against the NWO.

–by Blake Norton, TBR Editor

hollywood hogan

Our next president?

bret hart

The Excellence of Execution

scott hall

Coming back strong for '99?

lex luger

The total package!

bam bam

"Where's my career going?"

kevin nash

Former WWF and WCW Champion

the giant

Headed to the WWF?

My milk?
What provokes a wrestling feud? It's not the betrayals or the double crossings. It's wrestlers stealing other wrestlers milk. Milk is what every wrestler needs to be the best in the ring. And when a wrestler steals another's milk, that's worse than a flying elbow from the top of a ladder.

The Future of ECW

Looking back on the events of the past year in Extreme Championship Wrestling, it all seems like a blur. A canvas of faces, angles, and storylines – everything compressed into one chaotic image. There is, however, one theme that stands out from the disorder, not only from last year, but in ECW's history in general.

Survival.

The 1994-95 time period was an era many fans consider the finest ECW's had thus far, a period of excellence which may never be repeated. While the "big two" were otherwise occupied in Monday night combat and such, this small indy promotion possessed arguably the most phenomenal talent roster in the history of pro wrestling: Technical masters like Benoit, Guerrero, Jericho, and Malenko. (You'll never know what a true wrestling contest is until you've seen the Eddie vs. Dean farewell bout from August 6, 1995.) Then there was the heart of the company: Dreamer, Sandman, The Franchise, Mikey Whipwreak, and Sabu. The lineup was every promoter's fantasy and every genuine wrestling fan's dream.

Fast forward four years later and what is left? A few talented prospects, and the many of ECW's core workers, who are either worn down from years of taking insane bumps, or have departed for the green pastures of Atlanta or Stamford.

Beginning in January of 1998, if you were working in ECW without an injury, you were in the minority. This dangerous trend continued throughout the year, during which the ECW crew had sustained a longer list of ailments than "ER" has seen in its four-plus seasons: Broken limbs, broken jaw, torn biceps, fractured pelvis, fused vertebrae, stitches, concussions, the list goes on and on.

These wrestlers spend the better part of the prime of their lives pleasing the fans, bleeding, leaping off balconies, crashing through tables and getting hit over the head with whatever happens to be within their opponents reach – all for very little money. These men, and in some cases women, with themselves and/or families to support, literally put their asses on the line for the sake of our entertainment. And what do they receive in return?

When they decide to salvage what's left of their bodies and posterity, the same ignorant assembly who called them "hardcore," is now chanting "sellout." Is a wrestler somehow forever obligated to a company simply because that's where they got their "big break?" In la-la land, that kind of reasoning might make sense, but in reality, I must heavily disagree.

For example, if you're working for McDonald's and one day, Happy Foods approaches you with an offer to double your salary, you'll work half the time, and as a side bonus, you don't have to worry about carving up your face or having a hospital at the ready. You'll have more time to spend with your family. Can you seriously tell me you'd remain a faithful McDonald's employee?

So where does this leave the future of Extreme Championship Wrestling? With the basic core crumbling, will its hardcore style, which made them popular in the first place, eventually be the downfall of the world's most famous bingo hall? Can Heyman keep a fresh supply of young talent, and major box office draws to keep his buy rates up and his competition nervous into the new millennium? Some have said the return of Sid could be perceived as an indication that they are finally entering the big leagues, yet, with Sid Eudy's habit of contracting mystery illnesses, which can only be cured by playing softball every spring, that is not a long-term solution.

It is my suggestion that, while WCW may have the lineup, they haven't the slightest idea what to do with it, or how to handle the enormous egos.

This is where Heyman holds the advantage. Under extreme pressure (pardon the pun), within this ongoing game of blood, sweat, and broken bones, Paul E. has managed to create superstars so attractive, the big boys are tripping over themselves to snatch them up.

If Heyman can prepare for the long-term, as he has done in the past, without reducing his crew to five-second high spots that have ended so many careers prematurely, ECW can recover from the injuries and constant migrations to emerge as the No. 1 contender to the PPV throne.

If this can be accomplished, then as a fan who has seen the best ECW has to offer, the best could be yet to come.

You can E-mail the author at Galatea@excite.com

The Future of Shane Douglas

Speaking of Douglas, he's been heavily considering retirement. Douglas (real name: Troy Martin, 35) hasn't been too happy about the killing of his character; he's looked like a wimp against Taz in their recent angles. At the recent ECW show, the crowd was chanting "Please Don't Leave".... you have to love ECW fans! I'd like to add our voices to that movement.

If Douglas stays, look for him to be feuding with Chris Candido. You don't have to be an insider to figure that one out, since Candido turned against him at "Guilty As Charged." The latest word from Dave Meltzer's "Wrestling Observer Newsletter" said that he will indeed be hanging on, and that he still has four years left on his contract with ECW.

Also looking ahead to the next PPV, a guess would put Sabu in the main event against Taz. He almost walked out on the last PPV, and is said to be upset with his role in the company, for a variety of different reasons.

Reckless Youth in ECW?

Dave Scherer is talking about ECW boss Paul Heyman being interested in indy star Reckless Youth; he hadn't signed a contract at press time, but could be as you read this. Youth is a big name in the indies.

Next PPV...

The next ***ECW PPV*** will be ***"Living Dangerously"*** on the ***21st of March*** from Asbury Park, N.J. Check your local PPV outlet – if it's anything like "Guilty as Charged," it will be $25 well spent. The PPV will start at 8 p.m. Eastern (7 p.m. live at the Asbury Park Convention Hall).

Tickets went on sale February 1 through Ticketmaster (order by phone or on the Internet at www.Ticketmaster.com).

Van Dam on the Silver Screen

Rob Van Dam will be starring in a new movie, according to his Web site. He's already graced the silver screen in "Blood Moon" and "Superfights." From the site: "The rumors are true! Rob Van Dam is heading back to the silver screen and is in the process of starring in the film "Crunch...The Wrestling Movie."

RVD will play a laid-off auto factory worker who becomes an unexpected hero when he defeats a hated wrestling villain (former ECW superstar and current WCW heel Raven) in a bar brawl and the two become rivals."

by Dave Conroy, TBR Columnist

"Guilty as Charged"

January 10, 1999 / Kissimmee, Fla.

Coming off what some would call a lackluster "November to Remember" Pay-Per-View, ECW made an attempt at redemption with "Guilty As Charged" on January 10th. The general consensus is that they were successful, despite the fact that injuries prevented two of the scheduled matches to take place. The changes were handled extremely well, particularly the decision to give rising star Lance Storm a shot at the TV title in light of the scrapping of a three-way match.

Joey Styles made an insinuation just as the pre-game hype was ending that a former WWF champ that "tore through WCW" would be on the card. Just after going live, Paul Heyman came on the air, and in that overly excited manner of his announced that the card was changing, insisting that despite the absences, they were still going to put on a stellar show.

History has taught us that if any promoter can be believed when he tells us this, it's Paul Heyman.

Full Blooded Italians vs. Amish Roadkill & Danny Doring

As the match approached the five-minute mark, the shot widened and AC/DC's "Big Balls" began to play over the P.A., signaling the arrival of Axl Rotten and Balls Mahoney. Their appearance got a great response from the crowd, which sang along to their entrance music. Axl grabbed the mic and called the in-ring action a "homosexual dance party," issuing the challenge to turn the match into a three-way elimination match.

The pace of the match picked up. Huge fan favorites, Axl and Balls ignited the crowd whenever they became involved, even if some of the spots were sloppy. Tommy Rich nailed Doring with the Italian flag, setting up the fisherman's suplex by Smothers and Guido at 8:14. Just after the 10:00 mark, Balls and Axl finished off the FBI with each of their respective finishing moves. Big Guido and Sal rushed the ring for the save but were met viciously by Balls and Axl's PPV-logo-adorned chairs.

Terry Funk Interview

The interview was to further Funk's angle/feud with Tommy Dreamer. The pace of the interview seemed slow, and seemed to use a ton of words to say very little. Funk's ending to the interview, screaming at the cameraman to "get out" felt forced and out of place in the otherwise calm interview.

Super Crazy vs. Yoshihiro Tajiri

A five-star match all the way, with way too many moves to document. Despite a nice reaction from the fans at the outset, it died off to almost a dead calm by the midway point. At one point during the match, Tajiri locked in the tarantula, an impressive move, but it doesn't make sense, since most wrestling rules say you must break when in the ropes. Then again it's ECW, and their dictionary is missing the page with the definition of the word "rules." Tajiri got the win at the 11:38 mark with a nice dragon-suplex.

Sid vs. Kronus

Ex-eliminator John Kronus made his way to the ring, continuing his angle of a slide into mental instability that was hinted at before Saturn left for WCW. Former referee Jeff Jones told Kronus that in retaliation for attacking him, Jones would be judge, jury and he had a special executioner in store for Kronus.

Out from the curtain stepped none other than Sid Eudy! The monster made his first appearance in one of the big three federations in over a year. The former WWF champion made short work of Kronus, completing the squash at 1:30. He capped Kronus off with his trademark Powerbomb, one as well executed as he's ever done.

One interesting question to be asked of Eudy's return will be whether or not he can withstand the rigors of ECW. We saw Sid issue some brutal chair shots to Kronus here, but what happens when the injury-prone star has to receive those typically intense ECW bumps?

Dudley Boys

Apparently to fill some air time vacated due to injury, Joel Gertner's introduction of the Dudleys was particularly long, and unnecessarily raunchy. Buh Buh Ray next acquired the microphone, declaring that the Dudleys had done everything there is to do in ECW, except one thing – defeat the Public Enemy. Naturally, this was to set up P.E.'s possible return to ECW, as they try to recapture the dignity most would say WCW

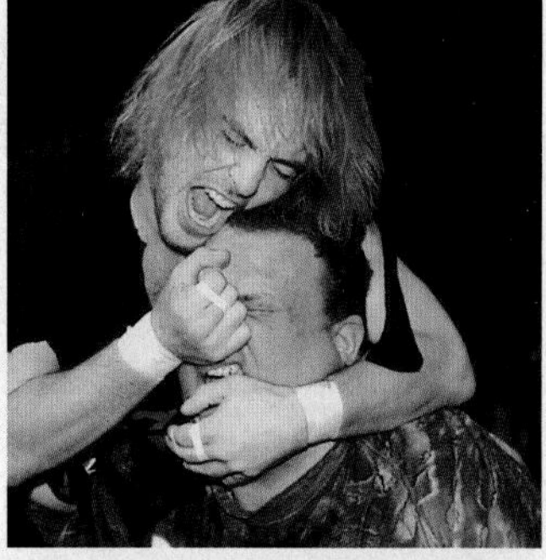

stripped from them.

The Dudleys issued an open challenge, and New Jack hit the aisle with trash can in hand. Following him is Spike Dudley. The unadvertised match begins, the typical mess that is a New Jack match. Plenty of weapons, massive blood loss, and just too much action at once for announcer Joey Styles to call.

Highlights saw Spike get tossed into the crowd much like he did at the hands of Bam Bam Bigelow, though this time the crowd surf did not work as effectively. There were a couple of nice guitar shots on Big Dick, but he no-sold the first one. The Dudleys tried the DDD on New Jack on the ramp, but messed it up. Their second attempt, on Spike, was more successful, ending the match at 10:07.

Television Title Match: Rob Van Dam vs. Lance Storm

The Television Title match between champion Rob Van Dam and Lance Storm became a game of "who could out-spot the other." The match saw plenty of high-impact and high-flying moves, winding up on the floor and in the crowd on more than one occasion. Some spots appeared to leave the combatants legitimately stunned, particularly Van Dam. At one point in the match Bill Alfonso attempted to attack Storm's valet, Tammy Lynn Bytch. Storm raced to stop him, although Bytch probably could have handled the scrawny Alfonso herself.

The ref went down when accidentally hit by Rob Van Dam's finisher, the "Van Daminator." Storm took advantage of the mistake to use the same finisher on Van Dam himself. Before Storm could use a chair, he was hit by the Van Daminator, but the recovering referee only counted to two. They went into a suplex trade-off, which Van Dam won when he got a three-count at 18:46, retaining his title.

"Stairway to Hell" Match (Ladder with a suspended Singapore cane)

Justin Credible hit the ring, posse in tow, sans Terry Funk. Lots of stiff spots and brawling. The highlight of the match came when about 10 or so minutes in, Dreamer introduced a second ladder into the mix. Ladders

placed side-by-side, the two climbed up, nearing the cane. When Credible attempted to move to Dreamer's ladder, he was caught by Dreamer while still straddling both ladders. Dreamer made him pay for the mistake with a "dream cutter," yet another variation of the move Steve Austin and Dallas Page made famous, off of the two ladders.

Dreamer reached the cane first, but Terry Funk appeared and attacked him with a trash can. Justin then grabbed the cane and went to town on Dreamer, topping it off with "That's Incredible" on a ladder. Three count seconds after at the 18:40 mark.

ECW World Heavyweight Title Match: Taz vs. Shane Douglas

The pace started off slow, but picked up quickly as the brawl spilled into the crowd. This is great for the fan's sense of involvement, but simply makes it difficult for the cameras to cover things well. Too often we see fans mugging for the camera, rather than the action.

The two fought their way to the back, whipping and suplexing each other into anything within arm's reach. Both men were juicing badly by the time they made it back to the ring. Table shots were exchanged before the lights suddenly went out. The entranceway to the ring lit up with pyro, and Sabu appeared. Sabu injected himself into the match by destroying both men in a flurry of moves. He exited as quickly as he appeared. Dazed, Douglas called for the Triple Threat.

Candido and Sytch appeared, but instead of helping Douglas, Candido engaged him in a war of words, as did their female companions. After the men separated the women, Candido discarded his Triple Threat T-Shirt and left. Upset and distracted, Douglas fell victim to Taz' kati hajime. Nowhere to go, Douglas passed out rather than tap out. The referee awarded the World Title to Taz.

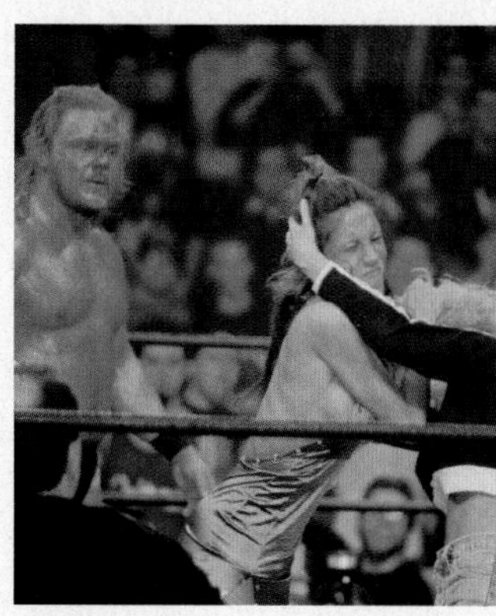

Epilogue

All in all, "Guilty As Charged" was a great Pay-Per-View, and as with all great PPVs, it raised almost as many questions as it answered. What will become of Douglas now that there is no more Triple Threat, and no more World Title around his waist? Three years ago, in an interview, Douglas made it well known that he would only wrestle a few more years. Is the injury-laden icon of ECW ready to retire? What role can/will Sid play? Will Tommy Dreamer ever take Terry Funk on? Are the PE returning? Well, we can all find out at ECW's next PPV, Living Dangerously, on Sunday, March 21 at the Asbury Park Convention Hall in Asbury Park, N.J.

ecw in the house

A roundup of house shows and other-PPV ECW TV events

By Sam Jerry, TBR Reporter

January 22, 1999

Sid d. Skull Von Krush

Sid demolished Von Krush, by Choke Slamming him over the top rope to the floor, and then hitting him with a Power Bomb. The crowd chanted "one more time," and Sid obliged with a second Power Bomb.

Super Crazy def. Tajiri

SC won the match with a Power Bomb and a Spinning Inverted DDT.

Taz v. Chris Candido

Taz's first title defense. Shane Douglas showed up and kicked Candido's head in, then asked for a rematch which Taz agreed to. It turned out to be a great high-impact match with action in the ring, at ringside, in the crowd and out into the street. They fought in the equipment and the announcer's position. In the end, Taz won after hitting a TazMissionPlex onto the table that Douglas brought into the ring. After the match the crowd applauded both men and implored Douglas not to retire, as has been rumored.

January 15, 1999

This program was the first since ECW's latest PPV, "Guilty As Charged," and was used to update the fans on it (See the ECW PPV Review on pages 96-97.)

January 8, 1999

This was the final TV program before ECW's next PPV, "Guilty As Charged," and was used as a promo for it. There was no original action on the show.

January 1, 1999 (Queens, N.Y.)

With ECW's next PPV, "Guilty As Charged" set for January 10, this program was used to showcase the people who will be there.

It began with Terry Funk coming to the ring during a match between Tommy Dreamer and Justin Credible. Tommy was on the mat and Funk began stomping and dissing him. He told Tommy to be a man and get up, then nailed him with the mic. Funk continued his verbal barrage and Tommy just took it.

Joey Styles said there was a problem with "Guilty As Charged" – there is no challenger for Shane "The Franchise" Douglas for the ECW Championship. Douglas said he told us so, that Sabu wouldn't make it to "Guilty As Charged" and that Taz did the job on Sabu that he was asked to. He then called Taz to the ring. Taz came in and Douglas told him he could have whatever he wanted for taking Sabu out, offering money, Francine, or a spot in The Triple Threat. Taz said he wanted a shot at the title and wouldn't show any mercy. Douglas tried to beg off, but Taz wasn't interested. Douglas was beside himself as Taz left the ring.

Yoshihero Tajiri def. Pablo Marquez

Tajiri won after he caught Marquez with a German Suplex, followed by a Brain Buster.

Super Crazy def. Anifaz Del

Crazy hit a Tiger Bomb and pinned Del Norte.

Rob Van Dam (Champ) vs. Skull Von Crush (TV title match)

Fonzie held a chair in front of Skull's face and Van Dam hit a monster Van Daminator, putting Skull's lights out and pinning him. This meant Van Dam would defend the TV Title v. Masato Tanaka at "Guilty As Charged."

December 25, 1998 (Philadelphia, P.A.)

Tajiri def. Del Norte

Tajiri hit a Dragon Suplex for the victory.

Rob Van Dam (Champ) def. Ballz Mahoney (ECW TV Title Match)

RVD nailed a major Frog Splash for the pinfall.

Sabu def. Taz

Taz laid down on the mat and pulled Sabu on top of him. The referee counted and Sabu won the match, although unconscious. Douglas was beside himself as Taz left the ring.

We saw Prazak following Taz into the parking garage asking him why he gave Sabu the win and title. Taz repeated his line about doing the hype and Douglas paying the price. He never gave a straight answer. Back in the ring, Van Dam was checking on Sabu and there was a crowd of people trying to help him. The program ended on that note.

December 18, 1998 (Tokyo, Japan)

Shane Douglas (Champ) def. Gedo (World Title Match)

Gedo is primarily a tag team wrestler and wasn't much competition for Douglas. His offense was limited to going after Douglas' left knee after Douglas missed a Leap Frog. He used a Figure Four that Douglas reversed. Douglas won with a Cradle Brain Buster to retain the title.

We saw a clip from the "November To Remember" PPV, of The Battle Of The Triple Threats. Taz had The TazMission on Douglas, when Sabu came in and nailed Douglas and pinned him for the win, igniting the latest feud between Sabu and Taz.

Jerry Lynn def. Mikey Whipwreck (from Ft. Lauderdale)

Storm hit Whipwreck with a chair to give Lynn the victory.

Masato Tanaka def. Mike Awesome (Heatwave '98)

It was won by Tanaka with a Tornado DDT on a chair.

The Dudley Boyz (C) v. Van Dam and Sabu (Tag Title Match)

It was shown highlight style and the action was fast and furious.The Dudley Boyz used their high-impact style of wrestling and the team of Van Dam and Sabu their high-flying and multiple attack style. Van Dam nailed Buh-Buh Ray with a Frog Splash, a Salto Suplex, and after Sabu threw a chair to Buh-Buh Ray, who caught it, a major Van Daminator pinned him to regain the ECW Tag Team Titles.

December 11, 1998

The program began with ECW Champion Shane "The Franchise" Douglas in the ring, along with Taz. He asked if the fans wanted to see Taz apply the TazMission, then said he was saving it for Sabu.

After the regular ECW opening, Joey Styles was at the announcers desk and gave a run down of late breaking news in ECW:

Douglas suffered a broken wrist in a match in Florida recently,but completed the match and will not miss any action.

Douglas lashed out at The Dudley Boyz, saying they had not held up their end of the agreement to take out Rob "Mr. Monday Night/The Whole F'N Show" Van Dam and Sabu.

A reporter in the crowd in Buffalo questioned The Dudley Boyz about not doing the job on Van Dam and Sabu and was attacked by them as a result. Charges have been filed against the Dudley Boyz.

A Three-Way Dance Tag Team Championship Match pitting The Dudley Boyz (Champs), Douglas and Taz v. Van Dam and Sabu, was won by Van Dam and Sabu after they dominated the match. They isolated Douglas, took him apart and Sabu pinned him to win the match, but not the titles.

The Dudley Boyz attacked Sabu after the match, nailing him with The 3-D (Dudley Death Drop) and then Taz struck again, once again injuring Sabu's neck.

The FBI (OMG and Little Guido) def. Chris Chetti & Super Nova

OMG hit a 747 Splash on Super Nova, knocking him out cold. As he was carried to the locker room, Smothers challenged Chetti to find a replacement and come back. Chetti returned with Tommy Dreamer. Justin Credible hit the ring and nailed Dreamer with his Singapore Cane and he was pinned by The FBI for the victory.

New Jack def. Rod Price

New Jack nailed Price across the skull with a stick, followed by a road sign and a telephone. After garroting Price with the cord on the telephone, New Jack jammed a piece of the stick, which broke when he nailed Price, into Price's face. He then placed what looked like a VCR over Price's privates and smashed the VCR with a hockey stick. New Jack went to the top turnbuckle and came down on Price's head with the hockey stick (or at least that's what it looked like), knocking Price into next week and pinning him.

Masato Tanaka v. Justin Credible (TV Title No. 1 Contender match)

Tommy Dreamer hit the ring and blasted Credible over the head with what looked like a Metal Tray. Tanaka hit a Rolling Whippersnapper and pinned Credible for the victory and the chance to meet Rob Van Dam for the ECW TV Title.

December 4, 1998 (Ft. Lauderdale, Fla.)

Spike, Sal E. Dreamer vs. Rod Price, Justin Credible, One Man Gang

His other partner, New Jack, covered Tommy, while Spike sat on top of the pile and the referee counted the pin. It was never explained which of Price, Credible, Graziano and The One Man Gang were the legal team, however the winners were Spike Dudley, New Jack and Tommy Dreamer.

Rob Van Dam (Champ) def. Mike Lozansky (TV Title match)

The end came after one of the Van Daminators and a Split Leg Moonsault. The match was classic Rob Van Dam, with moves only he is able to perform.

The Dudley Boyz v. Balls Mahoney, Masato Tanaka & Hack Myers.

The match ended when Buh-Buh Ray and D-Von nailed Myers with a 3-D (Dudley Death Drop) and pinned him. Balls took a 3-D also. Axl Rotten came to the ring carrying a barbed-wire-wrapped baseball bat. He massaged Buh-Buh Ray's face with the barb wire, turning it into a bloody mess, and did the same to D-Von when he tried to stop him.

Sabu def. Amish Road Kill.

Sabu took control of the match and hit several aerial moves. He put Road Kill through two tables during the match and won it after a Flying Leg Drop that put Road Kill through a table.

Kronus was in the ring and challenged Douglas to a title match. Douglas came in with Francine. He laid the ECW Championship Belt on the floor and dared Kronus to take it. Kronus started for it, but Taz came up from behind and nailed Kronus with a HardWay TazPlex, dropping him on his neck. He taunted Kronus, telling him to try and take the FTW Title Belt. He then stomped Kronus and followed with a TazPlex. The ring filled with ECW officials trying to protect Kronus. Taz broke through the crowd and applied The TazMission. The ECW officials were finally able to restrain Taz.

1. Taz (World Champion)

The man who defeated Shane Douglas for the ECW heavyweight strap. Taz has morphed from the "Tazmaniac" into one of the most feared, "No B.S." stars in wrestling. His array of suplexes are just awesome.

2. SABU (FTW & Tag Team Champ)

Said to be angry that he wasn't included in the Guilty as Charged main event ... Sabu is one of the most recognizable characters in ECW. Former ECW world champion, also briefly competed in WCW in '95 and has appeared on "RAW."

3. Rob Van Dam (ECW TV Champ & Tag Team Champ)

Van Dam has been on a tear since defeating Bam Bam Bigelow for the TV strap last April. "The one man in professional wrestling who truly is as good as he brags he is" commented Galatea of the "Figure Four Weekly" newsletter. "How annoying is that?"

4. Lance Storm

Youngster coming into his own as of late; hooked up with Tammy Bytch. Came close to beating Rob Van Dam at the GAC PPV in January. Look for him to be pushed into a title run in 1999.

5. Tommy Dreamer

Another ECW original, one of the "innovators of hardcore"... recently entered intriguing feud with mentor Terry Funk, who he helped win the ECW title at ECW's first PPV, "Barely Legal" in '97.

6. Super Crazy

Currently feuding with Tajiri, resulting in top class matches. International star looks to be hanging around in ECW a while, as ECW head honcho Paul Heyman is trying to get more fresh talent after recent departures to WCW.

7. Chris Candido

Formerly of the Triple Threat ... if Shane Douglas hangs around to feud with Candido, it will be a big push for his career ... Won WWF World tag team titles with Tom Prichard ("Zip") in 1996.

8. Jerry Lynn

Star coming into his own after beating Justin Credible several times last year. Currently out with injury, looks to get a sizeable push in the new year.

9. Justin Credible

"While it may be hard to imagine anyone's career going anywhere after you've spent the better part of a year with a groin support on your head, somehow P.J. Walker has done it" said one insider. "That in itself is just incredible."

10. Shane Douglas

If we knew he was staying, he may be No. 1 ... man who founded the "new" ECW in 1994 is now considering retirement ... "Franchise" character considered by most to be the most defined personality of 1998, recognized as the face of ECW. Douglas defines "Hardcore" by attitude.

Rob Van Dam

Age: *28*
Fed: *ECW*
Height: *5-10*
Weight: *232 lbs.*
Style: *High flyer/hardcore*
Highest Accolade: *ECW TV title*
Hometown: *Battle Creek, Mich.*

1989

Trained with The Sheik and his nephew Sabu (his current tag team partner). At the time, he'd already studied kickboxing, and had an interest in becoming a pro wrestler. The name Rob Van Dam would be given to him by Ron Slinker in the USWA.

1990

Made his debut, though only wrestled sporadically in lesser-known indies until entering the USWA in '91.

1992

Had first tour with "All Japan Pro Wrestling." He'd go in to work a lot with Baba's promotion over the next several years.

1993

Was brought in to WCW by Bill Watts and wrestled as Robbie V. However, he didn't stay long, as there was very little talent in the company at the time that wrestled his style according to Van Dam, and left soon after. Reportedly Sabu had the same problem.

1996

Paul Heyman called him out of the blue about working with ECW. He declined at first, but finally agreed in 1996, entering a program with longtime friend Sabu. He's spent the majority of his time since working with Sabu in some form or another.

1997

The biggest angle he's been involved in to date remains the "Respect Match" with Sabu, It fact, it still continues. The feud stems from Van Dam's refusal to shake Sabu's hand after the latter won a match. It led to a bitter feud for respect that spurned several excellent matches on ECW television.

1998

Teamed with Sabu to win the tag team championships from Chris Candido and Lance Storm. Defeated Bam Bam Bigelow for the TV title on April 4 in Buffalo, N.Y. He's held the title since, his first ECW singles championship. He and Sabu won the tag titles again on Nov. 6, defeating the Dudleys in the ECW arena.

1999

Van Dam remains in ECW, one of the top performers in the federation. Since he's had opportunities to go to the big feds, don't look for him to be making any moves in the near future—unless he's offered a contract that really works for him. He's also starred in several martial-arts movies, including "Blood Moon" and "Superfights"." He remains one of the most popular stars in WCW, and his battles with Sabu have been classified as classics.

–by Blake Norton, TBR Editor

spike dudley

Little sexy, the giant killer

taz

Finally World Champion

super nova

High-flying mayhem

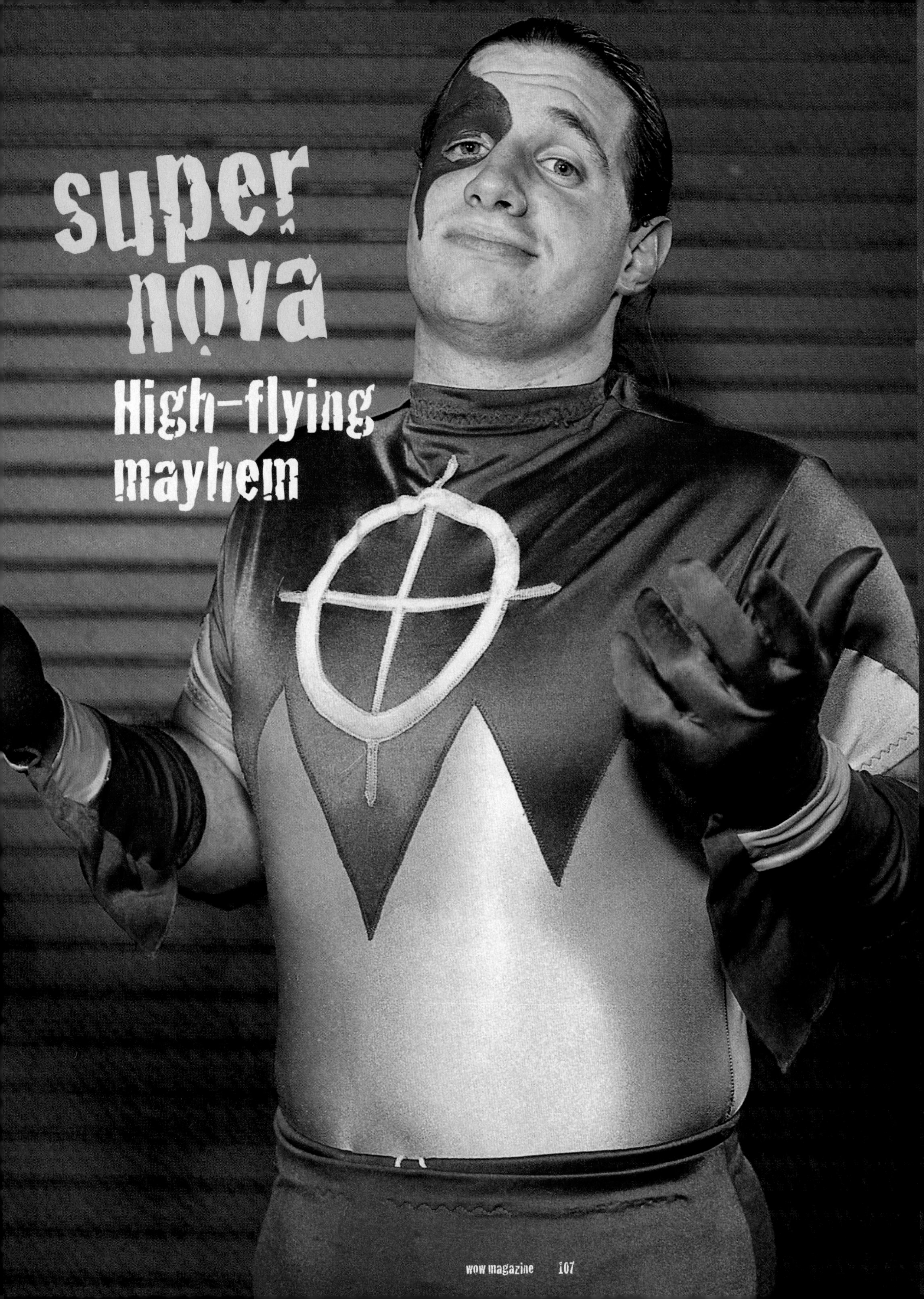

exposed...ecw

new jack

"This place got a balcony?"

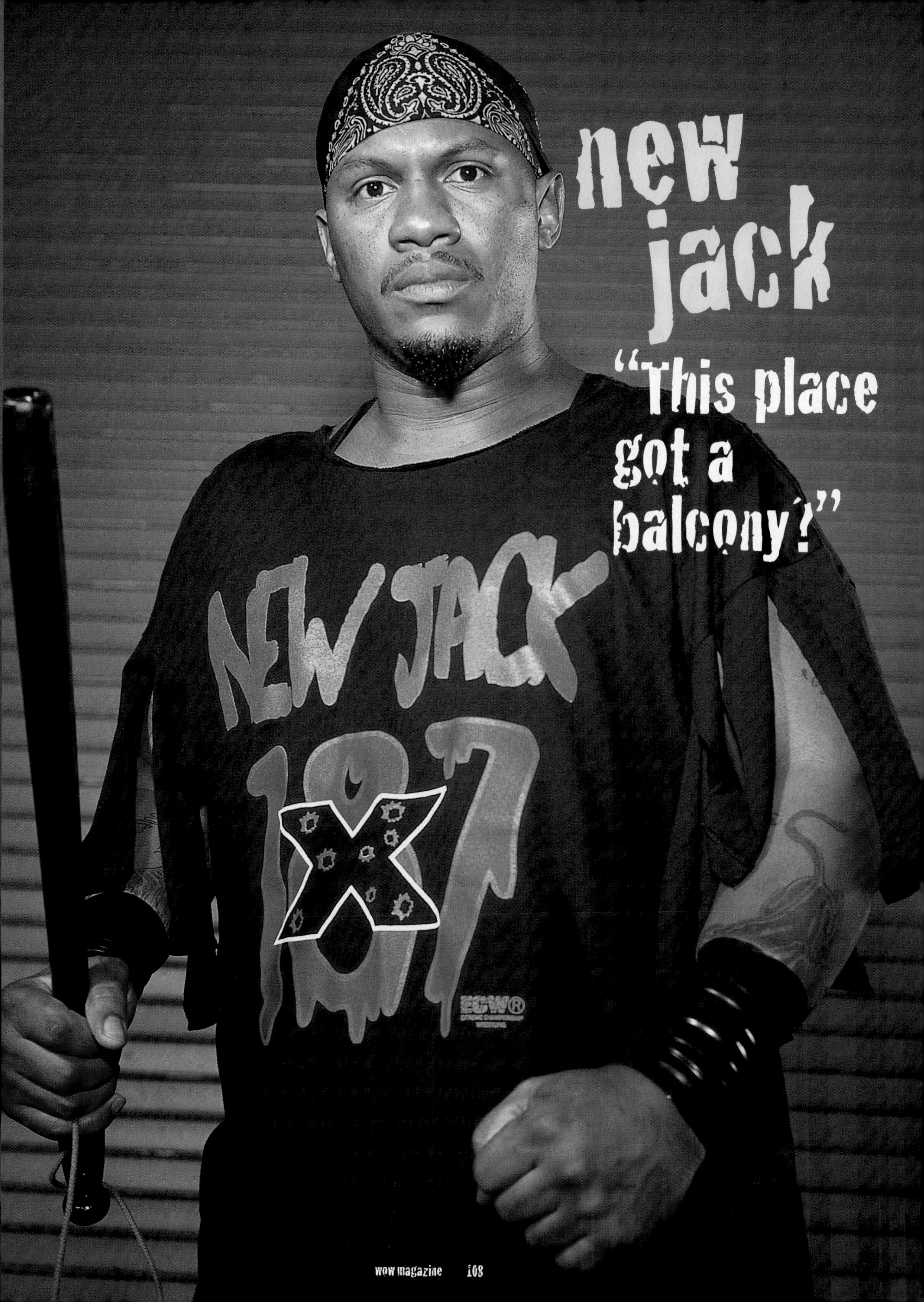

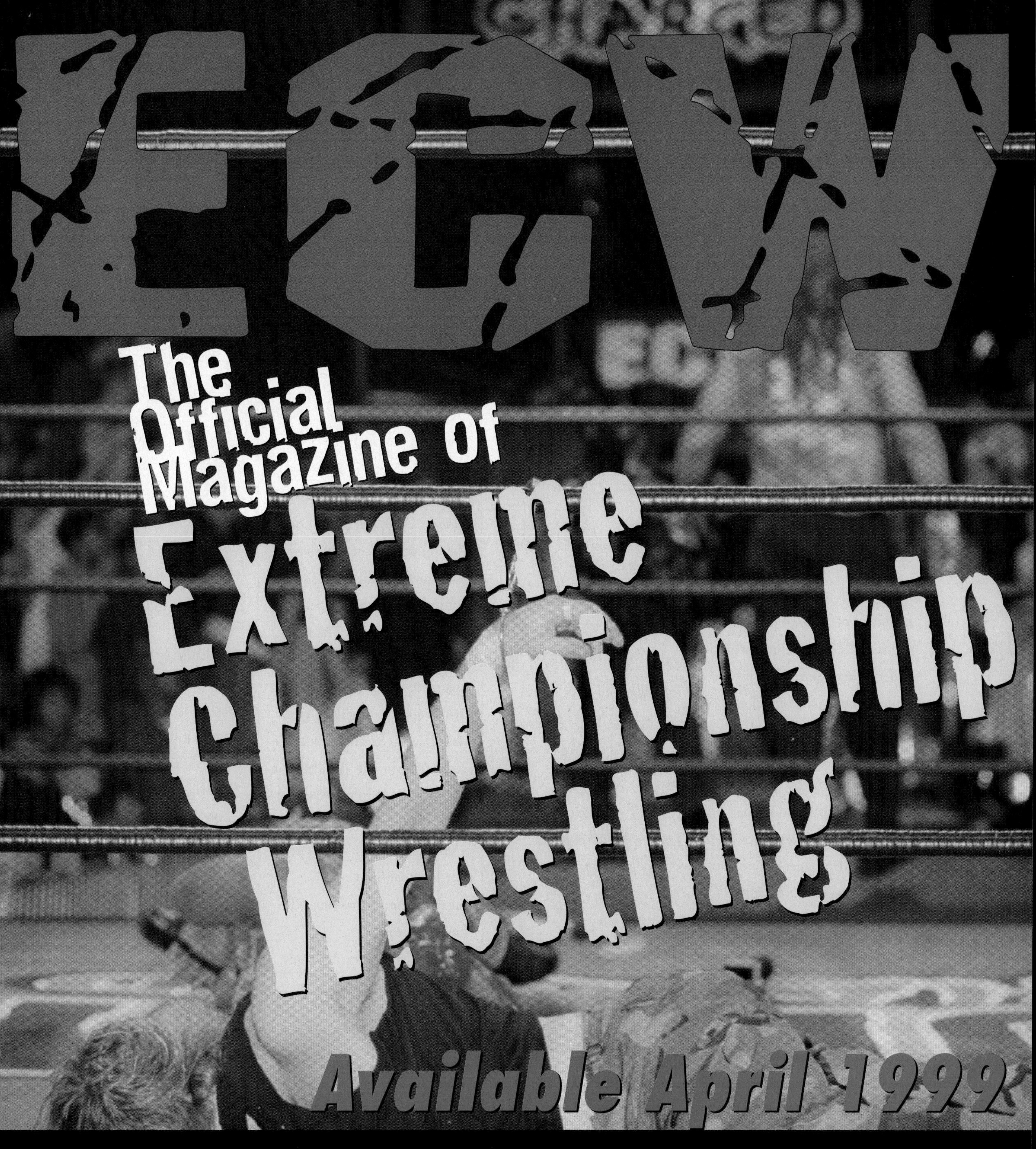

The ***most comprehensive,*** in-depth coverage of the ***wild world*** of ***ECW***!

• *Interviews* • *Features* • *Insider News* • *Schedules* • *Results* • *Color Action Photos* AND MORE!!!

The *International* Scene

by Sammy Eanes

New Japan crowns new champs

Three of New Japan's four championships changed hands on January 4, 1999, when the promotion presented its annual Wrestling World show in the Tokyo Dome, which drew a reported 64,000 fans. In the main event, Keiji Muto won the **IWGP** World Heavyweight Title, forcing Scott Norton to submit to the figure-four leg lock in just under 20 minutes. For Muto, it is his third reign as **IWGP** Champion, two under his real name of Keiji Muto and one under his alter-ego (The Great Muta), which more American fans would be familiar with.

Also in the Tokyo Dome show, the team of Kendo Ka Shin and Dr. Wagner, Jr., became the new **IWGP** World Junior Heavyweight Tag Team Champions with a win over Shinjiro Otani and Tatsuhito Takaiwa. Ka Shin made Otani tap out at the seven-minute mark with a juji-gatame. nWo members Hiroyoshi Tenzan and Satoshi Kojima won the **IWGP** World Tag Team Titles from Shiro Koshinaka and Genichiro Tenryu when Tenzan pinned Koshinaka after a diving head-butt. The only champion in the whole show to keep his gold was **IWGP** World Junior Heavyweight Champion Jushin Thunder Liger. He successfully defeated Koji Kanemoto with a super fisherman's buster.

Atsushi Onita was disqualified in his match against Kensuke Sasaki for throwing a fireball into Sasaki's face. Sasaki was very angry after the match and challenged Onita to an FMW-style exploding-ring death match in the future.

The New Japan vs. UFO challenge ended in a draw. Yuij Nagata (New Japan) made Dave Beneteau (UFO) submit in just over five minutes with a triangle choke. Don Frye (UFO) KO'd Brian Johnston (New Japan) in eight minutes. In the rubber match of the series, Shinya Hashimoto (New Japan) went to a no-contest with Naoya Ogawa (UFO).

Antonio Inoki's shoot-style UFO promotion ran its own show on December 30 in Osaka. The top matches of that show saw Naoya Ogawa defeat Gerald Gordeau and Don Frye beat Kazunari Murakami. The most interesting match of the show took place between Alexander Otsuka and the original Tiger Mask (Satoru Sayama). Otsuka scored the win. His popularity in Japan continues to rise. Otsuka, who wrestles for the Battlarts promotion, became very popular after he upset former UFC superstar Marco Ruas on a KRS show in October.

New Japan's next big show was held on February 6th in Sapporo with Scott Norton, Great Sasuke and Don Frye all scheduled to appear, plus Jushin Liger defending the **IWGP** World Junior Heavyweight Title against Dr. Wagner Jr. Wagner is the younger brother of **WCW** wrestler, Silver King.

Vader's dominance continues into '99

Vader continued to dominate all competitions in **All-Japan Pro Wrestling** through early 1999. His biggest test of this tour was a singles matchup against Kenta Kobashi on January 15 in Yokohama, but fans got a preview of that match on January 5 in Tokyo when the two went at it during a battle royal. Vader got the best of Kobashi, bloodying him up in the process.

Kobashi bounced back from the beating Vader gave him to team with Jun Akiyama to win the All-Japan World Tag Team Titles on January 7, conquering Toshiaki Kawada and Akira Taue. Kobashi scored the pin on Taue following a lariat.

The *International* Scene

Sammy Eanes is an international wrestling devotee from Virginia who has written a self-published book on the subject. A contributing writer to many Web sites, some of his work can be found at: www.geocities.com/Colosseum/Arena/2455.

WWF vs. WCW in Mexico

EMLL ended 1998 with its traditional Year-End Spectacular on December 18 in Arena Mexico. There were some problems leading into the show, with a lot of behind-the-scenes turmoil within **EMLL** due to the fact that they have struck a deal with the **WCW** to bring some of its talent into Arena Mexico, **EMLL's** home arena. The problem is that some of **EMLL's** top talent, namely Apolo Dantes, Negro Casas and the biggest name of all – Hijo del Santo – are all under contract with the **WWF.** This would lead to problems in the future, as neither the **WWF** nor the **WCW** would want their talent in the ring against the competition's talent, because it would look bad for a wrestler under contract to their company to lose a high-profile match to someone under contract to their rival.

The other problem was that the planned main event of Vampiro vs. Rayo de Jalisco, Jr., had to be scrapped because Vampiro left the promotion. The match was originally billed as a title match, but a few days before the show it was changed to a non-title match. Vampiro was angry at that and he left the territory, likely for good this time since he was supposed to start full-time in the **WCW.**

The main event of the show was changed to be the finals of a tournament to crown the new **CMLL (EMLL's championship)** World Trios (Three Man Teams) Tag Team Champions. The team of Dr. Wagner Jr., Black Warrior and Blue Panther won the titles, defeating the team of Scorpio Jr., Zumbido and Bestia Salvaje.

The semifinal on the show was billed as a **WWF** vs. **WCW** match. It pitted Hijo del Santo, Negro Casas and Felino against Los Villanos III and V and Silver King. Of these competitors, Santo and Casas are under contract to the **WWF** (as mentioned before) and Silver King and Villano V are under contract to **WCW.** Neither Felino or Villano III are under contract to either, although Felino has wrestled on **WWF** shows in the past. Santo, Casas and Felino won the match, so the **WWF** can put a notch in their belt for a victory of sorts in the ongoing war with the **WCW.**

Rambo returns to Europe

Rambo made his return to the Catch Wrestling Association **(CWA)** on their December 19, 1998, show in Bremen, Germany. In the main event of the show (**CWA's** annual big show of the year: the Euro Catch Fest), Rambo soundly defeated Big Titan of New Japan Pro Wrestling. American fans would recognize Titan as the second incarnation of Razor Ramon that the **WWF** brought in when Scott Hall and Kevin Nash left the promotion in 1996.

Rambo was the promotion's top star and perennial World Heavyweight Champion throughout most of the 1990s. He held the belt on three occasions, holding victories over Road Warrior Hawk, Vader and Ludvig Borga in the process. He vacated the title in 1997 when he left the **CWA** to join the World Wrestling Federation as Sniper of the Truth Commission. He is now back in Europe and has his eyes set on regaining the **CWA** World Heavyweight Title. To do that he must go through current champion Marshall Duke, who also formally competed in the **WWF** as Duke "The Dumpster" Droese. New Japan also sent nWo member Hiroyoshi Tenzan to Bremen for the show. He went to a 10-round draw with former **WCW** competitor, Ice Train.

Other results from the show saw the **CWA** World Junior Heavyweight Champion Karsten Kretschmer beat Shocker. Rhino Richards and Joe Legend successfully defend the **CWA** World Tag Team Titles against Ulf Hermann (who has appeared in **ECW** in recent months) and Rico de Cuban.

Tony St. Clair kept the **CWA** Intercontinental Title, defeating Robby Brookside. Franz Schumann beat Christian Eckstein in what was described by many as the best match of the entire show.

ECCW year-end awards feature Torch

Billy Two Eagles

Moondog Manson

Moondog Manson piledriving Tornado Tony Kozina

Extreme Canadian Championship Wrestling (a.k.a. the **NWA** Pacific Northwest) handed out their 1998 Year-End Awards, and one of their top stars, Torch, cleaned up. The former **ECCW** Heavyweight Champion really came into his own in 1998 with the introduction of a junior heavyweight division in **ECCW**, a division which better fits his size and style. He has held the **ECCW** Junior Heavyweight Title on two occasions since its inception in October. He also won the Most Improved and Most Popular awards and, in November, was involved in the **ECCW** Match of the Year, a four-way dance for the **ECCW** Junior Heavyweight Title, where he took on Strife, Tony Kozina and Ladies Choice. That match took place at Eagles Hall. The G.O.D. – Glamour Order of Discipline – took home Tag Team of the Year and Gorgeous Michelle Star was named Most Hated.

Toryumon's debut show

Ultimo Dragon's new Lucha-style promotion, **Toryumon**, debuted its show on January 31 in Tokyo. The show would feature Dragon students from his dojo in Mexico, including Magnum Tokyo, Dragon Kid, Shima Nobunaga, Judo Suwa and Sumo Fuji, all of whom have appeared on **WCW** television in the past couple of months. Michinoku Pro's Great Sasuke will also appear on the first tour. The group's first big show was set for February 7 in Yokohama. Look for details on these exciting shows in the next issue of WOW.

In other news, Ultimo Dragon announced that he will be vacating his **NWA** World Middleweight Title and a tournament will be held in Yokohama to determine the new champion. Dragon has held the title since 1994, when he beat Chris Jericho in Tokyo.

Eye on the Indies

by Richard Berger

Independent Leagues are a solid proving ground for young talent

Rick Patterson lay face down in a semiconscious state on the concrete floor. After 26 minutes, the hard-fought match for the North American tag team championship belts finally had come to a conclusion in Vancouver, British Columbia. Now, here in the babyface's dressing room, Patterson was in trouble. A deep gash in his head was bleeding freely, forming a pool on the floor. His blond hair was wet, matted and sticky as the blood began to coagulate. Suddenly, he started to jerk spasmodically and his body began to flail about.

Other wrestlers in the room grabbed various body parts in an effort to stabilize him. Patterson continued to twist and fight, smashing his head on the floor over and over until someone held him by the back of the neck. His tag partner, Jerry Morrow, turned and yelled to me, "Go get a bag with some ice!" I hustled over to a nearby concession stand and was accommodated. Upon returning, I could see Patterson was no longer in the same state of distress. He was now lying on his back as Morrow used a towel to apply pressure directly to the head wound. He accepted the bag of ice from me, and tossed the bloody towel aside.

Other wrestlers in the room grabbed various body parts in an effort to stabilize him. Patterson continued to twist and fight, smashing his head on the floor over and over until someone held him by the back of the neck.

After about 10 minutes, a few wrestlers assisted Patterson into the showers and cleaned him up. When I saw him later, he was still woozy and walking a bit unsteadily, but doing much better. The local ambulance people had arrived and put eight stitches into Patterson's head. His failed attempt to become a tag team champion was over. He would not be proudly wearing a belt that signified he and Morrow had reached the summit of tag team warfare in western Canada's ***Stampede Wrestling***.

Just another night, another crowd to excite and one more stop before the next town.

Such is life on the indy circuit. Far from the excessive glitz and over-the-top special effects of the so-called "big time," this is where it all really begins. I can speak from personal experience, for I was fortunate to work in many capacities for ***Stampede Wrestling*** in the mid-1980s. But this is not about me. When you "work the backwoods" (as smaller wrestling circuits are sometimes called), you keep your eyes and ears open if you're smart. Those who can incorporate what they take from the independent outfits will land in a much better position to advance in their chosen profession.

ECW star Nova put it bluntly: "Today, because there is no Smoky Mountain, no USWA, no territories, nothing like that you can go to for seasoning, you have to do the indies and learn how to work. It is that or nothing."

To illustrate this point, look no farther than Chris Benoit. In 1985, he had just completed his training at the renowned Hart Brothers Training Camp in Calgary. He then began his career (courtesy of ***Stampede Wrestling***), studying hard and becoming facile in the art of working a pro wrestling match. Combined with his natural talent, in no time he was good—in fact, very good. After almost a year of riding the buses in Alberta, British Columbia. and Saskatchewan, he went to Japan to attain his Ph.d. The rest is history.

It's in the independent

Richard Berger is a regular contributing writer for the Bagpipe Report.

groups that a focused wrestler can learn about ring psychology, how best to use transitions in the ring and the fine art of drawing heat. If a wrestler attends this school before applying his trade on a larger scale, he stands a much better chance of knowing his craft by the time he receives national and international attention. It's imperative to understand that it's necessary to learn to walk before trying to run. But make no mistake—life on the independent circuit is tough. It offers few amenities and an abundance of hardships. If the wrestling rookie enters with stars in his eyes, he quickly becomes disabused of that notion. His existence becomes little more than wrestling and traveling to the next town for very little pay or acclaim.

"I appreciate where I am now in **ECW** because I remember going to hundreds of indy shows and not getting paid," Nova says. "There were times I was getting next to nothing, and even losing money a lot of the time. It makes you thankful for where you are. Everyone in this business knows what I mean."

At this stage, the wrestler is akin to a gun for hire in a mutually beneficial arrangement. He needs to work to refine his skills, while the promoter needs young athletes to maintain steady growth. Most independents have a certain number of veterans who have worked at all levels of the business. In turn, the up-and-coming wrestler can take forward strides through the veterans' knowledge and experience. Mind you, some won't make it to the next level. Along with the ability to wrestle, the novice wrestler must learn how to relate to the fans through facial expressions, body language and verbal skills. The constant pounding his body takes causes him pain most of the time. There's little he can do but suck it up and learn to live with it. He has few days off to properly heal. And life on the road makes proper nutrition difficult to maintain, which means injuries often linger.

On the positive side, smaller venues permit greater accessibility to fans. They allow the crowd to enjoy a relationship with their favorite wrestlers—something that doesn't happen when the building is too large. Indies serve as the breeding ground for tomorrow's big names to learn how to relate to the audience in all facets of the business.
For every Mick Foley who reaches the pinnacle of his dreams, there are hundreds of Rick Pattersons who travel the miles, fracture their bones, spill gallons of blood, and yet remain as enthusiastic as when they began. Only so many are going to reach the heights of a Foley. But for those who give so much for so little in return, we tip our hat and acknowledge their importance to the future of professional wrestling.

"I appreciate where I am now in ECW because I remember going to hundreds of indy shows and not getting paid," Nova says.

Now, we're gonna party like it's 1999

gonna party like it's 1999

by Matt "Twiggs" Grill

Some people believe 1998 was the biggest year in pro wrestling history. Others consider it the best year in pro wrestling history. People can say what they want, but there's no getting around the fact that 1998 proved the most important year in the history of the sport of pro wrestling.

It was the year pro wrestling was put back on the map as one of the world's top forms of entertainment. Wrestling in general was taken to another level of not only performance, but also popularity. To be honest, pro wrestling up until this recent reemergence had been seen as a laughingstock by most mainstream media outlets. Now, wrestling can be seen everywhere—from Newsweek and TV Guide right on down to some of the lower-profile magazines and newspapers.

Wrestling has again become the talk of the office on Monday mornings and the discussion of school kids at recess. How can you help not being entertained by the ongoing trials and tribulations of these larger-than-life performers?

Pro wrestling has always had the right product; it just needed a year like 1998 to get it over the top. I don't think anyone thought it would happen like this.

Much of wrestling's recent success is due mainly to the two biggest wrestling names since Hulk Hogan. I am talking, of course, about Stone Cold Steve Austin and Bill Goldberg. The two most over-the-top competitors in wrestling history have turned the sport upside down this past year with some of the most memorable matches and storylines of 1998.

I'm sure we all know where we were when Austin beat Shawn Michaels at "Wrestlemania." What about when Goldberg defeated Hogan at the Georgia Dome "Nitro" and, of course, his unprecedented winning streak leading to that win? Don't forget the incredible Monday nights that Austin always seemed to get the upper hand on World Wrestling Federation owner Vince McMahon, no matter how outlandish the stunt.

Goldberg's winning match after match was getting a bit repetitive, though most of the fans enjoyed every second of it. The image of Goldberg walking

1998 proved to be the most important year in the history of pro wrestling.

down the aisle with 30,000 fans chanting his name will forever be linked with the rebirth of wrestling. Some people may say no two men have played a bigger role in wrestling than Austin and Goldberg. Though not liked well in storylines, there are two other men who in real life should be commended for their outstanding performance.

McMahon and World Championship Wrestling President Eric Bischoff deserve a lot of the credit for the rebirth of wrestling.

If it weren't for their amazing marketing skills and incredible creativity, wrestling would be nothing like it is today. McMahon has reformed the sport a little more than Bischoff by introducing a new style of wrestling—a style where the young and the charismatic thrive.

However, it's also a style filled with controversial storylines, some of which may be taking it too far. McMahon believes that's what sells, and how can you argue with his ratings? Since he moved into these racy storylines at the end of '98, his "Monday Night Raw" program on USA Network finished the year with 10 straight ratings victories over "WCW Monday Nitro," most by decisive margins.

Bischoff, on the other hand, has seen his shows come into a bit of a slump. He has vowed to never put on shows like the ones McMahon airs. Calling the WWF product "shock TV," he has compared the "Raw" program to the "Howard Stern Show." Bischoff's WCW show on TNT is a lot more tame than its competition. He bases his shows around the younger audience, and for the most part, uses no storyline that would even come close to being called controversial. He believes that's the best way to do things.

It's obvious both companies are looking to appeal to different audiences. The WWF seems to target teenagers and adult viewers, while WCW considers wrestling more for the enjoyment of kids.

If the end of '98 is any window into '99, WCW may have to push the envelope a little more to avoid monopolization by the WWF.

Bischoff has taken steps to freshen up his product and get a newer, more lively feel to his storylines. Toward the end of '98, he promoted Kevin Nash and

Wrestling can be seen everywhere.

everywhere

made him a booker in charge of the creative aspects of storylines. Also working with Nash is Diamond Dallas Page. Both seem to have some cutting-edge ideas that will hopefully liven up WCW programming.

The storyline at the end of '98 featured Ric Flair. The night he was inaugurated as president of WCW, Hollywood Hulk Hogan came out of retirement to have the WCW title handed to him by Nash. Let's hope this does not put WCW back into the boring, repetitive angles it had before Hogan's timely retirement on "The Tonight Show."

As of now, it appears WCW is trying to turn a new page and make its show more interesting. The Ric Flair heart attack storyline is the type of thing WCW needs to keep doing—adding interesting angles in the new year to try to regain the edge it once held over the WWF. In the meantime, the WWF is not looking back. It keeps running great TV shows and pay-per-views—and defeating "Nitro" in the all-important Nielsen ratings.

However, this may all come to an end soon. At press time, a WCW deal with NBC apparently was still on the negotiating table (WCW would not comment on the issue). The proposed deal would apparently entitle WCW to run as many as six prime-time specials on NBC throughout 1999. The idea would be to go head-to-head against the WWF pay-per-view

Cutting-edge ideas will liven up WCW programming.

events, which would truly be a huge step for WCW.

The WWF also wants to follow in WCW's footsteps and get its own program on the network level. To compete with WCW, it will have to strike a deal with one of the major networks. A network TV show reaches many more viewers each week than "Raw" and "Nitro" combined each week, opening up the leagues to a new market. It can be seen by fans who haven't seen wrestling since the WWF left network TV. Such a time slot (prime time Sunday night) would mean WCW garnering ratings five times higher than on the Turner networks. This is something that all three major promotions have been seeking for quite awhile.

Drawing Heat

The fans, now more then ever, play the most intricate role in wrestling. No longer do the promoters decide the good and bad guys—fan response does. Today, fans play a bigger role in wrestling than they may think. Entire storylines are now based around fan response to a wrestler. And, this has never been more prominent than in 1998.

Unknowingly, fans singlehandedly took Goldberg to the top. The same can be said for The Rock and Austin. Of course, they had great gimmicks, and in the case of The Rock and Austin, they both had great catch-phrases that won over fans. If it weren't for the incredible fan reactions night in and night out to all three of these guys, they would not be the main eventers they are today. In the business, we call that drawing heat—getting a fan reaction, whether it is face heat (being cheered) or heel heat (getting booed). It's the one thing wrestlers can't live without. If they don't receive heat from the crowd, promoters consider them useless.

More than ever, fans became smarter and more aware of what was going on in the ring during this past year. Years ago, fans used to get caught up in storylines of good versus evil, without knowing the actual circumstances. But now they know the lives of wrestlers better then they know themselves. The Internet and dirtsheets are always looking for a controversial story to print or an angle to give away. Though not always right, more dirt in the sport is revealed and known by most wrestling fans.

Wrestlers are now viewed under a microscope, with fans talking about their every move. This makes the wrestling world vulnerable to scandals. Though reporters are usually on top of everything in pro wrestling, an often-overlooked occurrence is the amount of illegal drug use that runs rampant throughout every major promotion.

Like it or not, it exists and I hope it doesn't take another controversy like the one McMahon and the WWF endured to realize it's a problem. Another scandal like that would set the wrestling industry back several years, overshadowing the recent boom in the industry. Steroids are far from the only problem these days.

Wrestlers ar under a microscope

Some wrestlers, due to the great stress they put on their bodies every night, are beginning to use painkillers for comfort.

After months of taking a painkiller (for instance, to work off an injury), an athlete can become dependent on the only thing that seems to heal his pain. The addiction sets in: a wrestler believes there's no way to go on without these pills. Who can forget the losses of Brian Pillman and Louie Spicolli, both due to fatal mixtures of drugs and alcohol? And don't think this problem is a thing of the past.

Fans play a bigger role in wrestling than they may think.

Entire storylines are now based around fan response to a wrestler.

These same addictions affected Scott Hall throughout 1998—and leave it to WCW to exploit his very real problems into a storyline. I have witnessed wrestlers using illegal drugs following shows. Of course, I will not give names for fear of repercussion, but believe me, it was done. I would not at all be surprised to see a drug scandal unfold sometime in '99, whether in the WWF, WCW, ECW or all three. The problem is by no means exclusive to one federation.

I just hope each promotion cracks down and cleans up its act—at least to the point that the problem isn't so visible to the public. With wrestling's mainstream media coverage of nearly all shows, one slip-up could open the door to a scandal that could kill the sport's newfound momentum.

Rising to the Top

Riding the breakthrough year of 1998, wrestling is now popular as ever in '99. If you don't think so, just take a look at the numbers. Not only did the WWF and WCW earn great TV ratings throughout '98, they caused other well-established programs to decline. "Monday Night Football," a mainstay at the top of the ratings charts for years, suffered from the wrestling boom. "MNF" ratings dropped 8 percent this past year. Though it still draws average ratings of 13, remember that the show has been on for 29 years. Also keep in mind that it airs on network TV.

'Riding the breakthrou[gh] of 1998, wrestling [is as] popular as ever'

Meanwhile, the combined ratings in '98 for "Raw" and "Nitro" in the fourth-quarter hour of "MNF" totaled 9.2—a huge jump from the previous year—and has exceeded an average of 10 so far this year.

Not only did the Monday-night ratings of each show jump, so did the pay-per-view buy rates. Now let's compare the 1997 WWF buy rates to the ones of '98. The 1997 "Royal Rumble" drew a 0.60 buy rate, compared with a 1.01 buy rate for '98. "Wrestlemania" saw the biggest jump in '98, mainly due to the incredible star power of a main event that included Shawn Michaels, Steve Austin and Mike Tyson. The '97 "Wrestlemania" drew a poor 0.73 buy rate, a number that was more then doubled by the 2.2 drawn by the '98 show.

The numbers speak for themselves and do not just tell the story of the WWF's success in '98. All three federations saw huge jumps in ratings and buy rates—not to mention the incredible revenue drawn by merchandise sales. It now seems everyone owns a piece of clothing with his or her favorite wrestling superstar on it. The WWF and WCW make thousands of dollars on merchandise at every show. The top sellers, of course, are the readily available Stone Cold shirts that seem to make their way into every clothing store. The Stone Cold videos also have climbed to the top of the videotape sales list.

Austin isn't the only man cleaning up on merchandising. Goldberg, Degeneration-X and NWO shirts are all generating incredible sales.

Let's not forget ECW; the numbers for its sales are also on the rise. On average, every person at an ECW show buys 1.3 T-shirts. Merchandise is a huge part of the profit for every ECW show. By far, ECW videotapes are most-requested tapes for sales and trade—whether via the Internet or through the promotion itself.

If you're not a believer yet, then you never will be. The numbers do not lie.

Looking Ahead

With '98 in the past, you may wonder what to expect in the future. Well, no doubt '99 will be filled with headlines that rival last year's huge stories.

Right now, the biggest story of '99 is shaping up as the big jump by the Giant to the WWF. McMahon will turn the Giant into a main-event talent by the end of the year and make him a superstar. You'll see the Giant become an indestructible big man and wreak havoc in the WWF.

And look for the WWF-WCW rivalry to escalate this year. As '98 was wrapping up, it became more and more evident that both federations were doing anything in their power to make their product outsell the others. This included the WCW giving away taped results of "Raw." 1999 is guaranteed to be filled with wars and mudslinging—the likes of which we have never seen.

The upcoming year also looks promising for a fad somewhat in a slump towards the end of '98. Look for ECW to come back in extreme fashion and again put itself right up there with the big two. One thing in ECW's future is a national television show. By the end of '99, it's more than likely that ECW will get a national cable show, thereby competing even more with the WWF and WCW.

We also may see the emergence of another federation, promoted by the Fox network, that will try to compete with the success and take some of the spotlight away from Titan and Turner. If the Fox promotion does form, it will already have a big edge on the WWF because it will, of course, have a network show right off the bat.

A promotion like this could really shake up the wrestling world. And, to be honest, I hope it does. This would cause everyone to up the ante and, in turn, give us a more entertaining show. 1999 will mark the biggest year for pro wrestling, by far surpassing the industry's record success in '98.

So, everyone strap in because it's going to be a long ride. Who knows where the curvy road of wrestling will take us in the upcoming year?

Matt "Twiggs" Grill is the owner of www.Ringsiders.com, where his top story and articles are featured every day. He can be reached via E-mail at TWIGGS316@aol.com.

h year
is now
n '99."
HOL

WOW
World of Wrestling
magazine

Direct from Cyberspace, and www.ScoopTHIS.com, home of the BEST wrestling parody on the Internet, WOW Magazine is proud to present ...

Ring-Zingers

"Because if you see it in print, it's got to be true!"

This is a Parody

More Stone Cold Look-alikes?

ATLANTA, GA – In the wake of Bill Goldberg's tremendous success, World Championship Wrestling is planning on repackaging several of its key wrestlers to look like the WWF's Stone Cold Steve Austin.

The company tried testing the waters where it's safe and nothing really counts – in other words, a house show – in front of an unsuspecting crowd in Atlanta, recently. Hulk Hogan, Kevin Nash and Bret Hart came out with shaved heads, black short tights, and had each grown a vandyke in the hopes of boosting their sagging popularity.

"I tried everything to get over in this @#$% company," confessed Hart after the show. "Whining, being good, whining, being bad, whining, apologizing, whining ... you name it, I tried it. Even whining. And none of it worked. But tonight ... did you hear that crowd? It was unbelievable. And that's the bottom line."

Hogan, who is planning a run at the presidency in 2000, couldn't believe it.

"I've heard loud pops, brother, but tonight was the motherlode. I didn't even have to work the mike. Just walking to the ring was enough. Usually, I get cursed out of the building for using the same three moves during a match, but not tonight, brother. Tonight, those three moves opened up a @#$% can of whoop-ass."

WCW is holding production on its next line of action figures. The new marketing strategy will save loads on production costs, since they can now include the same doll in every package and simply change the name it's advertised as.

As a result of the brilliant move, Ted Turner promoted Eric Bischoff to Senior Superior Executive of Elite Management Affairs, two levels above Turner himself.

WOW
World of Wrestling
magazine
wowmagazine.com
the
undertaker

Mr. McMahon

Big Poppa Pump Explodes!!

Stonecold Bret Hart

KNOXVILLE, TN – Thousands of fans in attendance and millions watching live around the world were witness last Monday to one of the most gruesome events in television history as Scott Steiner, a.k.a. "Big Poppa Pump," exploded on "WCW Nitro" following a match with Diamond Dallas Page.

As the match went back and forth, Vincent ran in, causing DDP to run into the referee. Buff Bagwell then threw powder in Page's eyes. DDP nonetheless nailed Vincent with the diamond cutter. Steiner then surprised Page with a chairshot, and strapped on the Steiner recliner for the win. Steiner then flexed for the audience in attendance, and exploded.

"It was one of the most gruesome, disgusting things I've ever seen," confessed one fan in attendance, too shaken up to elaborate.

"This is the greatest Nitro of all time," was announcer Tony Schiavone's only comment. "This is the single greatest moment in professional wrestling history."

"I've seen a lot of wrestlers," added color commentator Larry Zbyzsko, "and I've seen a lot of wrestling. But never ... EVER ... have I seen a man explode during a pose-down."

Scott Steiner had been gaining more and more muscle tone in the past year, which led to his nickname of "Big Poppa Pump." But ever since Hollywood Hogan's return at the helm of the New World Order, Steiner's been feeling a bit insecure.

"Scotty felt the pressure," said Marcus "Buff" Bagwell, "and tripled his bodybuilding efforts, just to keep up with the popularity of the reformed team and not get tossed."

Steiner will be away from action for an indefinite period of time, depending on the severity of the explosion.

"Enough is Enough, and it's Time for Some Change!"

ANAHEIM, CA –Owen Hart, who quit the World Wrestling Federation after accidentally injuring Dan Severn, was spotted in Anaheim, California last week.

The brother of WCW millionaire mid-carder Bret "The Hitman" Hart was seen washing car windows with a squeegee in exchange for "whatever people are kind enough to offer."

"Sometimes, people recognize me, and that's always kinda neat," said Hart. "Sure, some flee in terror at the very sight of me because of my reputation for accidentally paralyzing people, and I'd be lying if I said it didn't hurt me somewhere inside whenever that happens ... but other times – and those are the best times – wrestling fans will throw in an extra couple of bucks. There's no feeling like it."

Thirty-four complaints of accidentally broken windshields and scratched car exteriors have been filed before the The California State Automobile Insurance Commission against Hart, including 12 alleging physical injury. A court date has been set for May 14. •

Wrestling's king of kings, Hulk Hogan, has become legend with a 20-year-plus reign of dominance. But even the self-proclaimed "God of wrestling" has had to resurrect himself a couple of times over his career.

Today, the Hulk Hogan who invades our TV screens is a rippling reprobate. Clad chiefly in sinister black, he barks out his agenda of destruction to crowds all over the country. Hulk Hogan is wrestling's Darth Vader, a diabolical villain who uses his power to create chaos.

It's a far cry from times when Hogan stood for morality and truth. If the two personalities were to stand face to face inside a ring today, they would appear as different as day and night. But behind either version stands Terry Bollea, the man who breathes life into Hulk Hogan. As easy as it seems for Hogan to exist in the wrestling business, Bollea has had to live through the ups and downs to keep up that illusion.

In 1993, after a decade in the World Wrestling Federation as its signature star, Hogan was allowed to leave the company. WWF owner Vince McMahon decided that for some of the WWF's young, up-and-coming performers to reach the top, his older stars had to go. On June 13, 1993, Hogan made his last WWF title defense at the "King Of The Ring" in Dayton, Ohio.

He signed with Ted Turner's World Championship Wrestling nearly a year later after the longest time he had spent out of the wrestling spotlight. Just as it seemed Bollea had a fresh beginning in his career, an old issue threatened to destroy it. In July 1994, he was summoned to testify in federal court during McMahon's trial for steroid possession and distribution.

Bollea testified he had used various types of steroids himself from 1976 to 1989. This information contradicted statements he had made on the "Arsenio Hall Show" in 1991. Bollea said he "trained 20 years, two hours a day" to look like he did and that "I'm not a steroid abuser and I do not use steroids." During questioning, he admitted he did not tell the whole story on the "Arsenio" program and lied about his steroid use to the press.

While McMahon was acquitted later that month, Hogan's name became included in newspaper and magazine stories of steroid abuse. Though Hogan admitted to using steroids only while still legal in the United States, the public perception left his career in question yet again.

Hogan became wildly successful in his first few months in WCW. After winning the WCW title from Ric Flair in his first WCW

Resurrecting the Hulk

Hulk Hogan survives the ups and downs, ins and outs of pro wrestling

by THE STRAIGHTSHOOTER

Hulk Hogan
is wrestling's
Darth Vader

match, Hogan became WCW's most bankable star. Behind the scenes, Bollea was given significant power over the direction of his character. Having been brought in by Turner to impact the wrestling world on its behalf, Bollea reaped the benefits of Hogan's success. It was understood that Hogan called his own shots in WCW.

On September 4, 1995, WCW's confidence in Hogan resulted in the inception of "WCW Monday Nitro," a live wrestling program to run opposite the WWF's own show, "Monday Night Raw." Unfortunately, after six months of running neck-and-neck with "Raw" in the ratings, the numbers began to reflect the WWF's pulling away from its competition.

Recognizing that Hogan's name alone wasn't enough to help WCW climb over the WWF in the ratings, WCW Vice President Eric Bischoff began to use Turner's considerable resources to attract other big-name talent. WCW reached deep into its pockets to lure WWF superstars Razor Ramon and Diesel to the Turner organization. Going under their real names of Scott Hall and Kevin Nash, respectively, The Outsiders (as they were billed) operated under the concept that WWF stars were invading WCW. After a few months in the company, the two inspired a surge in "Nitro" ratings, but something was still missing.

Personality Change

Bischoff began to brainstorm about how this angle could be taken to the next level. It was then that he spoke to Bollea about radically changing Hogan's character. The idea would be for Hogan to turn heel and become the third member of The Outsiders. Bollea initially opposed tearing down all that Hogan's current character had built over the years. However, Bischoff explained that this move would refresh the Hogan character, not kill it. After much consideration, Bollea agreed to take a chance.

In an event considered one of pro wrestling's defining moments, Hogan became the third member of The Outsiders on July 7, 1996 at WCW's "Bash at the Beach" pay-per-view telecast. He emerged from the backstage area to attack Randy Savage, Sting and Lex Luger in a show of unity with Hall and Nash. Then, with one sentence, Hogan cemented his new role as villain by telling the fans they "can stick it!" On that night, The New World Order was born.

Almost overnight, the "Nitro" ratings skyrocketed past "Raw" and into unprecedented heights. As leader of the NWO and WCW champion, Hogan had his most visible platform for self-promotion since the zenith of his WWF tenure. With the NWO making WCW's box-office business white hot, Bollea became entrenched backstage as ruler of the roost. After Bischoff joined the NWO later in 1996, Hogan and those close to him received the bulk of the TV time and storyline angles. Hogan, though never considered a technical great on the mat, began to draw critical reviews from all over the industry.

At "Starrcade '96," Rowdy Roddy Piper—hardly in top wrestling shape himself—gave Hogan his first clean defeat in more than six years with a sleeperhold-submission victory in their non-title matchup. Critics, fans and even the WWF referred to the cage match as "Age in the Cage," calling it a poor offering for a pay-per-view main event.

Soon after, Hogan stepped away from WCW to work on projects in film and TV. While he spent time in Hollywood, WCW turned to Hall and Nash to carry the ball. Fans began to cheer the NWO, responding to the element of "cool" that Hall and Nash provided.

In July 1997, Hogan returned to WCW and announced nefarious Chicago Bulls forward Dennis Rodman had joined the NWO. Rodman's outlandish reputation appealed to WCW fans and helped Hogan regain some fame. Unfortunately, the team of Hogan and Rodman came up short in their match against Lex Luger and the Giant at "Bash at the Beach '97." The loss began Hogan's first slump as a professional wrestler. He lost the WCW title to Luger in August, but got it back a week later at "Road Wild." But then he lost to Roddy Piper yet again in a non-title cage match at "Halloween Havoc."

During Hogan's slump of 1997, WCW officials were spending the year building up a Sting/Hogan match for "Starrcade '97." It was believed that Sting would become the next centerpiece of the company with the planned title victory over Hogan. However, Hogan had other ideas. In a bout that ended with more confusion than crescendo, Sting defeated Hogan for the WCW title with help from new WCW arrival Bret Hart.

But once again, Bollea made sure the Hulk Hogan character would never be far from the top of the heap for long. In early 1998, Hogan recaptured the WCW title from Randy Savage, who had defeated Sting for the belt not long before. But this time the fans were neither glad nor upset that Hogan was the champion—just indifferent.

The fans' indifference to Hogan's victory was caused by another significant moment in wrestling: the feud between Stone Cold Steve Austin and McMahon in the WWF. Austin had become wrestling's No. 1 draw and successor to Hogan's role as most visible entity. The WWF was experiencing a renaissance, climbing out from under a massive winning streak by "Nitro" in the ratings to beat it on a semi-regular basis. Ratings for "Nitro" both on TV and pay-per-view dropped noticeably—something WCW executives did not take lightly.

By this point, a rookie performer by the name of Bill Goldberg had taken WCW by storm with an inconceivable undefeated streak and the roar of the crowds in most arenas. For the second time in his illustrious career, Hogan was about to be cast aside so younger talent could take his place.

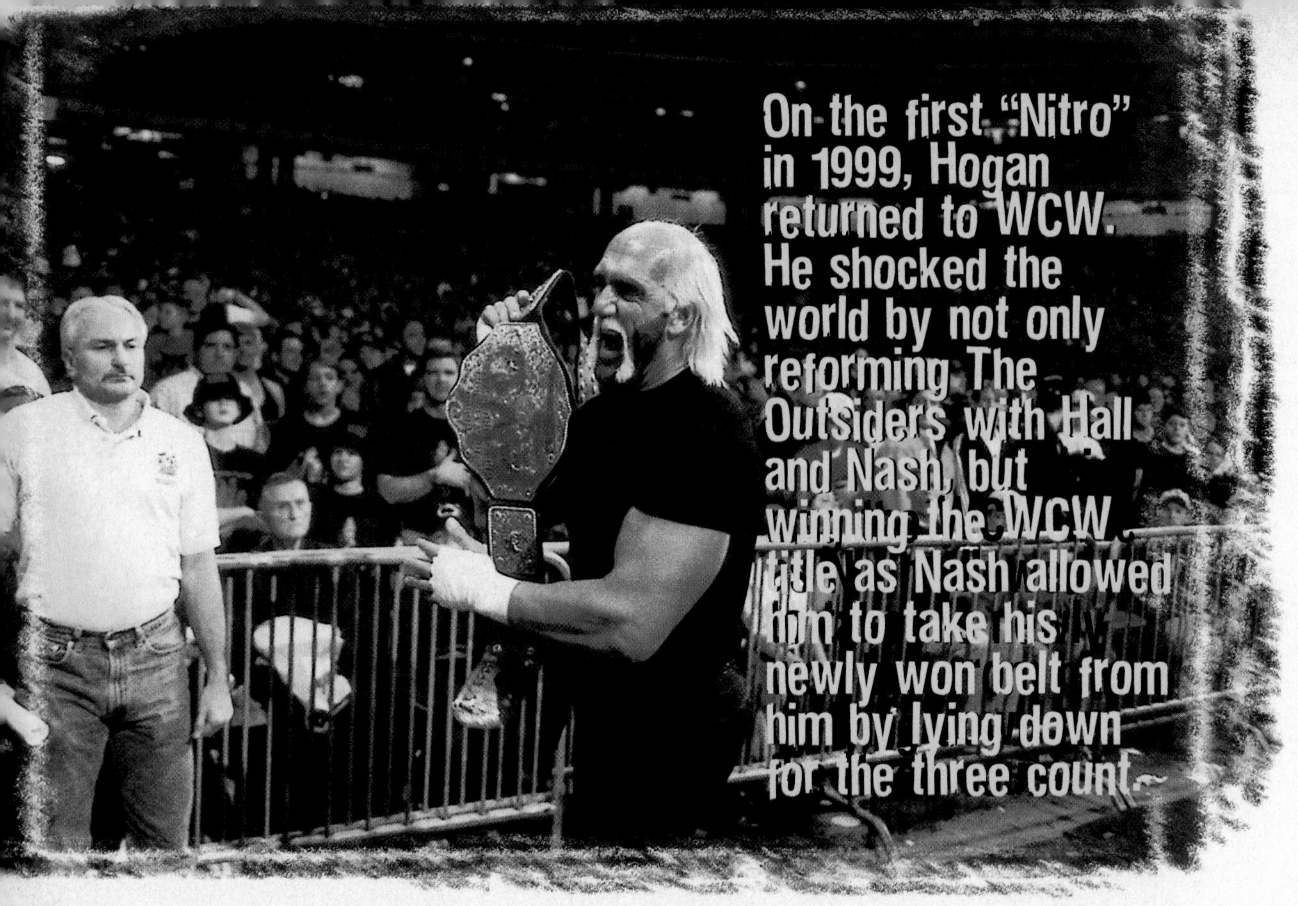

Another Fall

On July 3, 1998, Goldberg upset Hogan for the WCW title during a live "Nitro" broadcast from the Georgia Dome in Atlanta. Not only had Hogan been defeated in the ring, but Bollea was losing a political war backstage with Kevin Nash. Nash represented the new group of WCW stars who wanted to crack the glass ceiling and break out in the company. After a split in the NWO that saw Nash form his own Wolfpac apart from the black and white of the NWO, Hogan's career went into a free-fall that couldn't even be stopped when WCW brought in The Ultimate Warrior to face him.

After a disastrous pay-per-view buy for Hogan/Warrior 2 at "Halloween Havoc '98," WCW could no longer deny that Hogan couldn't carry the company. Bischoff, the man who helped Bollea revive his career in WCW, became the man who had to end it by telling Hogan to go home.

As a cover for Hogan's departure, Bollea decided to create a mock candidacy for president in the year 2000. With the stunning victory by former wrestling star Jesse "The Body" Ventura in the race for Minnesota governor, Bollea became jealous that Ventura was reaching heights that he had never reached. Fueled by jealousy and pride, Hogan announced his retirement from pro wrestling to pursue presidential aspirations on Thanksgiving night on "The Tonight Show" with Jay Leno. He used this farcical gimmick to extract the last few moments of glory from the public before he faded away.

With Hogan gone from the company, WCW used many of the younger stars who had lobbied for a chance to shine. Seeking ways to expand the visibility of his company, Bischoff negotiated with NBC about a possible series of network specials. NBC, haunted by the prospect of having the NBA lockout force a cancellation of its season and leaving lots of air time to fill, held serious discussions with Bischoff.

The last time NBC had aired pro wrestling was in the late '80s, when Hogan reigned over the WWF. Knowing that Hogan was property of WCW now, NBC insisted that any deal would include Hogan getting lots of time in front of the camera. The network still believed the name recognition of older stars like Hogan would draw a large viewing audience. While WCW had already decided those older stars could no longer help, the thought of reaching the network before the rival WWF was too attractive to pass up.

On the first "Nitro" in 1999, Hogan returned to WCW. He shocked the world by not only reforming The Outsiders with Hall and Nash, but winning the WCW title as Nash allowed him to take his newly won belt from him by lying down for the three count. Bollea had once again resurrected Hulk Hogan's career, with help from NBC.

Hogan is once again on top of the wrestling mountain. But while the WCW/NBC deal apparently still is on the table (WCW would not comment on the issue at press time), he knows that for WCW to move to the next level, it must keep him in the spotlight. "Hulkmania" may not live forever, but it will live to see another day.

THE STRAIGHTSHOOTER is a featured writer and regular contributer to www.RINGSIDERS'.com

For the second time in his illustrious career, Hogan was about to be cast aside so younger talent could take his place.

by A. Rettinger

i met with scott steiner backstage at the georgia dome a couple of hours before the monday nitro live television event. he was cordial, gave me a brief interview and posed for some of the photos you see here. we had several interruptions because he has a lot of air time and he was in demand so i was happy that superstar scott steiner could spend . . .

5 minutes with "wow"

5 minutes with "wow"

On January 4, 1999

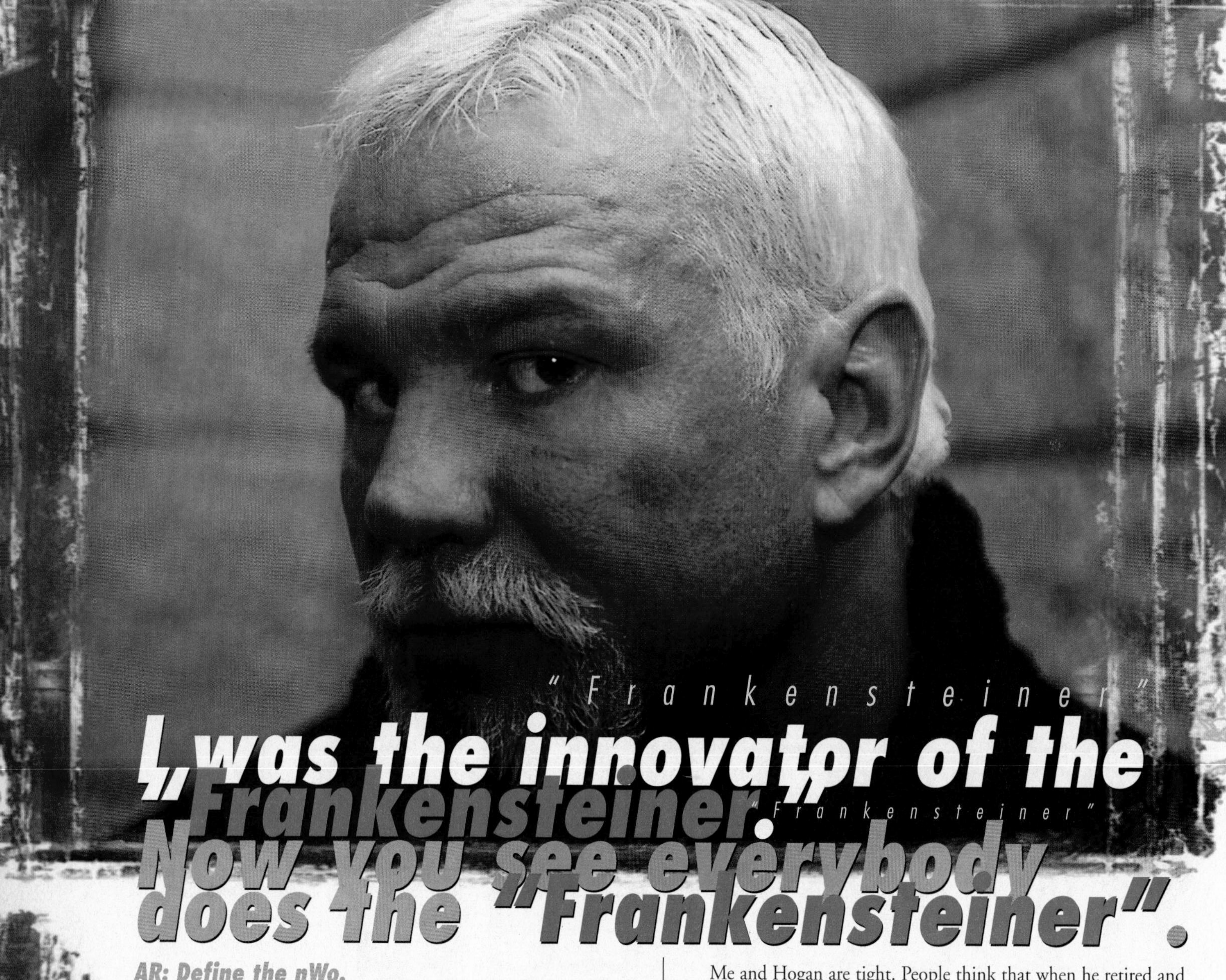

I was the innovator of the "Frankensteiner." Now you see everybody does the "Frankensteiner".

AR: Define the nWo.

SCOTT STEINER: We are a bunch of bad boys that only care about the nWo family. Our main objective is being the #1 organization in sports, which we already are. We've already achieved greatness and will continue being great until eternity (4 life).

The New World Order is an organization that Hollywood Hulk Hogan started up two years ago and he made it the greatest organization. He chose me to take over when he retired. He made me the spokesman. Hulk Hogan was the originator of the 24" pythons (biceps). Everybody knows that. At this current time I have the largest arms in the world. It's just a natural progression. He was the originator and I'm just carrying on tradition.

Me and Hogan are tight. People think that when he retired and passed the torch on to me, that was it. I have always stayed in contact with Hogan. It's no secret. Everything we do in the nWo Hogan has approved. He has approved of my attitude and my attitude change in the nWo. He knows that I'm all about the nWo.

AR: How did it feel wrestling your brother?

SCOTT STEINER: I've beaten up my brother my whole life. In this instance (regarding joining the nWo), he did not see the light. He did not want to joint the nWo, but stay with the WCW. I was the leader of the Steiner Brothers since day one. He did not want to follow my lead. So he brought it upon himself (the Steiner vs. Steiner match) and basically I put him out of wrestling.

I was the innovator of the "Frankensteiner." Now you see everybody does the "Frankensteiner." I taught my brother other moves and we were the first tag team to do the "Bulldog" off the top rope, the "DDT" off the top rope, invented a lot of great moves. I made the Steiner Brothers great and I'm going to make the nWo great because I'm great.

AR: How do you feel when another wrestler steals one of your moves, like the "Frankensteiner?"

SCOTT STEINER: It's like imitation is the best form of flattery. If they can't use their own minuscule minds and come up with something new, you know I don't care. It's more a testament of me being 285 pounds doing the "Frankensteiner," then you see the Mexicans at 150 pounds doing it. So it shows what type of athlete I really am.

AR: Describe your whole style of wrestling now versus tag team style. Seems like you do a lot of power moves now and you finish off an opponent quickly.

SCOTT STEINER: It's hard to withstand the power of force. Scott Steiner is a powerful force in wrestling. So opponents don't last as long. If I can hurt somebody before I beat them, then I'll hurt them. When I finally get them in the "Steiner Recliner," there's nothing better than hearing them submit. That's when you are breaking some guy's will. It's a great feeling.

AR: Another form of power you hold is over the people.

SCOTT STEINER: I've come to realize that most people suck. That's a part of life. That's my personality and if people don't like it they can kiss my (bleep).

AR: When you go into a town for an interview, you bury their sports team or hero. Like in St. Louis, ribbing Mark McGwire.

SCOTT STEINER: ESPN buried him for two-and-a-half weeks. I just put my own spin on it. Too bad if the St. Louis fans can't take a joke. Mark McGwire brought the baseball fans back to that sport this year. I heard a lot of the St. Louis fans and some of the people in the organization were kind of pissed off but whatcha gonna do?

AR: Does the nWo have something to do with the resurgence of professional wrestling?

SCOTT STEINER: Most definitely. The nWo is a group of elite athletes that no one has ever seen before. People pay to see great athletes. I'm a freak of nature. There is nobody's body that is as good as mine in professional sports. They pay to see me.

AR: Your new look is similar to Superstar Billy Graham. Did he have influence on you?

SCOTT STEINER: The look is similar. I'm not exactly the same. His hair was long. He was an innovator back then, like I am now. He was one of the first guys to have a great physique in professional wrestling back in the sixties. I actually never really saw Billy Graham wrestle. I've seen pictures of him when he was older in the WWF, when he was done wrestling. I think my new look goes hand-in-hand with my aggressive style. If you look at me you can tell I'm not a nice guy. And I'm not a nice guy. So, I'm not trying to fool anybody.

AR: What is your relationship with Buff? Has it taken the place of your relationship with your brother Rick?

SCOTT STEINER: No. I'm on my own. I'd rather be on my own. We're the nWo. Buff is like a brother in the nWo. We work together good. We are just getting the job done and spreading the word. Buff had a serious neck injury last year. Accidents happen, injuries happen. It could happen to anybody, so as a wrestler in general, I think everybody was concerned, but I tell you one thing, if Buff wasn't in the nWo as soon as he got better I would kick his (bleep). You don't like to see injuries, but once you get better all the condolences are out the window.

AR: Getting up for a live event . . .

SCOTT STEINER: On live TV, everybody wants to be on TV. All the fans want to be on TV. They definitely are a lot more vocal. So you notice a difference in the crowd, in their enthusiasm, and such. It's a lot easier to get up but also it is more strenuous doing it week after week after week.

AR: Do you see nowadays in professional wrestling the fading of the "team" vs. the "gang" style?

SCOTT STEINER: Yes, we are thugs, criminals. Society is a lot more jaded. I've always been a tough guy. Wrestling in college, All

It's hard to withstand the power of force

It's hard to withstand the power of force

American. I've always had that persona. Throughout life you realize certain things, you know.

AR: Was professional wrestling a fulfillment of a childhood dream?

SCOTT STEINER: No. I didn't start watching professional wrestling until I was in college. I started watching it then and saw some of these lame wrestlers like Tully Blanchard, the Midget, the Rock and Roll Express . . . these guys are like 5'6"? If these guys could beat somebody up — well, we (the Steiners) proved a point. We kicked everybody's (bleep).

AR: Greatest moments in wrestling?

SCOTT STEINER: Every time we (The Steiners) won the Tag Team Championships it was a great time and also when we won them in Japan. Wrestling in Korea in front of 106,000 was a big thrill, too.

AR: After 10 years in the business, are you in your prime?

SCOTT STEINER: What do you consider prime? When we (the Steiner Brothers) went in here (to the WCW), we won the World Tag Team Championship. I've always been in my prime, better than anybody else. Yes, then I am in my prime because I beat everybody up. But as soon as somebody comes along and kicks my (bleep) then I'm not in my prime, and if anybody wants to prove me wrong—prove it!

A. Rettinger is a well-respected wrestling photographer, journalist and friend to wrestling superstars too numerous to mention here. Look for her work in future editions of "WOW"

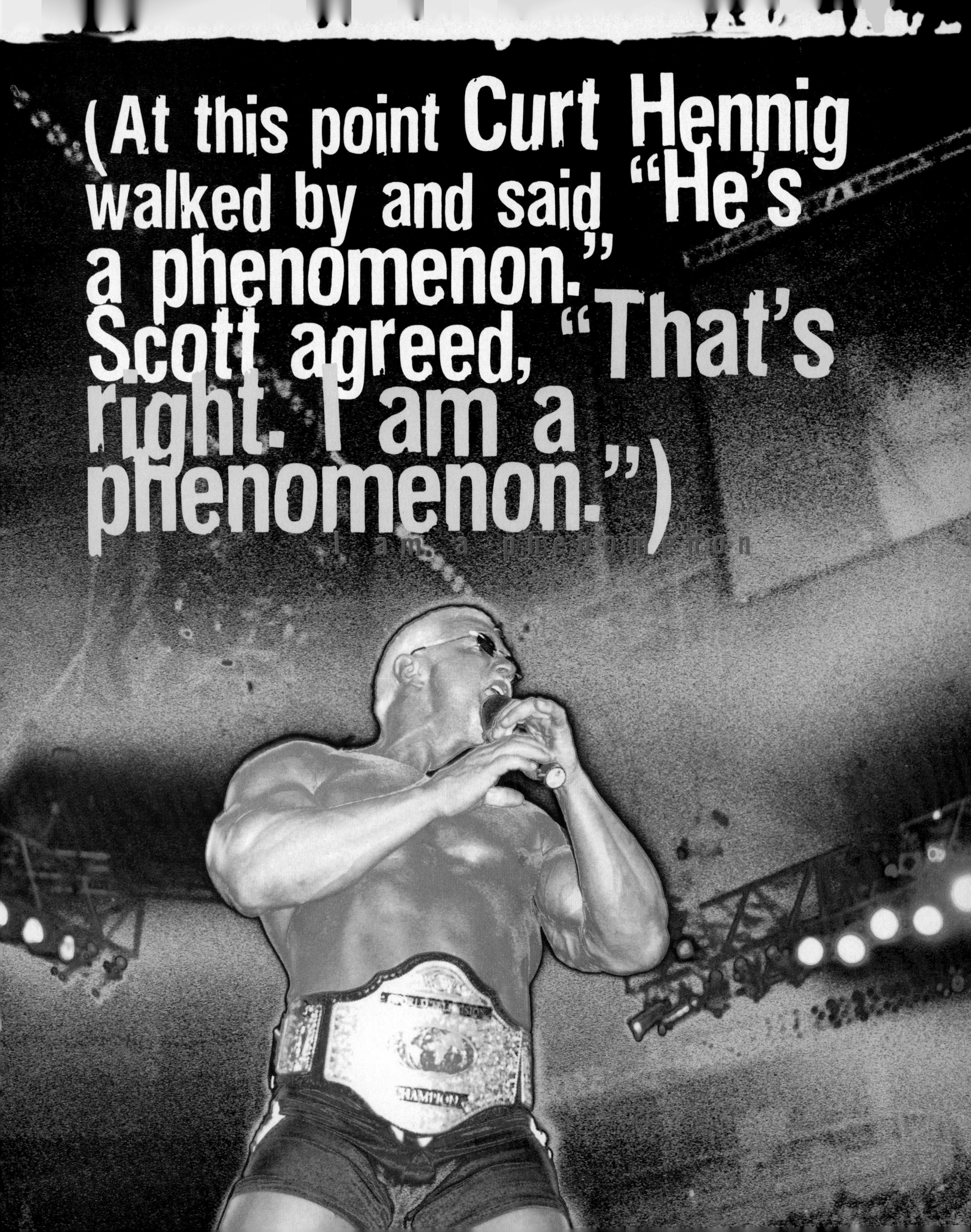
(At this point Curt Hennig walked by and said "He's a phenomenon." Scott agreed, "That's right. I am a phenomenon.")
I am a phenomenon

A Wrestling Dictionary of Terms

Angle - (n) The storyline of a wrestling match or feud. **Face** - (n) The good guy. **Gimmick** - (n) Any prop or persona used in wrestling. Mortis' Skull on a Stick (Yorick) or the Goddwins' Slop Bucket are gimmicks, while their personae are also gimmicks (v) To change or rig something. "They gimmicked the ring mat so the Undertaker could break through it to grab Diesel." **Heat** - (n) The crowd response, or the response from other people in the business. The entire purpose of a face or heel is to generate heat from the crowd. Heat is not necessarily always meant negatively. Sting or Shamrock can get a lot of heat, even though they are faces. "Shawn Michaels got a lot of heat from other people in the WWF because of his arrogant attitude." **Heel** - (n) The bad guy, and I don't mean Razor Ramon. **Job** - (v) To lose the match. "At Starrcade, we saw Hulk Hogan job to Sting." (n) The loss of a match. "Before the match, the booker told the new guy he was going to do the job tonight." **Jobber** - (n) A person who typically loses their matches and doesn't have a gimmick. These are the nameless people who are beaten up each week. They are roughly the equivalent of the no-name guys in the red shirts who would beam down to the planet with Captain Kirk on Star Trek only to die a quick and horrible death.

Kayfabe - (n) The reason why wrestlers will not admit that anything is staged. Kayfabe is the code of silence practiced in the business to keep the trade secrets within the business. **Mark** - (n) A person who believes everything in wrestling is real. Also a term used by wrestlers to refer to any fan or anyone watching. There are several degrees of marks. Whether you like it or not, we are all marks—otherwise, we wouldn't be watching. It is possible to be a mark for only certain feds or wrestlers. "nWo mark" or "Shawn Michaels mark." (v) To lose control during a wrestling event. "Did you see that guy completely mark out when Kevin Nash came into the bar? It was embarrassing." **Over** - (adj) To be popular with the crowd. "I can't believe how over Steve Austin has been since Wrestlemania." Another term you will hear is "put over." This commonly refers to a star or veteran who loses to a new talent or takes them under their wing to help the newcomer establish their career. "Chris Benoit really wasn't big in the business until Kevin Sullivan put him over." **Shoot** - (n) An event that is not planned or is a surprise to the participants involved. Despite popular belief, shoots do happen. They are not always in matches, but most often they are in the form of interviews on live television where wrestlers will say things they are not supposed to in order to put pressure on people in the business. (v) The act of committing a shoot. "I couldn't believe it when Brian Pillman decided to shoot on Kevin Sullivan by leaving the match."

Smart - (n) Any person who understands the business behind professional wrestling. The majority of people who think they are smarts are not. As a matter of fact, when someone comes out and says they are a smart, there is a very good chance they are not. Knowing that there is an element of entertainment to it all is not enough. Being able to understand the logic behind the business decisions in the business is a big part of it. You don't decide if you are a smart—other people do. **Turn** - (n) To change from heel status to face status or vice versa. **Tweener** - (n) A wrestler who doesn't fit into the traditional heel or face role. This is becoming more and more common these days. A good example of a tweener is Kevin Nash (and to a lesser degree, Scott Hall) of the nWo. While these men have committed heel acts, they still are very popular with the fans and often get a face reaction from the crowd. **Work** - (n) A staged incident or act. "People are saying that Woman and Chris Benoit are having an affair, but I bet that it is a work."

WOW Magazine would like to thank RichInKC and Al Isaacs for granting their permission to run this feature. Al's work can be found at www.scoopscentral.com. RichInKC can be found at www.scoopscentral.com/RichInKC. RichInKC also works on the Official Diamond Dallas Page Web site at www.thediamondmine.com and the Official Bill Goldberg Web site at www.jackhammer.net. You can E-mail RichinKC at RichInKC@wws.net

bombshells bombshells

The Women of Wrestling

1. Chyna

Why is Chyna No. 1? Well, she spoiled WWF owner Vince McMahon's plan. On a recent RAW is WAR, Chyna eliminated Vince to become the 30th participant in the annual PPV, "The Royal Rumble."

2. Tammy Sytch

Tammy and Chris Candido, two ECW employees, had taken a little time off from ECW. But they returned at ECW's January PPV, "Guilty as Charged." She and Chris made their return during the Shane Douglas vs. Taz Heavyweight Title Match. They were the key factor in Taz finally winning the ECW title.

3. Debra McMichael

Some may not think it's right, but Debra's exposing herself during Jeff Jarrett's matches sure pays off. Her teasing Jeff's opponents has led Jeff to many key wins.

4. Sable

Sable recently captured the WWF Women's Title. It had been defunct for some time, but now seems to be worn with pride ... by Sable.

5. Chastity

Chastity recently made the move from ECW to the WCW. In my opinion, this will be a great move for Chastity, because she should get more exposure in the WCW.

6. Jackie

Jackie left Mero ... but formed PMS (Pretty Mean Sistas') with Terri Runnels. Jackie looks like she could do something good with this angle and be productive now in the WWF. The Mero/Jackie angle just wasn't working for her.

7. Terri Runnels

I don't like the "Baby dead" angle, but I do like the PMS angle with Jackie. Terri seems to be providing good entertainment now that she's left Val Venis and Dustin Runnels alone.

8. "Justin Credible's Mystery Woman"

As of press time, no name has been announced for this woman. But, she appears ringside with Nicole Bass, Jason and Justin Credible. From what I've seen, she can take the ECW style, and help Justin and Jason in their matches. Definitely made an impact.

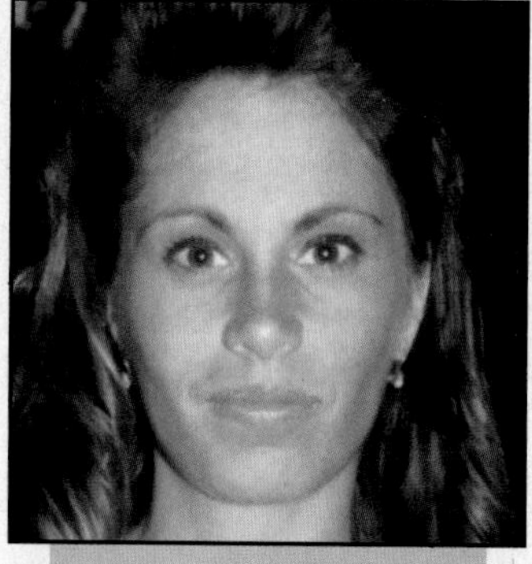

9. Francine

Talks of her leaving ECW have surfaced. But she still provides something nice to look at, and great ring work. Her "feud" with Candido and Sytch, if it follows through, could be something to watch. Francine has something most people like in ECW, the good looks and the hardcore style.

10. The Nitro Girls

Ah, some say they're a waste of space and are getting boring and old. In my opinion, they're still a reason to watch WCW Monday Nitro each week.

Francine leaving

There have been increasing rumors of Francine leaving ECW. Many ECW employees have left ECW recently for the "Big 2" promotions. Chastity, who was a member of Justin Credible's entourage, recently left ECW and made her debut in WCW on an episode of Thunder. Also, rumors of Francine's man, Shane Douglas, retiring are in the air.

Sable Bares all in Playboy?

Sable's big "Playboy" pictorial is done. She will appear on the cover of the popular men's magazine in April of 1999. Word has it that Sable had full control over what appeared in the magazine and what photos were taken.

Debra McMichael, understandably, is ticking Steve McMichael off with her antics in the WWF. Steve, currently employed by the WCW, reportedly was upset at Debra for "stripping" and "exposing" herself on WWF TV.

Miss Elizabeth has returned to WCW. She was the main reason Goldberg didn't get his WCW Title rematch and that Hulk Hogan won the title.

Justin Credible and Jason Credible have a new female added to their stable. On the indy circuit, she was called **"Jasmyne."** She was brought into the ECW by Rod Price. You may have seen her: so far, she looks like she can take a beating – and dish them out, too!

Find out more about the following Women of Wrestling on the Internet:

Chris Candido and Tammy Sytch Online
http://www.CandidoSytch.com

Sable Online
http://www.WWFSable.com

Dawn Marie's Homepage
http://www.wrestlingman.com/dawnmarie

The Official Francine Fournier Homepage
http://www.outsideredge.com/francine

The Nitro Girls Online
http://www.nitrogirls.com

bombshells

Sable Revealed

WOW Magazine would like to thank Sable for taking time out of her busy January schedule to chat with Marc Middleton. Here is what she had to say . . .

by Marc Middleton

MM: You recently made the choice to pose for "Playboy." Most everyone is aware of that now. Is there any chance of another spread in "Playboy?" Do you hope to pose nude again?

SABLE: This is something I have been negotiating for two years. I really don't think I would pose again, but I never thought I would pose this time! I just found out that I am going to be on the cover of the April '99 issue.

MM: What are your thoughts on the abuse some women seem to take in Extreme Championship Wrestling? Would you ever consider going to ECW?

SABLE: I really don't get a chance to watch their show. I am under a long-term contract with the WWF, so I don't see myself going anywhere soon.

MM: For those that don't know, please state your REAL relationship with Marc Mero.

SABLE: Well, it's no secret we are very happily married.

MM: What are your thoughts on The Nitro Girls? Do you think they're just something pretty to look at?

SABLE: I think they're very entertaining. It gives the show sex appeal!

MM: Who, other than Marc, inspired you or pushed you to get involved in pro wrestling?

SABLE: Nobody pushed me to get into pro wrestling. When Marc left WCW, I flew with him to Stamford (Conn.) to sign his contract. When I met Vince he asked me at that time if I would like to be part of the WWF, and it has sort of taken off from there. I don't regret my decision one bit.

MM: What is your response to all the criticism and negative comments that you receive from many critics?

SABLE: If I let negative comments bother me, I would never be able to continue in this business. No matter how much you succeed, there is always someone who wants to put you down. Everyone is entitled to their own opinion.

MM: While you and Tammy Sytch were in the WWF at the same time, you two were always being compared somehow by someone. What are your thoughts on Tammy, and what do you have to say about the comparison?

SABLE: Tammy has been in this business a lot longer than I have. I think she is talented. I really don't pay much attention to anyone who compares me to other people. I'm happy with who I am, and I try to be my own person. She has her talents and I have mine.

MM: Do you and Marc agree on or like the angles where you and him are against each other? Do you wish this could change and you two could be "on the same side" once again?

SABLE: Marc and I are very professional.

I think they're very entertaining. It gives the show sex appeal!
bombshells
bombshells
EVERLAST
M
M

We have no problems separating this business from our personal life. We do what the company thinks is best for business.

MM: Would you ever leave the WWF? If so, what would be a good enough reason for you to leave?

SABLE: I have no plans on leaving the WWF. I just renewed my contract for three years. I will see how things are at that time in my life and reassess from there.

MM: What is your thought on the whole WWF/WCW ratings war? Do you feel you typically help the WWF win the ratings?

SABLE: I think we all work together as a company to win the ratings.

MM: If you had the chance to step in the ring with any female or male in the sport, who would it be? Why?

SABLE: There is no any one in particular. I will defend my belt against anyone.

MM: When you think of WCW, or someone mentions World Championship Wrestling and its leaders, what do you think of?

SABLE: We still have a lot of good friends that work there. I think competition is good for wrestling. It's the fans who are winning!

MM: Many know you appeared on an episode of "Pacific Blue" and an upcoming special, Pen and Teller's "Sin City." Is acting a big thing to you? Are you interested in pursuing it full time?

SABLE: Acting is something I have always wanted to do. I am very thankful that the WWF has given me an opportunity to pursue this. I had a great time doing "Pacific Blue," and I am looking into further acting opportunities.

I think we all work together as a company to win the ratings.

MM: Female participation in pro wrestling is a big thing these days. It's a big part of ratings, merchandise, cards, pro wrestling in general. How long do you see things like Women's Titles and women in wrestling lasting?

SABLE: I think women in pro wrestling are here to stay.

MM: What does Marc Mero think about you appearing in "Playboy?" Could you give us a brief description of your experience with the photographers and the whole "Playboy" empire?

SABLE: This was something we discussed and both agreed upon. Marc has been extremely supportive. The people at "Playboy" were very professional and I had a great time. Going into it, I had no idea how things were going to work – do the shoots start off with nude shots or what? They made me feel very comfortable since we progressed from bathing suit and lingerie shots to the actual pictorial shots.

MM: Lastly, where do you see yourself in 10 years? Still in the sport? The "Sable" thing still alive?

SABLE: I see myself just enjoying life with my family.

MM: Alright Sable. Thanks alot for participating with "WOW Magazine."

SABLE: No problem.

(Don't forget to check out the official Sable Web site at www.wwfsable.com)

Marc Middleton is the Webmaster for the official Web site of Chris Candido & Tammy Sytch, at www.CandidoSytch.com. You can reach Marc via E-mail at MMiddl01@aol.com.

bombshells

Sable (Real Name: Rena Mero)

Wrestling Debut: Wrestlemania XII, March 30, 1996
Birthdate: August 6
Birthplace: Jacksonville, Fla.
People managed: Hunter Hearst Helmsley, The Oddities, Marc Mero
Height: 5 foot, 6 inches
Titles held: WWF Women's Title; Dressed to Kill (Slammy); Mrs. Slammy
Finishing move: "Sablebomb"
Memorable feuds: Marc Mero, Luna Vachon, Jackie

Rena Mero first appeared as a valet for WWF wrestler Hunter Hearst Helmsley at Wrestlemania XII. She was just another "property" of HHH until "Wildman" Marc Mero came to her rescue. Mero also made his WWF debut that night.

Sable and Mero soared to new heights in the WWF. But eventually, Sable's popularity got to Mero. Marc had a streak of jealously and took it out on Sable. The two eventually split up. The break resulted in many situations where Sable defeated Marc in a match or humiliated him on TV.

But Marc made a bet with Sable. Sable lost the bet at WWF's In Your House Over The Edge and was forced to leave the WWF. But WWF owner Vince McMahon brought Sable back shortly after.

Marc would then pair up with WWF valet Jackie. This pairing made the Marc/Sable feud grow. Jackie and Sable's feud was one of Sable's most memorable. Sable had a similar feud with Luna, which was just as crazy, but ended eventually.

Sable soon managed The Oddities with Luna. But with Sable's growing popularity and with Sable winning the WWF Women's Title at the WWF Survivor Series in 1998 after beating Jackie, Luna too became enraged with jealously. Luna recently attacked Sable on WWF RAW, so the Sable/Luna feud looks to continue on.

But is Sable alone in the WWF? You may have seen a woman appear many times on RAW, either in the crowd or at ringside. She usually gets involved in Sable's matches or segments. Her name is Terri Powers. There were rumors recently of the WWF bringing her in as Sable's sister ...

Rena recently posed for "Playboy," one of the world's most respected men's magazines. This highly-anticipated release reportedly has Sable gracing the cover of the April issue, which will also include a pictorial and feature story inside. Happy reading!

—by Marc Middleton

bombshells

debra
wwf

Legs, Legs, Legs

nitro girls Body, mind and soul!

bombshells

9:24

TAMMY LYNN

ecw

These guns are loaded!

OH MY GOD

TAMMY LYNN

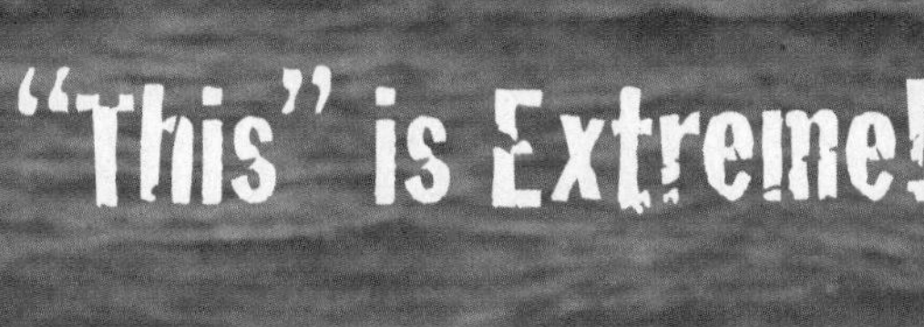

"This" is Extreme!

TAMMY LYNN

ecw

Leader of Champions

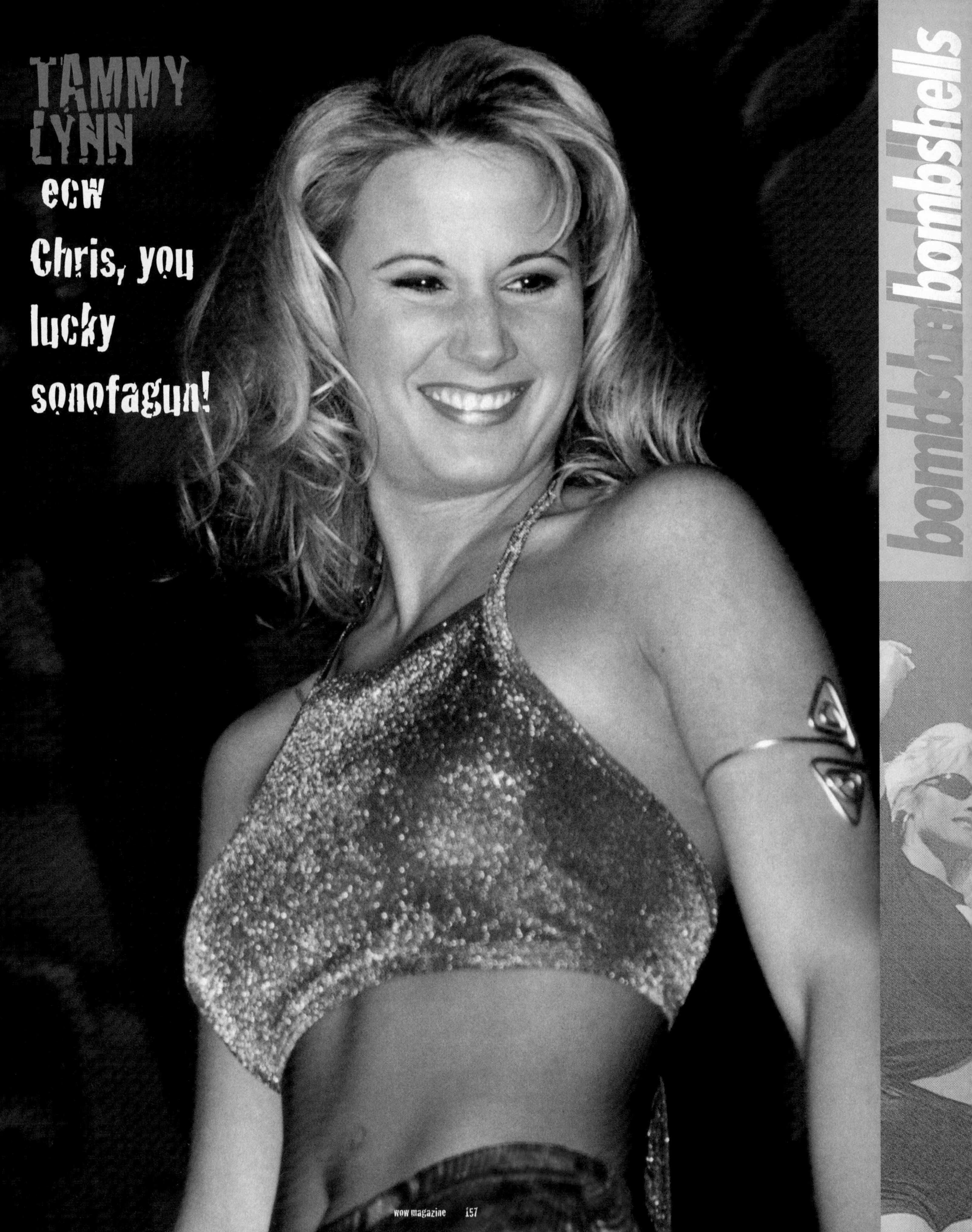
TAMMY LYNN
ecw
Chris, you lucky sonofagun!
bombshells

bombshells
TAMMY LYNN
ecw
What Tammy
wants,
Tammy gets!

Francine
ecw
Thinking of you.
bombshells

bombshells

Elizabeth

WCW

Feeling lucky today?

Jacqueline

wwf

On top of the World!

bombshells

Chyna

wwf

You want me? Come and get some!

Luna
wwf
I'm just a little
crazy today!
bombshells

austin vs. goldberg:

The Match You Never Thought You'd See

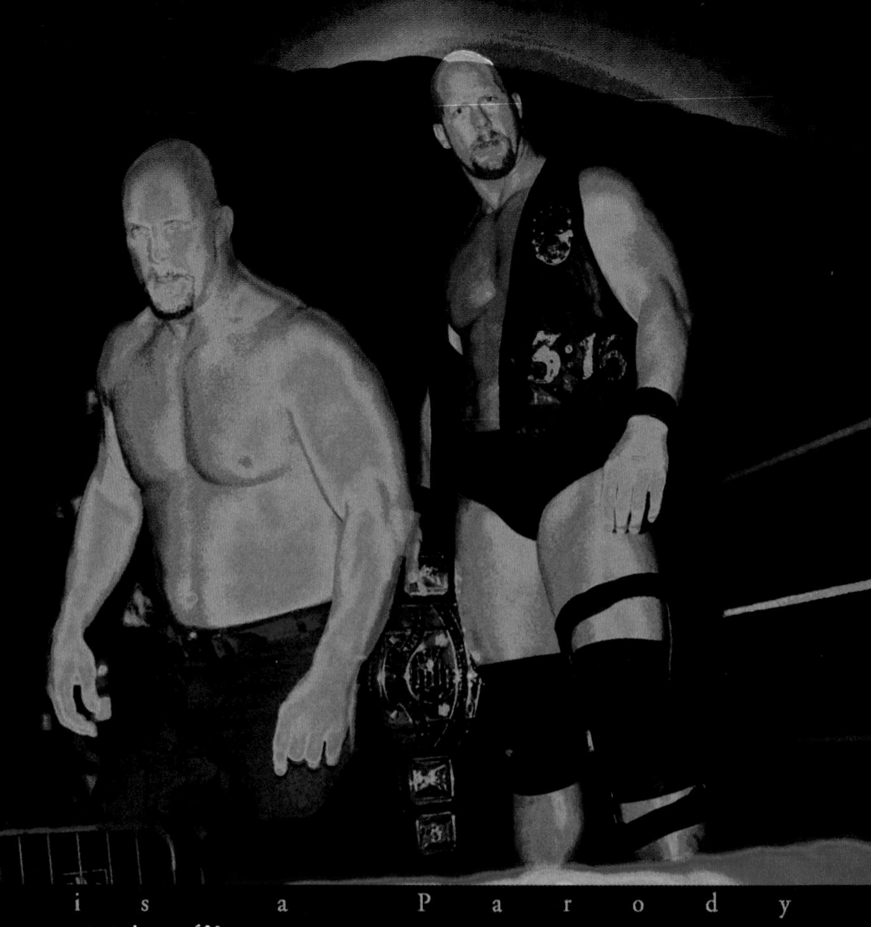

T h i s i s a P a r o d y

Direct from Cyberspace, and www.ScoopTHIS.com, home of the BEST wrestling parody on the Internet, WOW Magazine brings to you a transcript of the highly-anticipated main event for a truly unbelievable card – as the World Wrestling Federation's Stone Cold Steve Austin faces World Championship Wrestling's Bill Goldberg.

Your announcers for tonight's event are – Jim Ross, Tony Schiavone, and Larry Zbyzsko.

Schiavone: "Welcome, ladies and gentlemen, to the greatest matchup in the history of this great sport!"

Ross: "This one's gonna be a slobberknocker, folks!"

Larry Zbyzsko says nothing, slowly getting up from his chair, looking high as a kite, and salutes the crowd.

Mark Madden immediately rushes the broadcast booth to take Larry's spot, but is wrestled down by security and escorted out of the building.

Schiavone: "Goldberg lost the pre-show beer-drinking competition, so he'll come out first."

Goldberg walks out of his dressing room, only to find that all of his security guards were missing. This match is being held for charity, after all, and additional expenses had to be cut down.

Confused, Goldberg tries to make his way to the ring on his own, but gets lost somewhere in the arena's basement levels.

Ross: "I'm not sure what's going on back there, Goldberg's not coming out."

Zbyzsko, in awe before the largest crowd he's ever seen, slowly walks closer to the fans to shake their hands.

Schiavone: "Folks, this is the longest wait of all time! Don't touch that dial!"

Ross: "Hold on a minute, there ... what's that on the left side of the ring? Something's coming out of that air duct! It's ... it's Goldberg!"

Schiavone: "UNBELIEVABLE!!"

Ross: "Bill Goldberg is coming out of the sub-level air-ducts!"

The crowd reacts to Goldberg's arrival as he crawls out of the opening with a confused look about him.

Schiavone: "WHAT A MOMENT!"

Mesmerized by the huge crowd before him, Zbyzsko is slowly lured into them, with a spaced out look about him, as they lift him above their heads ... Zbyzsko body surfs the crowd in peaceful bliss and is never seen again.

Ross: "We've lost Larry."

Suddenly, the sound of breaking glass booms through the arena as Stone Cold Steve Austin's entrance music begins – and the crowd goes wild.

Ross: "It's the rattlesnake! Business is about to pick up! Listen to that crowd!"

Schiavone: "I... don'thearanything."

Confusing him for Goldberg, the pyro techs light up the spark shower on the walkway as Austin approaches the target zone. Caught off-guard, Austin freaks, realizes what just happened, and runs to the east side corner of the arena to beat on the techies responsible for the light show.

Ross: "Oh, my. In the WWF, a mistake like that would have cost those gentlemen their jobs."

Schiavone: "Here in WCW, mistakes like those are considered creative booking."

Austin makes his way to the ring, climbs up to the mat, yells his favorite cookie recipe at Goldberg, and then goes up a ring post to salute the crowd, both arms extended.

Stone Cold climbs back down and walks up to Goldberg, nose to nose, and finishes yelling that cookie recipe at him. Goldberg just keeps staring him down, wishing he had paper and pen in hand.

Schiavone: "Look at that raw intensity in both men's eyes ... intensity like we've never seen before, and likely will NEVER SEE AGAIN, FOLKS!"

Austin pushes Goldberg back.

Schiavone: "WHAT A MOVE!"

Goldberg pushes Austin right back.

Schiavone: "That's it. This match is over. Stick a fork in him, he's done."

Ross: "uh ... Tony, those are just shoves."

Schiavone: "Sorry, it's just more action than I'm used to seeing in a main event."

Both men lock up!

Schiavone: "Uh-oh."

Ross: "Oh, damn. I was afraid this would happen."

Schiavone: "They ... locked up, Jim."

Ross: "I know that, Tony."

Schiavone (whispering): "I lost sight of who's who."

Ross: "So did I. Just wing it."

Schiavone: "The ... bald guy gets the upper hand!"

Ross: "And the ... goateed wonder is down on one knee!"

Schiavone: "uh ... one of them just got a boot to the mid-section!"

Ross: "..."

Schiavone: "uh ... YES! I think I see a tattoo!"

Ross: "Oh thank God."

Schiavone: "It's Goldberg! Goldberg throws Austin over the top rope!"

Austin lands on the guard rail, and cuts himself mildly on the forehead while doing so. A tiny drop of blood makes its way down his brow.

Schiavone: "OH MY GOD, WHAT THE @#$% IS THAT?!"

Ross: "Calm down, Tony. It's just a bit of blood. This is a contact sport, it's perfectly nor..."

Schiavone: "MAKE IT STOP! BY GOD, MAKE IT STOP!"

Jim Ross slaps Tony Schiavone across the face.

Ross: "Get ahold of yourself, for Heaven's sake!"

Austin pulls Goldberg out of the ring by his feet, as both men beat up on each other with closed fists.

Then, the crowd turns its attention towards a dark figure looming in the rafters high above the arena.

Schiavone: "Look! It's Sting! IT'S STING!!"

Ross: "And he's got a bird with him!"

Sting signals for the bird to fly to the ring to deliver his message, but it instead flies down into the crowd and attacks a fan.

Schiavone: "Oh my..."

Ross: "er ... was that supposed to happen?"

Security finally succeeds in restraining the bird, as medics are called in to carry its victim to the back for some medical attention.

Sting slides down a cable toward the ring below, but gets stuck about a third of the way down.

Ross: "uh ..."

Schiavone (whispering): "Ignore the problem, it'll go away."

Everyone forgets about Sting as Goldberg hurls Austin onto the nearest ringpost from the outside. He then picks him up and tosses him back into the ring.

Ross: "I've never seen Stone Cold dominated this way!"

Goldberg climbs in and crouches as he prepares to deliver his spear. The crowd reacts accordingly.

Schiavone: "Listen to that crowd! This is the GREATEST crowd in the history of this great sport!"

Goldberg lunges forward and delivers the spear on Austin!

Ross: "Austin is down! Austin is down!"

Schiavone: "INCREDIBLE! Not since I was last up for a raise has someone gone down so fast!"

The fans then once again turn their attention to the rafters atop the arena ... this time, it's Mankind!

Ross: "Up in the rafters! It's Mankind!"

Schiavone: "THIS IS THE GREATEST MOMENT IN PROFESSIONAL WRESTLING!!"

Mankind suicide-jumps to Stone Cold's aid ... says hi to Sting on the way down ... but ends up falling clear through the ring mat.

Schiavone: "OH MY GOD! OH MY GOD!!"

KER-PLAT!

Ross: "Oh my goodness – Mankind has just jumped over 200 feet and gone right through the mat!"

Shiavone faints.

Ross: "...Tony?"

Distracted by the loud thud and the Mankind-shaped hole in the center of the ring, Goldberg doesn't see Austin walk up behind him. Austin turns Goldberg around, kicks him in the mid-section, and applies the Stone Cold Stunner!

Ross: "This is it!"

Austin goes for the cover! As the ref begins his count, the ring fills with smoke ... when the smoke dissipates, both Goldberg and the ref are gone, and Warrior stands with a microphone at hand. The ref rings the bell to signal a no-contest finish for cause of ethereal kidnapping via teleportation.

Warrior speaks: "Stone Cold Steve Austin ... throughout time, warriors have stepped forward and risen to the challenge. Men and women who set their vocational locale in stone; using their lifetime to achieve what most others only reve about. In the optics of the reveur, successful achievements always seem as if they are done effortlessly, unaccompanied by travail, but rather, companioned by luck and happenstance..."

Austin looks around at the crowd to see if anyone else understands what this man is saying. The audience starts flooding the ring with debris, as one soft drink container accidentally knocks Warrior's hidden earphone out, which falls and rolls into the gaping hole at his side created by Mankind's freefall.

Warrior now just stands with a blank look on his face, a mix of confusion and dumbfoundedness about him.

Ross: "Tony, wake up! Something's happened to the Warrior!"

The crowd, as well as Austin, wait for Warrior to finish his thoughts. But all Warrior can do is stare blindly ahead of him, with a little spittle making its way down the side of his mouth.

He then begins to snarl...

And then grunt...

And then snarl again...

Austin had heard enough – and delivers the Stunner as the crowd erupts! The rattlesnake's music booms through the arena as he bends down to share more of his mother's recipes with the Warrior.

But the arena turns red, as Kane's entrance theme replaces Austin's.

Ross: "Through Hellfire and Brimstone! It's Kane!"

Kane walks to the ring, painfully stepping over the top rope despite the fact that it would evidently be far easier for him to go over the second, but Austin jumps on him and unmasks him before he can make a move.

Ross: "Good Lord, it's ... the Blue Blazer!"

The crowd gasps as Austin unmasks the Blue Blazer...

Ross: "It's ... it's Rey Mysterio Jr!"

The crowd gasps again as Austin unmasks Rey Jr...

Ross: "What the.. it's Max Mini!"

Austin takes off the Mini mask, and finds nothing. Only a heavy pile of accumulated costumes and masks at his feet.

An awkward silence takes over the arena.

That is, until the next interruption, as Hollywood Hogan's ego rushes the ring, quickly followed by Hogan himself, Kevin Nash, and Lex Luger. That's all the encouragement the other wrestlers backstage needed to invade the ring as well. Every single wrestler in the arena is now in the ring in a gigantic screwjob battle royal! From Road Dog to Ric Flair, they're beating the tar out of each other ... except for Too Much and Perry Saturn, who remained backstage, complimenting each other's attire...

Ross: "We're out of time! This one's over, folks! On behalf of the unconscious Tony Schiavone and Larry Zbyzsko – wherever he may be ... have a good night!"

"Titan" Tim Washington (center) of the New York Enforcers executes a block on David Gletty (right) of the Florida Sundogs while setting up a whip with Enforcer teammate Jr. Weidner (left).

This isn't your daddy's game anymore!

by Joe Bush

Think back to the days when NFL, NBA and Major League Baseball players had to work in the off-season to make ends meet. You've seen film clips. Most of them were like the guy next door; there were more beer bellies than chiseled physiques. Toughness, not skill or speed, saved the day.

The same is true with Roller Derby and RollerJam. Old film or videotape of Roller Derby – a nationwide success in the 1960s and early 70s – reveals skaters with more mean than lean. No one cared about muscles or miles per hour, just good guys and bad guys, winners and losers.

As the P.A. announcer screamed before the first RollerJam competition Jan. 15 on TNN, "This is not your father's Roller Derby!"

A super-charged hybrid of professional wrestling and antique Roller Derby, RollerJam (Fridays on TNN, 8 p.m. Eastern) is proud of its skaters' strength, quickness and size. Before the first Jam was unleashed, viewers learned that Florida Sundog skater Debbie Rice was the world-record holder for downhill in-line skate speed with a 62-mph run.

Later in the show, a side story gave an inside look at New York Enforcer Tim (Titan) Washington, a 6-foot-4, 275-pound menace who flirted with an NFL career, has won a division of the 1996 Yukon Jack Arm Wrestling Championship, and is undefeated in his first year of pro boxing.

Among the World Skating League's six teams are also a former pro ice hockey player, an alligator wrestler, bodybuilders, a martial arts expert who appeared on "American Gladiators," former Roller Derby competitors, and a creamed-corn wrestling champion.

Not your father's Roller Derby? More like your father's worst nightmare.

The first showdown – the Enforcers versus the Sundogs – was a blast. The Enforcers won 25-24, ending the fracas with a controversial hit from captain

Denise Loden (right) women's team captain of the Florida Sundogs maneuvers past tough competitor Karen Magnussen (left) of the New York Enforcers.

Mark D'Amato, a bald, goateed bouncer at an alternative bar who skated in the Roller Derby days and was the only skater wearing the old four-wheel skates.

D'Amato stunted the Sundogs' sixth-period rally with his "Screamer" move, a flying body kick from which he says "no one has survived."

D'Amato is the perfect representative for a team which the P.A. announcer introduced as from "the rotten side of the Big Apple." The Enforcers wear black and silver, scream at the crowd and include Heather Gunnin, a former national speed-skating team member who took the time to pull a crutch from an injured Sundog who was minding her own business on the sidelines.

Here's how the no-holds-barred game is "supposed" to be played: each team puts out five skaters for each of six periods. Men face men three periods, women versus women three periods.

Each team has three "blockers" and two "jammers." At the start of each 60-second "jam," (there are six jams per period) the jammers (wearing black helmets) break from the pack, and upon catching up with it, try to pass as many skaters as possible. The blockers try to stop the opponent jammers from passing. A jam ends when the time's up, or when a jammer who has gotten ahead of the others puts his/her hands on his/her hips.

That's strategy for "I've scored quite a bit, I'm not gonna let anyone else score."

Blockers, like Washington and D'Amato – or their female teammate Jannet Abraham (the Minister of Pain) – can stop jammers almost any way they choose. The referees aren't supposed to allow tripping, fully-extended arms or flying elbows, but hey, they can't see every thing, can they?

Besides, the jammers can do enough damage to one another as they chase the pack. In the Florida-New York scrap, more bodies were flying over the railing during chases than within the pack. Most of the blockers'

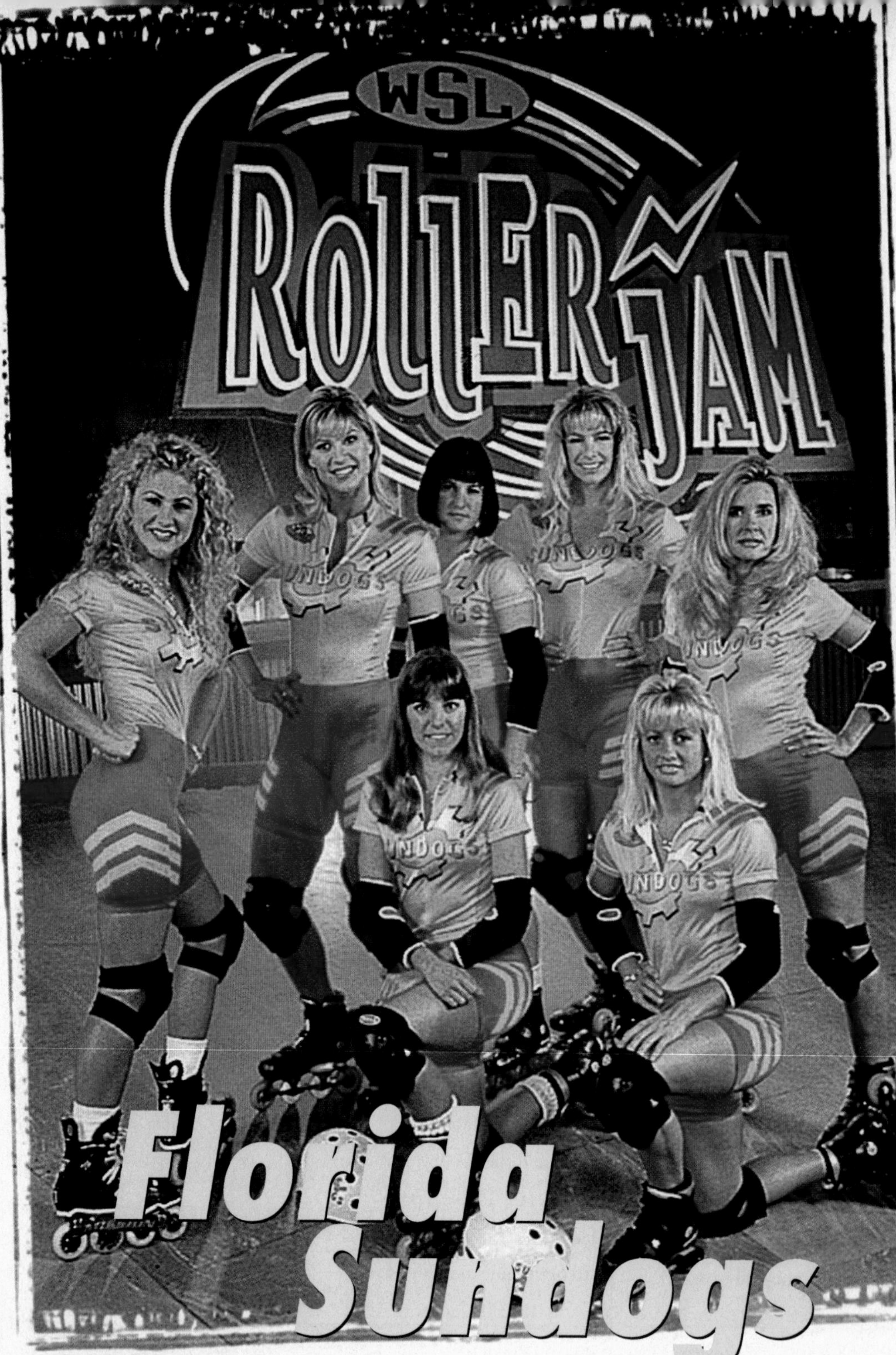

the noise a few notches whenever Rice and Gunnin jammed at the same time. Also that night, Washington readied his "redneck radar," otherwise known as a massive left elbow – for the head and chest of Sundog David "Gator" Gletty, who is a mountain-climber, tree surgeon and alligator wrestler.

It was Gletty upon whom D'Amato unleashed the "Screamer" to end the event in the Enforcers' favor.

The World Skating League's other teams are the California Quakes, the Illinois Riot, the Texas Rustlers, and the Nevada Hot Dice. The Quakes just might become the league's top attraction.

Led by blocker Sean Atkinson, whose grandparents and parents competed in the original Roller Derby, the Quakes feature general manager Heather Moore's beach-babe "Bod Squad" of Stacey Blitsch, Jamie Conemac, and Cindy Zimmerman. Watch for their taunting victory dance, "The Quake Shake."

You can keep up with the excitement in between contests at www.rollerjam.com. If you want to get even closer to the action, you could become a RollerJam skater. The Web site will let fans know when and where they can try out.

Treat yourself and your action-starved curiosity to a night of RollerJam. If you can remember your father's Roller Derby, you'll soon forget!

damage knocks jammers flat to the track, followed by the blocker, who tries to add an elbow to the fallen jammer's helmet.

There are penalties, minor and major. Minor infractions – when the offender has to sit for one jam – include (according to the official rules) "holding, illegal blocking, stalling, tripping, illegal use of hands, and grabbing. Major fouls – those requiring the offender to sit two jams – include fighting, intentional roughness, and unsportsmanlike conduct.

Funny, it didn't seem like Gunnin sat for a second after pulling the crutch from the unfortunate opponent. Must be judgement calls.

Finally – and judging by the first game, someone is bound to test this part of the rule book – there is banishment. Any player who racks up six penalties in a game will be tossed.

If the Enforcers-Sundogs showdown was any indication, the mere point-scoring competition between the teams won't be the only focus for the viewer.

Rice and Gunnin, it turns out, were roommates in the past. It was a relationship that ended ugly. The two got into a fistfight after an argument. When the two were interviewed before the matchup, Gunnin recalled that Rice "was so plastered, she had to ask other people about the fight."

The rowdy crowd kicked up

X marks the spot

ESPN's Winter X Games puts Shaun Palmer back in the spotlight

By Joe Bush

Shaun Palmer

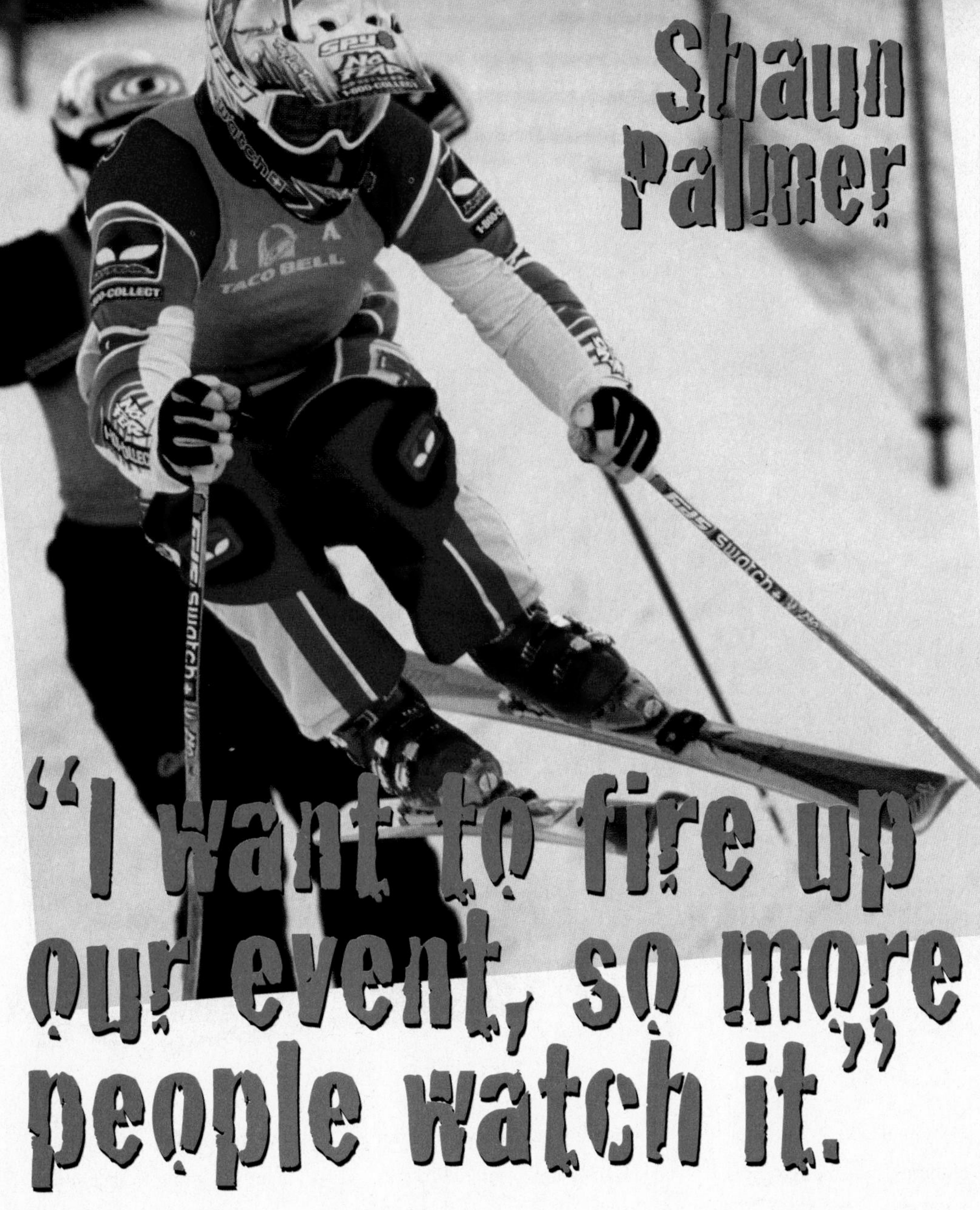

"I want to fire up our event, so more people watch it."

Ah, extreme sports.

Or rather, EEEAAHHHH-HHH! Extreme Sports!

The most visible of these 1990s-hyped competitions are snowboarding, street-luging, inline-skate tricks, skateboarding, and mountain biking. Strap yourself to anything with wheels or a flat surface, and head to the nearest ramp, pipe or impossibly-steep incline.

The reason these injury- and death-defying feats are nearing mainstream media coverage is marketing. Sponsors find the best of these daredevils – with their independent, rebellious styles and attitudes – attach their names and target the valuable youth demographic. Presto, you've got rich, crazy guys.

ESPN hops on board for the Summer and Winter X Games. Even the Winter Olympics are allowing for non-traditional skiing events such as freestyle, mogul and snowboarding.

Extreme sports have arrived, but you know what? They've been here all along. Remember surfing? Skydiving? Motocross? Mountain-climbing? Any kind of car racing? That's pretty nutty stuff, and it's been going on for half of this century, and more than a century in the case of mountain-climbing.

It's time for something new, something fresh, something like Shaun Palmer.

The 30-year-old Palmer was one of the first snowboarders to go pro, and has long been one of the best shredders. The tattooed platinum blonde with a jones for Cadillacs just won his third straight ESPN Winter X Games Boarder X gold medal.

He's wealthy, brash and infuriatingly cocky, and more often than not, able to back up his snide remarks. There's a method to his mouthy madness.

"I want to fire up our event, so more people watch it," Palmer told ESPN.com during the 1999 Games in January. "I want to get these athletes fired up to want to beat me. Stir it up a little bit. I want to get it going. I like to talk a little smack and get these guys fired up, so everybody will be trying hard.

"I don't talk unless I'm winning. If I'm not winning, you won't hear a word from me. But I like to win, and when I win, I'm a big mouth. That's just the way I am."

World-class mountain-bikers know. Someday, so might pro snow-mobilers and skiiers. A few years ago, "The Palm," as he likes to be called, stumbled into mountain biking, and before you can say "competitive fire," was entering and winning races. A year after acting on a whim, Palmer turned pro at a World Cup event in Spain, and though he didn't qualify for the downhill final, he finished eighth at the World Cup's next stop, in Italy.

In the same year, he rose to the No. 2 ranking in the National Off-Road Bicycle Association (NORBA) National Championship series in the dual-

3 of the top five World Cup half-pipers are American

slalom event and the No. 8 spot in the downhill. He won NORBA downhills, and placed second in the World Championships. Sponsors soon followed.

"He doesn't have the pedaling skills or the cadence like the guys with road-racing backgrounds," Intense Cycles president Jeff Haber told Snowboard Online. "He's just total aggression, and he takes some insane lines."

With his snowboard wealth Palmer had bankrolled all but his equipment that first year in mountain-biking, but after his stunning success, he signed a $250,000 deal, plus incentives, with the Specialized/Mountain Dew team.

At the 1997 Winter X Games, Palmer won the Boarder X competition as well as the Snow Mountain Bike downhill. He may not be the world's best in snowboarding, he may not be the world's best in mountain-biking, but no one has crossed the line like Palmer.

That's fresh. And he's not done yet.

In addition to the snowboarding and mountain-biking events Palmer entered in the 1999 X Games, he also competed in the snow-mobiling and Skiing X competitions. He placed 14th in the mountain-biking and sixth in the skiing. The snow-mobiling? That was his biggest risk. He'd only had two races under his belt before the X Games.

And he's not done yet. After his double gold in the 1997 X Games, iBike.com asked Palmer what was next.

"I'm going into (Grand Prix) racing (motorcycles), doing some road racing," he said. "Then I'm going to race supercross West Coast 125, till I qualify for all the mains. I'll probably do that for a year, because it's always been my dream. A serious goal is to road-race for the rest of my life.

"It's a thing where I want to be the best athlete in the world, and I think I am. I think Deion Sanders and all these Bo Jackson guys are pretty talented, but they ain't no Shaun Palmer. They can't do everything. I can. That's what I'm here to do – show the world who I am. It sounds bold and cocky, but that's

what I'm here to do."

Enough about one maniac. Let's look at some of the other crazed competitions and their major loonies.

Snowboarding:

Probably the first sport you think of when you think "extreme sport." It has progressed from being shut out of most ski resorts to barely being tolerated to propping up those resorts when skiing hit a down trend.

Now, more than 90 percent of U.S. resorts welcome snowboarding. It's a culture, with speed-metal and punk and ska music in the background; baggy, bright clothes on the boarders; air-grabbing, half-pipe-tricking attitudes on their brains.

There are men's and women's World Cup competitions in half-pipe (for tricks) and giant slalom (for speed and handling). Boardercross – in which several boarders race together over a twisty, jumpy course – is snowboarding's newest tweak.

Currently, three of the top five men's and women's World Cup half-pipers are American: Ross Powers, Tommy Czeschin and Zach Horwitz; Tricia Byrnes, Kim Stacey, Michelle Taggart.

In the giant-slalom and boardercross disciplines, European riders dominate. Must be the American taste for flair. Two boarders who are separate from the pack, and who pick and choose their events rather than compete in series—Palmer and Terje Haakonsen. Haakonsen, considered the "Michael Jordan of snowboarding," blew off the 1998 Olympics because it didn't fit his idea of fun.

Skiing:

The most common winter sport besides pond skating, skiing has always been extreme at its top level (remember the wild ski-jump crash at the opening of the original Wide World of Sports?).

Competitive downhill skiing is flat-out crazy to people who ski recreationally. Steep courses with enough bumps and turns to send edge-of-control skiers flying in spectacular spills. Ski-jumping? It's been around forever, but the premise is still the same: fly down an incline with a lip on the end and try to land as far from the lip as possible.

Events have been added in the past 10 years which prove that life can be wild outside of downhill and jumping. Mogul skiing is done on a knee-busting course of close-together bumps (moguls); freestyle skiing is simple – it's like ski-jumping, but the ramp is shorter and the competitor earns point for tricks he or she does while in the air.

Finally, there is extreme skiing. Skiers bored with the most difficult courses at resorts go to mountains with no resorts—just snow and inclines and treacherous rocks and avalanche risk.

The Ninth World Extreme Skiing Championships will be held March 31 through April 6 in the Chugach Mountains near Valdez, Alaska. The average snowfall on the Thompson Pass exceeds 400 inches, while the inclines range from 35 to 55 degrees and descend 2,000 to 3,000 feet. Last year's men's division champ was France's Adam Arnaud.

Arnaud is the world's top-ranked extreme skiier, with Americans Miles Raney and Greg Morris in second and third. The women's rankings are topped by Switzerland's Francine Moreillon and France's Raphaelle Monod, followed by Americans Wendy Fisher and A.J. Cargill.

Winter X Games:

The younger brother of ESPN's Summer X Games, this collection of six sports includes snowboarding, snow mountain-biking, ice-climbing, skiboarding (skiing with shorter, wider skis), snowcross (snowmobiling over a challenging circuit), and free(style) skiing.

There's no guarantee that the world's best in each sport is at these games, because the World Cup series is happening at the same time.

Ultimate Fighting:

This five-year-old phenomenon has done well on pay-per-view and in videotape sales, though cable giant TCI has dropped the sport.

The bloody battles in an octagonal ring are a stew of the world's martial arts and artists. Any style is allowed, so long as it doesn't include eye-gouging, biting, or elbows to the back of the head. In a chart compiled by Ultimate Fighting Championship, the most successful fighting styles are shoot-fighting (a 28-11-2 record), wrestling (44-21), and Jiu-jitsu (31-22-1).

Other styles include: Boxing, Sumo, Muay Thai, Sambo, Luta Livre and Trapfighting, to name a few. Fights can end by knockout, referee stoppage, doctor stoppage, corner stoppage, or a fighter "tapping" the mat in submission.

Some of the UFC legends include Tank Abbott, Vitor Belfort, Jerry Bohlander, Mark Coleman, Randy Couture, Don Frye, Royce Gracie, Bas Rutten, Dan Severn, Frank Shamrock, Ken Shamrock, and Oleg Taktarov.

BMX & Mountain-Bike Racing:

BMX racing began in the 1970s as a non-mechanized imitation of motorcycle dirt-course racing. Today, the National Bicycle League, the sport's largest not-for-profit sanctioning body, sanctions over 3,000 races per year, including 16 U.S. Open events and 23 National events.

The NBL awards over $225,000 in yearly prizes. Over the years BMX has grown in style to include trick riding out of half-pipes (vert riding), riding a bike on flat surfaces without touching the pedals (flatlanding), doing tricks in the air after launching from a ramp (dirt jumping), and maneuvering and doing tricks off of various everyday obstacles (street riding).

It is this skateboard-style trick riding which attracts the most sponsors and produces the most famous names. Inclusion in the ESPN Summer X Games helps, too. The best-known BMX tricksters include Dave Mirra, Trevor Meyer, Jimmy Walker, and Ryan Nyquist.

For the nearly-out-of-control, bone-jarring thrill of mountain-biking, the best ride is National Off-Road Bicycle Association (NORBA) events. The National Championship Series is a seven-site set of races (downhill, cross-country, and dual slalom) held from May through September.

The sport's finest include the colorful and pierced Missy Giove, as well as Cheri Elliott, Steve Larsen, Alison Sydor, Ruthie Matthes, Brian Lopes, John Tomac, and Leigh Donovan. Lance Armstrong, the former world 10-speed cycling

champion who had to take a 16-month break in the prime of his career to recover from cancer, signed with a pro mountain-biking team last season.

Skateboarding:

One of the most enduring and most common of the "fringe" sports, skateboarding gets its best mainstream exposure during ESPN's Summer X Games and Mountain Dew commercials. The most spectacular form is vert, or tricks out of a half-pipe, though the most spectacular wrecks come from street riding (anytime you see a kid trying to ride a railing or jump an obstacle).

There are mostly regional legends in this sport, which has few if any national competitions besides the X Games. Dominant X-Gamers include Tony Hawk and Andy Macdonald in vert – they've traded the X Games vert singles title since 1995 and teamed for the doubles crown the past two years – Rodil de Araujo Jr., Chris Senn, and Macdonald in street.

In-Line skating:

It was inevitable that this once leisurely, exercise-oriented activity has been twisted into extremism. There's roller-hockey, the return of roller derby, downhill, marathon, speed, vert, and street (just like BMX and skateboarding street).

Once again, the main vehicle for nationwide exposure has

been the Summer X Games, which invented downhill, a five-wheel-per-skate hybrid. There are three sanctioning competitive bodies – the National In-Line Skating Series, Aggressive Skating Association, and USA In-Line Racing.

The ASA introduced an amateur circuit in 1997, a move which makes it easier for skaters to find a path to turning pro.

"Before it was who you knew," ASA executive director Todd Shays told ESPN.com. "Now it clearly has more to do with how you do in competition. Having a performance-based measurement has raised the bar in the competitive world and legitimized the pro class. It's been a wake-up call for the industry and a great way for new skaters to rise in the ranks."

There has been no dominant skater – man or woman – in most of the X Games's in-line events. In the women's vert, however, Fabiola DaSilva has claimed the last three golds. Chris Edwards has twice bronzed in the men's vert and men's street, while Gypsy Tidwell won the women's downhill in 1996 and 1997.

Rollerblade has started making an all-terrain in-line skate, so look for some sort of cross-country or mountain-skate sort of event in the near future.

Summer X Games:

Responsible for much of the exposure given to extreme or underground sports. Begun in 1995, the summer version includes skateboarding, in-line skating, bicycle stunts, sport-climbing, big-air snowboarding, skysurfing, street luge, and watersports.

Sportclimbing involves separate disciplines: difficulty and speed. Each is done on man-made walls. The men's difficulty event is the only one without a dominant performer. American teenager Katie Brown is the three-time defending champ in the women's difficulty; Hans Florine claimed the first three men's speed events; in women's speed, Elena Ovtchinnikova has won three of the four competitions.

Big-air snowboarding debuted at the 1997 Games in San Diego, and the most important aspect was, of course, making it snow in Southern California. Thirty-eight hours of snowmaking, nine semi-truck loads of liquid nitrogen, 200 tons of snow and more than 500 man-hours later, the necessary jump was finished. Peter Line beat out Kevin Jones in the first men's event, while Jones moved up a notch last year. Tina Dixon and Janet Matthews have won the women's division.

Skysurfing – in which a pair of teammates jump from a plane, perform tricks on a snowboard-like board and videotape them for judges – is the most expensive and least attainable sport for the masses. A pro U.S. team averages $40,000 to $50,000 to train, equip and travel to events – and the most it can win is less than half that. There are less than 30 professional competitive skysurfing teams in the world.

Street luge owes its popularity – indeed, its continuing existence – to the X Games. After its debut at the 1995 Games, the sport – downhill racing on mountain roads on boards a half-inch above the ground and with no brakes – grew to a three-sanctioning-body phenomenon.

Dual, or one-on-one, racing has been dominated by Biker Sherlock, who also has ruled the mass-racing event. Sherlock has claimed two titles in each discipline, and one in the super mass event. Rat Sult is close behind; he's the defending champ in mass and super mass.

Watersports include barefoot jumping, and men's and women's wakeboarding. Of the three, barefoot jumping is the most interesting. There are less than 500 people in the world who competed in barefoot events in 1997.

"Barefoot jumping is not for the recreational barefooter," Brian Heeney of the American Barefooters Club told ESPN.com. "It's so heavily scrutinized. It's so selective and radical. It's only the water, your feet, and the ramp."

The X Games added more difficulty by putting obstacles in the water before the skiers get to the ramp. Trick points helped Ron Scarpa win the title in 1996, while Peter Fleck chose to score by jumping as far as he could. He didn't land his jumps in 1995 and 1996, but he did the past two years, and the result was a gold medal each time.

This year's Summer X Games are set for the end of June through early July in San Francisco, California.

The most spectacular form is vert, or tricks out of a half-pipe

The Winter X Games consists of 6 sports, including ice-climbing

Extreme sports have arrived, but you know what? They've been here all along.

Strap yourself to anything with wheels or a flat surface, and head to the nearest ramp, pipe or impossibly-steep incline.

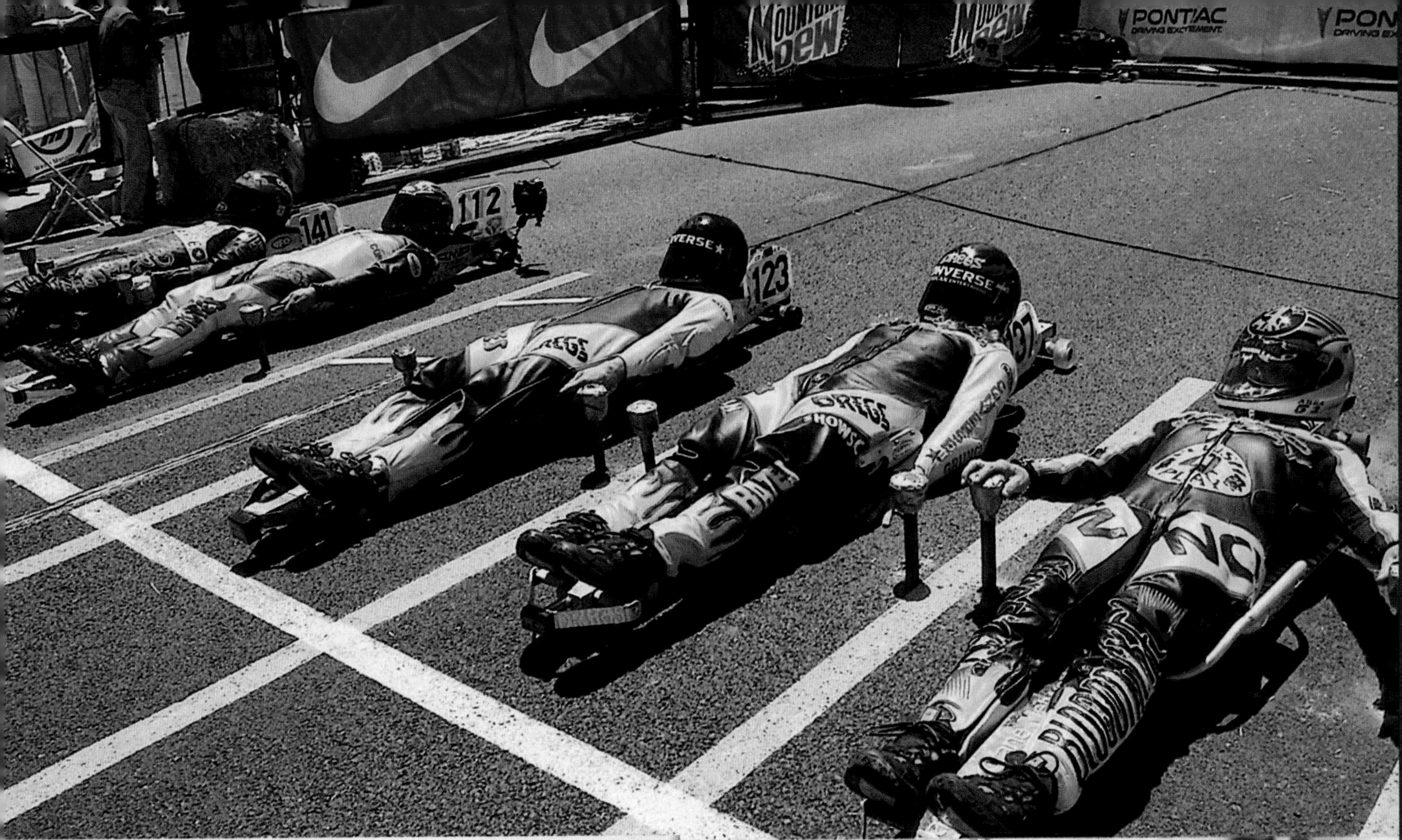

TEAM ARCTIC
PSI
STUD BOY
ACTION
FINISH LINE
MICRO BELMONT
ARCTIC CAT
PSI

Lowe alpine
PETZL

raw sports

raw sports

Ranking the Top 5 Playstation and Nintendo 64 Wrestling Games

#1 "WWF: War Zone"

(For Nintendo 64)

This is the best wrestling game on the market today and really shows off the 64 bits of power which makes up the Nintendo 64. The big standout in this game is the unprecedented graphics. This has got to be the most impressive-looking wrestling game to ever enter your home. Each wrestler is realistically motion-captured with silky-smooth movements that only the N 64 can handle. There are over 300 different moves between the wrestlers, including signature moves which are all executed with vivid realism. "War Zone" features 20 official WWF wrestlers, in addition to some bonus players. It also has different modes of play, including Tag-Team, Royal Rumble, WWF Challenge, Versus Mode, Steel Cage Match, and even a training mode which is great for getting different moves down. Another big plus: you can create a wrestler. The possibilities are endless. You can change your wrestler's height, weight, skin color, costume, etc. I did have one minor gripe with the game: for some reason, you cannot choose your opponent, and I still haven't figured out why Acclaim left out that option. Nevertheless, "WWF War Zone" has got to be one of the best fighting games on the system, and if you're into wrestling, you can't lose with this one. Nice job, Acclaim!

Between the PlayStation and the Nintendo 64, there is a wide variety of wrestling games available. Below is a top-5 list of the best wrestling games offered for both systems. Whether you have a PlayStation or a Nintendo 64, you simply can't go wrong with these great wrestling titles:

#2 "WWF: Warzone"

(For PlayStation)

Hey, Nintendo 64 owners can't have all the fun! "Warzone" for PlayStation is virtually identical to its N 64 counterpart; the only difference is that the 32-bit graphics are not quite up to par with Nintendo's 64 bits. But the great game play and the motion-captured wrestlers move smoothly and play just as well as they do on the Nintendo 64. Since this version is on a CD, the sound is much better than the N 64 version. Each fighter is introduced with an inspiring introduction, rockin' music and an awe-inspiring crowd, which was somewhat ignored on the Put You At Ringside. This game's music was meant to be cranked up. "Warzone" features 20 official WWF wrestlers. The big plus, as is the case with the Nintendo 64 version, is that "Warzone" has a Create-A-Wrestler option. You can change your wrestler's clothes, hair, weight, mask, and many other attributes, which really give your wrestler a personality of his own.

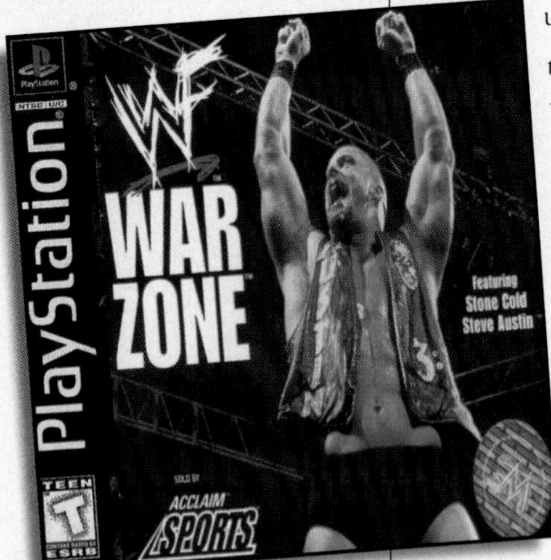

#3 "WCW/NWO: Revenge"

(For Nintendo 64)

"Revenge" is the sequel to THQ's "WCW/NWO: World Tour." This time around, THQ did the right thing by adding more wrestlers (50 in all), better

game play, more rings, and most importantly, better graphics. These new graphics include new animations and textures. The players themselves got a major facelift, look more realistic and have a less blocky look than they did in "World Tour." The realistic shots to the face are brutal, and the battered, fatigued wrestlers are inflicted with the most blood ever seen in a wrestling game. The game also plays remarkably smoothly. Even with four wrestlers on the screen, the game has virtually zero slow-down. Multi-player modes are great, especially if you have some buddies playing the game with you. And while there is no Create-A-Wrestler feature, "Revenge" features a Costume mode. This mode allows the players to change their wrestlers' clothing to suit their liking. You can change masks, colors, design, etc. In regards to the sound, "Revenge" is pretty basic. Cartridge-based games are limited as to what they can offer the game player. The sound effects are good, including the crowd and the actual fighting noises, but there is no color commentary, and the music leaves much to be desired. Aside from mediocre sound, "WCW/NWO: Revenge" is a worthy successor to "World Tour" and is easily worth the price of admission.

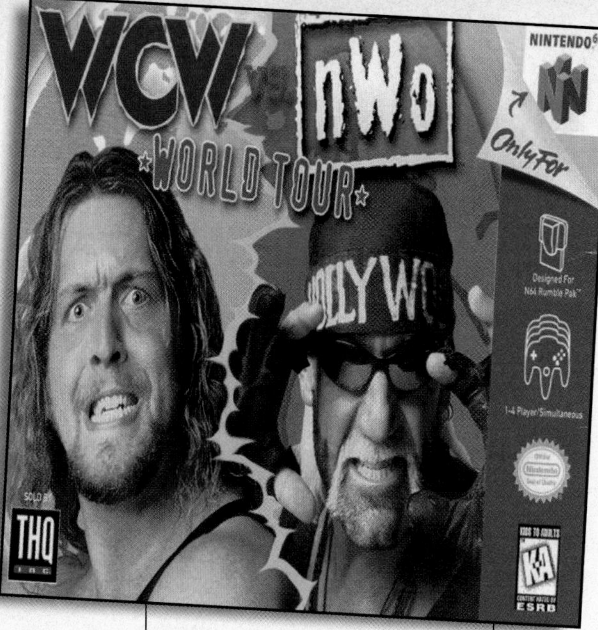

#4 "WCW vs. NWO: World Tour" (For Nintendo 64)

"World Tour" is the first wrestling game THQ made for Nintendo 64. Even with THQ's worthy successor, "Revenge," on the market, "World Tour" is worth a serious look. "World Tour" features more than 40 wrestlers. It has five modes of play, including League Challenge, League, Tournament, Exhibition, and of course, WCW vs. NWO. Compared to "War Zone" and "Revenge," the graphics on "World Tour" certainly will not blow you away. The wrestlers themselves are animated nicely, but they are somewhat flushed out and their faces are barely recognizable. Another drawback is the dull crowd graphics, which are unanimated. These are the worst-looking crowd graphics you will find on the Nintendo 64. (And this is 64-bit?) The sound is acceptable, the crowd stays involved and the sound effects in the ring are well done, but there is no announcer and no voice sample of any kind from the wrestlers. THQ needs to take notes from Acclaim on how to compress voice effects to a N 64 cartridge. Games like "Quarterback Club '99" and "South Park" have a substantial amount of voice effects, and THQ needs to do the same thing for their wrestling titles. Aside from the sub-par graphics and sound, "World Tour" is a good wrestling game, especially in multi-player mode. Bring three of your friends over and you can have an instant royal rumble.

#5 "WCW Nitro" (For PlayStation)

THQ knows wrestling, and next to "Warzone" on PlayStation, this is a decent wrestling title. "WCW Nitro" features 16 wrestlers from the WCW. It offers 5 game modes of play, including Exhibition, Tournament, 2-Player Versus, 1-Player Tag-Team and 2-Player Tag-Team. The graphics are not going to blow you away and the wrestlers look decent, but they appear to have more of a cartoon-like look in comparison to other wrestling titles. But they are animated nicely and the game plays fast and furious. A big surprise was the sound: even though this is on a CD, there is virtually no commentary. On the brighter side, "Nitro" offers some jammin' wrestling music from Korn and White Zombie and the sound effects in the ring are right on. The decent graphics are excellent for game play. Next to "Warzone," this is the wrestling game to get for your PlayStation.

John Spangler is a Web page designer and video game enthusiast who reviews Nintendo64 and Playstation games independently on the Internet. You can find his reviews for these and other video games at http://205.212.144.133/index.htm. You can E-mail John at Reviewer24@aol.com.

Testosterone Rock

"Music With Balls"

by Jim DeRogatis
WOW Rock Music Critic

I don't know about you, but I'm sick and tired of the unending onslaught of gutless wonders—alternative wankers who are alternative to nothing but good rock 'n' roll, pretentious ninnies who talk about rocking hard but never deliver the goods (Courtney Love, are you listenin'?), and music that claims to be heavy but is really about as substantial as a freakin' feather pillow.

You can keep your Lilith Fair! I am not ashamed to say I long for sounds that embody the same sweaty, loud, obnoxious, testosterone-powered, no guts, no glory, kick-out-the-jams ROAR to be found in the ring with the wrasslers profiled elsewhere in these pages.

I'm talkin' about music with balls, if ya haven't caught my drift.

This column will be devoted to keeping you abreast of such new and exciting sounds, whether or not they're directly involved with professional wrestling. (In fact, most wrestlers oughta stick to what they're good at rather than trying to make music, judging by the pathetic and hoarse crooning of Jesse "the Governor" Ventura, Hulk Hogan and "Mean" Gene Okerlund on "The Wrestling Album," recently released by Koch Records.) What we'll deal with here are sounds that pack the wallop of a full-on body slam, the neck-breaking intensity of a vice-like half-nelson, and the breathtaking urrggghhh!!! of a well-placed scissors kick.

In other words, without further ado... let's get r-r-r-r-ready to r-r-r-r-r-rumble!

When it comes to heavy, "Jerusalem" by the late lamented **Sleep** nearly redefines the term. This CD consists of one dense, disorienting, 52-minute monstrous monolith of a stoned-out jam painstakingly recorded in the trio's rehearsal room. Originally intended for release on London Records, that company just didn't have the guts to actually unleash the thing on a rock-deprived public. It was left to the adventurous indie label The Music Cartel to see that Sleep's unstoppable sounds finally flowed forward with the red-hot intensity of a lava flow. Matt Pike's searing guitar solos scorch everything in their path as Al Cisneros' rumbling bass and even deeper voice o' doom vocals bore through yer eardrums so that the brain fluid runs down yer neck and ruins yer favorite T-shirt. But you better believe the mess is worth it! The trio's inspiration is obvious—the back cover features a cute lil' pic of a homemade bong. But just listening to this heaviosity is enough to make ya feel zonked outta yer gourd. **Rating: Two giant f''''''' balls!**

"Time Traveling Blues" by British sludge merchants **Orange Goblin** is another fine release from The Music Cartel, this one the sophomore outing by a quintet devoted to updating the vintage heavy-metal stomp of powerful progenitors such as Black Sabbath, Deep Purple, and Mountain, with a bit of Pink Floyd's interstellar overdrive and some of Hawkwind's science fiction revelry thrown in for good measure.

"When the dream is over,

blue snow will fall on you," leather-lunged vocalist Ben Ward bellows on the opening track. And though I have no freaking idea what he's talking about (is blue snow anything like Frank Zappa's yellow snow?), the band's mix of retro grooves and here 'n' now high-energy has me banging my head and screaming: "Let it snow, let it snow, let it f****** snow!" **Rating: Two big balls.**

Speaking of the mighty, mighty **Sabbath**, you probably know the original quartet of Ozzy Osbourne, Tony Iommi, Geezer Butler, and the heart attack-plagued Bill Ward have reunited for the unimaginatively titled "Reunion" album (Epic). Far be it from me to dis the boys (who are now rather paunchy lookin' middle-aged men), since they pretty much invented heavy music.

But it's worthy mentioning this soggy double-disc collection for two reasons. One, if you've heard it and it prompted ya to consider skipping the Reunion tour, DON'T! The band is a million times better live than on this crappy disc (they musta met with Satan at the crossroads somewhere and resold their souls for rock 'n' roll).

On the other hand, if ya saw Black Sabbath recently and were rightfully blown away by

their evil awesomeness, don't buy the live album, 'cause they clearly hadn't shaken the rust off yet when this was recorded. Invest in another copy of any of the first seven albums instead. And any of youse kids who don't own "Black Sabbath," "Paranoid," "Master of Reality," "Sabbath Bloody Sabbath," etc.—what the hell are ya thinking? Go out and buy 'em right this second! (I'll wait till ya get back.) **Rating for "Reunion": One shriveled 'n' shrinking little ball.**

In death-metal circles, the aptly named **Death** is another much-revered name, having been one of the founding noisemongers of this unrelenting and coolest-of-the-cool underground metal genres. On "The Sound of Perseverance" (Nuclear Blast), guitarist/vocalist Chuck Schuldiner returns with a new lineup and the band's sixth album, its first since 1995's "Symbolic."

While it most definitely does not suck, the band has been leaner, meaner, faster, 'n' heavier in the past. Chuck's either gettin' old and slowin' down, or he's anxious to get on with the more mainstream metal sounds (a la Queensryche and Iron Maiden) that he's been promising from his side project, "Control Denied." The coolest moment here is a metal classic: "Painkiller" by Judas Priest. The rest has gotta take a back seat to what Death has done on other discs. **Rating: Two medium-sized balls (they really shoulda been bigger).**

I was likewise deflated by "Meet Your Evil Twin" (Radio Mafia) from the L.A. foursome **Doppelganger.**

I originally had high hopes for this 'un, based primarily on the cover: One very hot babe squats over her band's fiery moniker while wearing this latex strap ensemble, her boobs bared but for her long raven locks, a sultry come-hither look upon

her face, and two big devil horns atop her head. Got my own horn rising, if ya know what I mean, but the grooves inside didn't live up to the promise.

Said seductress (one Joan Sceline—a surname that may or may not be a pun on this famously surly French philosopher named Celine) is joined by two equally bodacious babes and one lame, wussy-looking dude onstage and in the studio. They proceed to churn out a rather anemic brand of what useta be called hair metal—essentially a mix of glam, goth-rock and the odd wanky guitar solo. Plus, there's synthesized keyboards. As a rule of thumb, it's a good idea to never trust a band with synthesized keyboards. **Rating: No balls.**

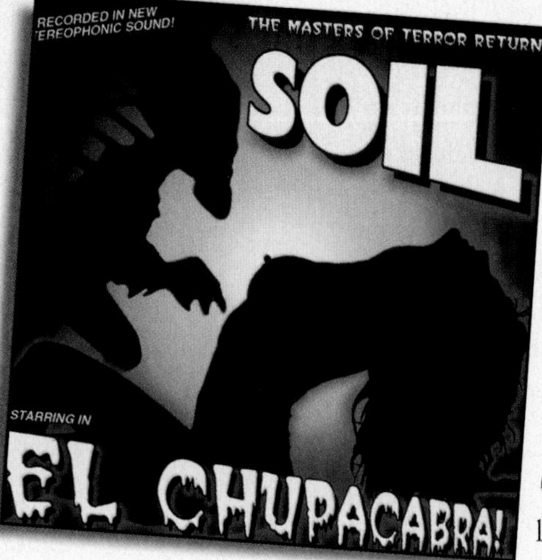

A lotta folks seem to be going back to metal's roots these days. Another case in point: the Chicago quintet **Soil**, which makes its second appearance on shiny disc with the five-song "El Chupacabra EP" on MIA Records. In addition to a bounty of '70s metal influences, these boys throw in hints of classic Southern rock (I hear subtle touches o' Lynyrd Skynyrd and Molly Hatchet) and more than a bit o' Harley-ridin' bad-boy biker attitude on tasty hard-rock nuggets such as "Broken Wings" and "F-Hole."

Things are propelled by the intertwined two-guitar pummeling of Adam Zadel and Shaun Glass, as mighty a pair of six-string mofos as I've heard of late (no keyboards to be found here, brother!). With a long-player in the works produced by Steve Albini (Nirvana, Bush, Page & Plant), Soil sounds like one to watch. **Rating: Two pretty big balls.**

I wanna leave ya with two more primo slabs of great greasy garage rock. "Supershitty to the Max!" (Man's Ruin Records) is a collection of 13 fuel-injected barn-burners by The **Hellacopters**, an amped-up quartet from Stockholm obsessed with good ol' fashioned all-American stomp 'n' grind. They deliver it in big heapin' helpings via tunes such as "(Gotta Get Some Action) Now!," "Random Riot" and "Fire Fire Fire." Those song titles (plus the creepy cool cover art by the famous poster artist Kozik) kinda say it all. Ditto the lyrics from "Every Shitty Thing," my favorite track on the uncompromising "Broken Bottles Empty Hearts" (Sub Pop) by Seattle's **Murder City Devils.** Sings vocalist Spencer Moody: "Every shitty thing that I've ever done / Waits for me underneath the wool of the covers / It's not a lie but still I can't sleep at night / And I'm the only one that knows every shitty thing that I've ever done!"

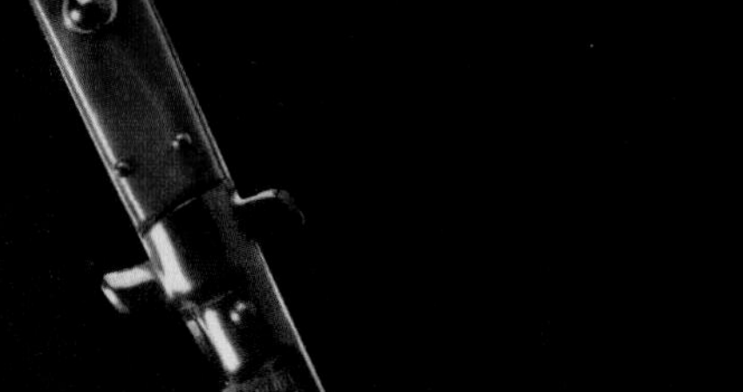

Meanwhile, things are kicked into high gear by a pounding rhythm section, a swirling Farfisa organ, and a wave of fuzz-tone guitar straight outta Detroit 1970 (the original Murder City and home o' these boys' obvious heroes, the Stooges and the MC5).

Ya gotta love that.

Ratings for the Hellacopters and the Murder City Devils: Two sets o' big balls (one pair for each)!

Jim DeRogatis is the Rock Music Critic for the "Chicago Sun-Times." He has written for numerous publications, including "Rolling Stone," and is the author of a number of critically-acclaimed books on music.

The World According to Dutch

by Dutch Mantel

The Man They Call Dirty Dutch

Who is Dutch Mantel? If you don't know, your ass better call somebody! Dutch is the man who gave Steve Austin his name; he's been held up at gunpoint with the Undertaker, wrestled in prison, fired by Jerry Lawler for "Being one of them;" and his picture is hanging in the Smithsonian Institute. For the last eight months, he's contributed more than 30 stories about his 20-plus years in the wrestling business to The Bagpipe Report online. And now his work comes to the pages of WOW magazine for the reading pleasure of all the "Dutchaholics."

When we went to track him down about WOW, he was in Puerto Rico; we talked to his wife, Kay, who informed us that he'd had his butt kicked the previous Saturday when a riot broke out at the matches. Just another day in the life of Dutch Mantel. Without further ado, we present some classic examples of Dutch's work, kicking off with a few words on one of his recent trips to Puerto Rico in '94, so you REALLY know what he's been up to. Enjoy!

Greetings, New Dutchaholics

Sometimes in Puerto Rico in the wrestling business, it's not the most esteemed company you can work for. They have a history of not paying or paying late. It's very dangerous, and it is very dangerous in Puerto Rico. They're Latin, they're hot-blooded, the security isn't very good...if they had security, it'd be OK. They serve beer and they sell whiskey at the matches, a very dangerous place. And, kids, they throw things and they'll knock the hell out of you! They'll throw anything—from spark plugs, to rocks, to empty rum bottles.

As far as me going back? Hell, yeah, I'll go back in a minute! I like having people take target practice on me! I like being hit with bottles and sticks, people dropping damn fire extinguishers on your head. It's great! It makes you really appreciate getting back to the dressing room!

I brought Greg Valentine down there for a weekend deal and we had a riot. People were beating the doors down. I got 12 stitches in my eye. Hell, it took 18 cops to get me out of the building. I got back at 6 a.m. I had to go to two hospitals: one hospital stitched up my eye and I had to go to a better one to stitch up my left eyelid. Anyway, Greg Valentine was there. He was supposed to come back the next week...Never heard from him again.

Are Any of You Men on Drugs?

Several years ago, I worked a show in Memphis for Jerry Jarrett just about the time he was going to the WWF. In those days, WWF had a fairly strict drug-testing system in place. Before the show started, Jerry called all the wrestlers together for a pre-show meeting.

During the meeting, Jerry announced he had accepted a position with the WWF and stated he would like to take some of the Memphis wrestlers there with him. He explained that the WWF had a drug policy and he said the drug policy included illegal drugs as well as anabolic steroids. Memphis was in one of its notorious dry spells and nobody was making any money. Plus, Memphis had a history of paying like s**t anyway.

Jerry then asked the question: "Are any of you men on STEROIDS?"

The dressing room looked like a survivor scene from "Schindler's List." So, I don't think it would have taken a Ph.D. to figure that one out. No one said a word except me. I said, "On....steroids? Hell, Jerry, we ain't even ON FOOD!!!" (The pay packet wasn't the best at that time.) Needless to say, I didn't work Memphis again for three years. I don't think Jerry thought that was too funny. But hell, I thought Jerry's threshold for humor was higher than that.

Dirty Dutch's Top 5 List of Worst Drivers

5. Barry Horowitz

Barry really doesn't like to drive, and since he wears corrective lenses, he has a saying: "I have very poor night vision." Well, that's like saying he doesn't drive at night. I used to travel on occasion with Barry and I didn't believe him until witnessing his attempts to kill me on the Santa Monica Freeway in the daytime while we were headed to Anaheim, Calif. I believed him then. Barry couldn't drive a nail straight. He not only has poor night vision, he has poor day vision, too.

4. Tracy Smothers

Tracy likes to talk when he drives. Not only does he like to talk, he likes to have interactive talks. Plus, he likes to look at the person he's talking to. It doesn't matter that the person is in the backseat. Tracy just turns around and keeps on talking. I used to dare him to look at the road every couple of minutes or so.

He got yanked over one night in Knoxville, Tenn., and after shining his light in Tracy's face, the cop asked him if he was drinking. Tracy said "no. "The cop then asked was he under the influence of drugs. Tracy again replied "no." The cop then wanted to know why Tracy was driving 35 mph in a 65-mph speed zone and weaving all over the road. Tracy just said, "Hey, man...I can't drive too good."

The cop must have believed him as he didn't give him a sobriety field test and let us go. The cop just said to pay more attention to the highway. Hell, I could've told him that.

3. Harley Race

Harley drove fast, hard and wild—120 mph was everyday fare for him. He liked to run up on other guys' bumpers and give them a nudge or two with his car...all the while doing 90 mph. I didn't find this too amusing myself, but Harley thought it was hilarious. If you've been paying attention to my "Top Five" lists, you may have noticed that Harley also finished in the Dirty Dutch Top Five Drinkers List. So, combine speed and alcohol, then you'll have some inclination as to what Harley's driving consisted of. I tried to stay clear of any vehicle that had Harley behind the wheel or within 50 feet of it.

2. Dr. Tom Pritchard

(formerly one half of the Body Donnas with Chris Candido and Sunny)

Tom doesn't drive fast…Tom doesn't drive reckless…Tom just can't drive worth a flit. I've taken many trips with the Good Doctor and Tom has a tendency to float all over the road while traveling 80 mph, then he'd drop down to 45 mph. Consistency was not his strong point, but crossing the center line apparently was. Plus, he can't see the side of a barn.

One night, Tom, Bradshaw and I were leaving Bethlehem, Pa., after the matches in a fog so thick that you could hardly see 10 feet in front of the car. Tom ran over something like a ditch, blew out his tire and completely ruined the tire rim. I've never taken over the driving duties of the assigned driver but after this display of NDE (near death experience), Bradshaw and I conducted a mutiny and fired Tom from driving.

To say Dr. Tom is dangerous with a moving heap of metal is to understate it. Damn...reliving these events makes me think how lucky we all were to have survived them.

And the No. 1 worst driver (that I've ever run across) is…

"See, I still don't know where we were headed. How we ever got there still amazes me."

Paul E. Heyman

1. Paul E. Heyman

You know the old saying, "Friends don't let friends drive drunk?" Well, we're going to change that saying for Paul. For Paul, it should read., "Friends don't let Paul drive…period." One time, Paul, the Undertaker and I left Chicago very, very late for a Sunday afternoon show somewhere in Indiana. See, I still don't know where we were headed. How we ever got there still amazes me. We had three hours to get there, but unbeknownst to us at the time, we also had 300 miles to cover with 100 miles of it on a two-lane highway. You know, it wouldn't have hurt if one of us had taken five minutes to look at a Rand/McNally road map, but we didn't because Paul said he knew how to go. I have only myself to blame for this one, though.

Paul started driving, and I swear to God that boy missed his calling. He would've given Jeff Gordon of NASCAR fame a run for his money. He drove like a bat outta hell…I was screaming, "Slow down" and "Whoa" and "Watch out" about every 30 feet and stomping the floorboard on the passenger side like I could actually brake the car. At one point, he had the speedometer completely buried. Not only is he dangerous to let drive, he's also lucky as the Irish, as an Indiana state trooper pulled us over on the two-lane segment of the trip. I thought to myself,

"Yes…YES…there is a God." But the trooper turned out to be a huge wrestling fan and let him go without even a warning. I begged Paul to let me drive. (The Undertaker, who had tied on a big drinking binge the night before, slept the entire way so he missed the whole incident. I wish I could've been so lucky.) Needless to say, when we got to where we were going (we were only 90 minutes late, plus we also had to go on to Cincinnati) I found myself another way to Cincy.

When I got there, I needed a couple of things. One was a Valium (to calm down), another was an EKG (surely I had suffered heart damage), and I needed a gun to shoot Paul.

I asked Paul E. how we survived the trip, and he said that God was with us. I told him that he should let God ride with someone else…he was gonna kill him. Paul E. should never drive a car—at least one with me in it. And to this day, I've never stepped back into a car with Paul at the helm.

Parting Shots

Well, I've rambled on enough. Hope you've enjoyed this latest "bulls**t" edition of "The World According to Dutch." If you got any questions and/or just a funny story, send me an E-mail. Also, if there's a special topic that you're partial to, let me know. And remember: if you can't dazzle them with brilliance, befuddle them with Bulls**t. As for the next edition, who knows what the f**k I'm gonna write? I don't even know. Hell, I never write what I say I'm going to anyway. I just write what I'm thinking at the time. Hell, whoever heard of "organized bulls**t?"

Later…

Dirty Dutch Mantel's column can be found on the Internet at www.bagpipe-report.com.